Memories War Stories and STANS

(Shoot That Ain't Nothing)

OLIVER HURT

ISBN 978-1-68197-985-4 (Paperback)
ISBN 978-1-68197-986-1 (Digital)

Christian Faith Publishing, Inc.
296 Chestnut Street
Meadville, PA 16335
www.christianfaithpublishing.com

Printed in the United States of America

Dedication

To my beloved wife, Laura.
You have always been my wings.

—My love always,
OJ

And

To all those service men and women whose achievements in peace and war built our great nation. To those who stepped up to meet the challenge. Their bravery in battle continues and is an inspiration to us all.

To all veterans, who are ready anytime and anyplace.

Authors Note

There may be some who read of my war time experiences that will disagree with my perspective. That's OK with me. There are those that endured much more than I did, and their perspective will be based on their experiences which will have differed from mine. I am proud to call any veteran a brother or sister in arms no matter their perspective.

I was privileged to serve in military intelligence and my career was not taken lightly. I served with the finest group of intelligence professionals in the Army. I would like you to know your intelligence services are very active and the war against terrorism actively engaged. You can be proud of America's finest intelligence professionals.

Here are my only disclaimers: You'll have to cut me some slack because some of my stories are over 30 to 50 years ago, and my memory may be a bit fogged by time. Because of this time lapse, my dates may be off. My other disclaimer is that my stories and experiences are not endorsed by any employer. I wrote the stories as I remember them. As I look back; I think really! Has it been that long? I read once that the reason time goes faster as we age, is that as we age, we have more life experience. The more life experience, the faster time flies. That may be true, but I do know that time has stolen my youth. That said, I don't feel old, I feel I am just wise in the way of life. Age is not the flight of years, but the dawn of wisdom. To me, age is an asset. Our minds do not age. Dr. Michael DeBakey, the person who developed the first roller pump for blood in 1932, described his philosophy on turning 90; "As long as we have challenges and are physically and mentally able, life is stimulating and invigorating". I'll end this disclaimer with a thought by Dr. Joseph Murphy, Ph.D., DD, who said; "Old age really means the contemplation of the truths of God from the highest standpoint. Realize that you are on an endless journey, a series of important steps in the ceaseless, tireless, endless ocean of life. You are a child of infinite life, on a path which knows no end, and you are an heir to eternity".

Contents

Foreword

by Chief Warrant Officer 4
David F. Berry

If you knew OJ Hurt, you would know him to be a quiet and reserved man. You will not find him boosting about his life experience and accomplishments at the local tavern. He is not prone to complaining. Nor is it likely you will hear him raise his voice in anger or discontent. I've been a friend of OJ's for 20 years, and I've known him to be a fine officer and gentleman. But don't let his quiet demeanor fool you. He is a man committed to his family, faith and country with a resolve seldom observed in today's America. He has that internal strength more common to American men and women born in the late 1940s or 50s that is not often identified in America's younger generation today. It is that common strength, courage and "get it done" attitude passed on to us by our parents, grandparents and great grandparents that is characteristic of Americans since the signing of the Declaration of Independence. It is the strength and courage to choose one's own path, one's own goals, and live the "American Dream". OJ chose his path, pursued his dream, and is still living it today.

You will enjoy this read; especially if you are a "Baby Boomer" for it will bring back precious memories and remind you of where you come from and who you are. Born in 1948, OJ walks you through his life path and goals starting with his childhood days in the farming community of Clay Center, Kansas; his first paying job, his hobbies, his early heroes and his hopes and dreams, fears and concerns. You'll enjoy his stories as a kid with cap pistols, bb guns, outhouse adventures, and the dangers of monkeying around with .22 caliber pistols, just to mention a few. He'll take you along his journey through the Army, from Private E-1 to Chief Warrant Officer 4; his enlistment into the Active Duty Army and his tours in Korea and Germany and his service with the US Army Reserve including a tour in Iraq.

OJ provides his personal insight into the life of a Law Enforcement Officer on the streets and in the air; from Patrolmen to Police Helicopter Pilot to Chief of Police. He will also introduce you to his career as a Special Agent Investigator for DIS (Defense Investigative Service).

Love and commitment to family and friends, his faith in God, and loyalty and service to country is not taken lightly by Oliver J. Hurt. He will share these thoughts with you too.

All Americans have a story, and those stories are unique, regardless if you arrived in this country yesterday or you are a descendant of the 1776 patriots. There is something common to each of us that binds us together as Americans and makes our Nation exceptional. It is not always easy to identify in yourself or others, but there is a good chance you'll find it in Oliver J. Hurt's story.

Enjoy,
David F. Berry
Chief Warrant Officer Four (Special Forces Retired)
Military Intelligence

Preface

This is a story about a typical guy who grew up in small town rural America. I am nobody special and certainly nobody important. I grew up on country and gospel music; Ernest Tubb, Hank Williams, Red Foley, the Carters, Johnny Cash, Bill Monroe, Little Jimmie Dickens, etc. My tastes have changed over the years to the blues now, but I'm still fond of country music. I grew up instilled with integrity, character, and a moral foundation. This is my story. I'm just a man, conscious of the responsibilities and duties God has placed upon me. I did my duty as God gave me the light to see it.

I am one who has fulfilled many boyhood dreams and one who is thankful for the many blessings God has bestowed upon my family and me. All the little pieces (stories) of the pie that make the whole made me the person I am today. I put this book of stories together as a promise to our daughter Janelle who, after hearing some of my many stories over the years, said, "You should write a book, Dad." Well, here it is. I cannot write all my stories in this book but will relay a few—the good, the bad, and the ugly.

I am the culmination of every person I have ever met and everything I have ever done or seen. I have had many mentors in my life, too numerous to mention. However, they are a part of me and had a lot to do with my career. I think often of them all, even though some have no idea as to their impact on me. My military and civilian careers have taken me around the world and to almost every state in the Union. I have met many wonderful people: astronauts, famous pilots. I have investigated scientists, physicists, generals, admirals, and individuals associated with Operation Paperclip. I have been to places and seen things I am unable to talk about. I have followed my dreams, accomplishing more of them than I thought possible. I wanted to become a pilot. I did, both fixed wing and rotor. I wanted to become a police officer. I did. I wanted to become an investigator. I did. I wanted to be in the military. I did and had the honor and privilege of leading men in combat operations. I'm not proud of some of my actions or behavior as I grew up, but they are a part of me. As I progressed in my life, I completed tasks that some folks have only dreamed of. Some have been downright challenging and difficult. My thinking was that when I retire, I do not want to look back and say, "I could have done that." I want to look back and say, "I did that." And I think I have. I never look in the rearview mirror of life because that is not the direction I want to go. I have accomplished most of what I set out to do. My advice: if you think you can or think you can't, you will. So follow your dreams, because if you can dream it, you can do it. Remember that once you reach the top, realize the most important thing is the journey. Never forget how you got there or who got you there. My second piece of advice is this: the difference between you and someone you envy is that you settled for less.

I have held our Daughter Janelle on my knee and held her tiny hands and fingers in mine. I have lived to see her grow and laugh and run. I have held our Granddaughter Emily on my knee and held her tiny hands and fingers in mine. I have lived to see her grow and laugh and run. And I told them stories of a vanished time in a far-off land—the way it used to be.

Aknowledgements

To the many people who have influenced me, and helped me understand a career that has spanned over three decades. Colleagues, mentors, and friends, who inspired a journey full of adventure and allowed me to work with them. You have helped me find the truth.

To my Family and Friends, without whom I would not be the person I am today. I wish to thank our daughter Janelle and her family, who without her sometimes asking, this book would not have been written, and I wish to thank my beautiful wife Laura, always an inspiration, who has been with me every step of my journey. She is a true hero. I love you all.

Acronyms and Jargon

I am inserting a few pages of Acronyms because aviation, military and police jargon is sometimes difficult to understand if one is unfamiliar with some terms. Below are some Acronyms I used throughout this book.

AVIATION JARGON

ATC - Air Traffic Control

A & P - Airframe and Power Plant Mechanic (Aircraft Mechanic)

AGL - Above Ground Level

ANTI-TORQUE PEDALS - The anti-torque pedals are located in the same place as the rudder pedals in an airplane, and serve a similar purpose. The pedals control the direction that the nose of the aircraft points. Applying the pedal in a given direction changes the tail rotor blade pitch, increasing or reducing tail rotor thrust and making the nose yaw in the direction of the applied pedal.

CHINOOK CH54 – is a Sikorsky twin-engine heavy-lift helicopter designed for the U.S. Army. It is named "Tarhe" after an 18th Century chief of the Wyandot Indian Tribe. The Chinook is also known as "The Hook."

CAVU – Ceiling and Visibility Unlimited. This is a Pilot saying that's been around since at least WWII. It simply means, there is a clear sky, no clouds, with visibility as far as you can see. Listen for CAVU in a 1949 movie, High Noon, starring Gregory Peck. President George H.W. Bush, 41, used it as a motto. As a Pilot, one always tries to fly in CAVU. It's not fun flying in heavy rain unless you absolutely have no choice. If you are a Pilot, you know what I'm talking about.

COLLECTIVE – The collective pitch control, is normally located on the left side of the pilot's seat with an adjustable friction control to prevent inadvertent movement. The collective changes the pitch angle of all the main rotor blades collectively (all at the same time) and independent of their position. Therefore, if a collective input is made, all the blades change equally, and the result is the helicopter increases or decreases its total lift derived from the rotor. In level flight this would cause a climb or descent, while with the helicopter pitched forward an increase in total lift would produce an acceleration together with a given amount of ascent. The change in pitch changes the angle of attack into the wind and creates lift.

COMPASS HEADING - In an aircraft one flies by a Magnetic Compass known as a Mag Compass or Mag North, verses flying True North. I won't go into the difference here, but depending on where you are at on the earth, there is a big difference between the two.

CYLIC - The cyclic control is usually located between the pilot's legs and is commonly called the Cyclic. On most helicopters, the cyclic is similar in appearance to a joystick in a conventional aircraft. The Cyclic changes the pitch angle of the rotor blades cyclically. That is, the pitch, or sometimes called the feathering angle of the rotor blades, changes depending upon their position as they rotate around the hub of the main rotor system. The cyclic changes so that all blades have the same incidence at the same point in the cycle. This change in cyclic pitch has the same effect of changing the angle of attack into relative wind, thus, lift is generated by a single blade as it moves around the rotor disk. This causes the blades to fly up or down in sequence. Something you may find interesting, is that lift is generated by approximately the last three or four feet of each individual rotor blade. The result is to tilt the rotor disk in a particular direction, resulting in the helicopter moving in that direction. If the pilot pushes the cyclic forward, the rotor disk tilts forward, and the rotor produces a thrust vector in the forward direction. If the pilot pushes the cyclic to the right, the rotor disk tilts to the right and produces thrust in that direction, causing the helicopter to move sideways in a hover or to roll into a right turn during forward flight, much as in a fixed wing aircraft. I hope my explanation is not too technical?

LANDING FLARE - a maneuver during the landing of an aircraft. The flare follows the final approach phase and precedes the touchdown of the aircraft. In a flare the nose of the aircraft is raised, slowing the descent rate, and proper attitude is set for touchdown. You basically level the aircraft, and in the case of a helicopter, come to a hover. When flaring a helicopter to land, you reduce both vertical and horizontal speed to allow a near zero-speed touchdown to hover.

ICT - Wichita Airport, now known as Eisenhower International Airport (EIA)

ROTOR - Helicopter

TRACON - Traffic Control

TRANSPONDER – A Transponder is short for transmitter responder. The Transponder is an electronic device inside the aircraft that produces a response when it receives a radio-frequency interrogation from the ATC handling the airspace the aircraft is flying in. Aircraft have transponders to assist in identifying them on air traffic control radar and collision avoidance systems that have been developed to use transponder transmissions as a means of detecting aircraft at risk of colliding with each other. There are certain frequencies that a Pilot inputs into the Transponder that identifies that particular aircraft. An aircraft flying VFR, would be squawking

1200, which is standard for VFR flight; meaning the transponder would be indicting 1200, unless the Pilot has been assigned another code. ATC uses the term "squawk" when they are assigning an aircraft a transponder code. As an example, outbound ATC may advise the Pilot to "Squawk 7421". Meaning select the number 7421 into the transponder code. By doing this, ATC then would have an exact location of the Pilot's aircraft on their radar. This allows the individual ATC controller to either guide the aircraft out of their airspace, or would let the ATC know exactly where the aircraft is within their controlled airspace. There are Transponder codes the Pilot can input as a frequency to alert the ATC he is experiencing an emergency without having to use the radio. There is a standard frequency the Pilot inputs for flying IFR, etc.

VOR - Visual Omni Range. A VOR is a radio beacon put out from a radio tower to aircraft.

VFR - Visual Flight Rules. VFR are a set of regulations under which a pilot operates an aircraft in weather conditions generally clear enough to allow the pilot to see where the aircraft is going. Specifically, the weather must be better than basic VFR weather minimum. Verses IFR when operation of an aircraft under VFR is not safe, because the visual cues outside the aircraft are obscured by weather or darkness. IFR flight rules must be used instead.

Vr Rotation (lift off) Speed

Vtocs Take-off climb out speed (helicopters)

MILITARY JARGON (and terms used associated with my military career)

C2 - Command and Control

C3I - Command, Control, Communication, and Intelligence

C2PC – Command and Control Personal Computer System

CO – Commanding Officer

DFAC – Dining Facility

DoD – Department of Defense

DOG TAGS – A term for the identification tags worn by military personnel, because of their resemblance to actual dog tags. The tags are primarily used for the identification of dead and wounded soldiers, they have personal info about the soldiers; such as blood type along with religious preference. Dog tags are usually fabricated from two pieces of a corrosion-resistant metal. This allows half the tag (or one of two tags) to be collected from a soldier's body for later notification, while the other half (or other tag) remains with the corpse when battle conditions prevent the body from being immediately recovered. While in Iraq, I wore one tag around my neck and one in the bottom boot string on my right boot. I will stop explaining here. I could write another story on how dog tags are used.

FATWA - a legal opinion or decree handed down by an Islamic religious leader, known as a Mufti. A Fatwa was usually a death sentence, however, not all Fatwa's are sentences of death.

FNG - Flippin New Guy (I'm cleaning that up by the way)

GAYAGEUM – or Kayagum is a traditional Korean Zither-like string instrument with usually 12 strings.

HUMINT - Human Intelligence

ICF – Intelligence Contingency Fund

IED - Improvised Explosive Device

EFP - Explosively Formed Penetrator EFP is a special type of shaped charge designed to penetrate armor.

IMIR - Iraqi Military Intelligence Regime

JWICS - Joint Worldwide Intelligence Communications System (pronounced JAYwicks), is a Top Secret/SCI network run by the Defense Intelligence Agency to transmit especially sensitive classified information. This computer system is only operated from a SCIF and is primarily used by members of the intelligence community.

KIMCHI- Also spelled Kimchee or Gimchi, is a traditional fermented Korean side dish made of vegetables with a variety of seasonings. The traditional preparation of Kimchi was stored underground in jars to keep cool during the summer months and unfrozen during the winter months. There are hundreds of varieties of Kimchi made from Napa, Cabbage, Radish, Scallion, or Cucumber as the main ingredients.

MITT – Military Intelligence Training Team. In civilian speak: Mobile Instructor Training Team

MTOE – Modified Table of Equipment

OCONUS - Outside Continental United States

OIF II - Operation Iraqi Freedom 2d Iteration

OMT - Operations Management Team (This term refers to the management of TAC HUMINT teams under one umbrella.

OMT OIC – Operations Management Team, Officer in Charge. This position is equal to a Director or Regional Director in civilian speak. My OMT was a split based operation, meaning that I had THT Teams working out of the Green Zone, Baghdad, to include Sadr City, and also had THT Teams working out of Camp Victory, Iraq.

OPERATION PAPERCLIP (OP) – For you history buffs. Operation Paperclip was the codename under which the US intelligence and military services extricated scientists from Germany, during and after the final stages of World War II. The project was originally called Operation Overcast, and is sometimes also known as Project Paperclip. Since the paperwork of those Germans selected for transfer to the United States was indicated by paperclips, those Germans involved in the mission became known as Operation Paperclip. Operation Paperclip employed many German scientists who were formerly considered war criminals or security threats. The individual I conducted an investigation on, who was actually a German Scientist (now a U.S. Citizen) involved in Operation Paperclip, was involved in the German V1 and V2 Rocket Program, and was forced into the Nazi Youth Program when he was 12 years of age through 17 years of age. I will not go into any other personal history information on this individual. As a side note, the V-1 Flying Bomb (German: Vergeltungswaffe), also known to the Allies as the buzz bomb or doodlebug, was an early pulsejet powered cruise missile. The V2 (German: Vergeltungswaffe), or "Retribution Weapon", with a technical name of Aggregat 4, was the world's first long-range guided ballistic missile. It was fueled by a liquid-propellant rocket engine. The V2 was designed to attack Allied cities as retaliation for Allied bombings against German cities. Of note is that the V2 was the first artificial object to cross the boundary of space.

OSINT - Open Source Intelligence

SIGINT - Signals Intelligence

PIR – Priority Intelligence Requirement

SCI – Sensitive Compartmented Information is usually only briefed, discussed, and stored in an accredited SCIF.

SCIF – Secret Compartmented Information Facility (pronounced "skiff") in U.S. Military, security and intelligence parlance, is an enclosed area within a building that is used to process Sensitive Compartmented Information (SCI) types of classified information. Access to SCIFs is normally limited to those with a Top Secret clearance. When entering a SCIF you are required to surrender recording and other electronic devices to include telephones. All of the activity and conversation inside is presumed restricted from public disclosure.

SOP – Standard Operating Procedure

SAW - Squad Automatic Weapon

TAC – Tactical

THOPS – Tactical HUMINT Operations. The Officer in Charge (OIC) of THOPS is equal to a Director or Regional Director in civilian speak.

THT – TACHUMINT Team

THT Team Leader – Is equal to a Special Agent in Charge (SAC) in civilian speak

TTP – Techniques, Tactics, and Procedures

TOC – Tactical Operations Center

SAEDA – Sabotage and Espionage Directed Against the Army. SAEDA is now known as

TARP, Threat Awareness and Reporting Program.

UCMJ – Uniform Code of Military Justice

WAR – Here is my definition of War; War is killing people and breaking things until the enemy surrenders. I value life and I want peace.

I do not like war, no one does. War is a last resort, and is fought by men and women who least of all want to be on the battlefield. On the other hand, we must keep our swords sharpened because there will always be an enemy who despises our way of life. A life given to us by the Grace of God, and a Country founded on religious principles through our Constitution. If an enemy pushes us with steel, we have to respond with steel. Men and women willing to sacrifice their life if necessary to preserve our freedom. This is what stops an enemy advance.

Our founding Fathers gave up their livelihoods, their homes, even their families and their lives to gain freedom from oppression. Almost every generation since has had to contend with tyrants who have tried to take our freedoms. Tyrannical men who are weak in character, values, and morality. Men who think their way of life, their ideology and religious beliefs are the only way to live. We prevent harm by recognizing the threat and remaining cognizant of the fact that we are in a dynamic risk environment. It's simply common sense to protect our homeland, and illogical to think otherwise. We are at risk of being targeted because we are seen as soft and weak. You cannot just wish for peace. You have to be willing to earn it.

> "War is an ugly thing but not the ugliest of things; the decayed and degraded state of moral and patriotic feeling which thinks that nothing is worth war is much worse. A man who has nothing for which he is willing to fight, nothing which is more important than his own personal safety, is a miserable creature and has no chance of being free unless made and kept so by the exertions of better men than himself".
>
> - John Stuart Mill

The Prayer known as General Patton's Weather Prayer.

I include this prayer, as I mention it in this book. One must remember, we were at War when this prayer was written. General Patton's Weather Prayer, written by BG Msgr James O'Neill, who at the time was COL Msgr O'Neill. General Patton's Third Army Headquarters was located in the Caserne Molifor in Nancy, France, 14 Dec 44, at the time the prayer was written.

"Almighty and most merciful Father, we humbly beseech Thee, of Thy great goodness, to restrain these immoderate rains with which we have had to contend. Grant us fair weather for Battle. Graciously hearken to us as soldiers who call upon Thee that, armed with Thy power, we may advance from victory to victory, and crush the oppression and wickedness of our enemies and establish Thy justice among men and nations."

I proudly took the following Oaths while in the Military, they are;

Oath of Enlistment (May 1968)

I, Oliver J. Hurt, do solemnly swear that I will support and defend the Constitution of the United States against all enemies, foreign and domestic; that I will bear true faith and allegiance to the same; and that I will obey the orders of the President of the United States and the orders of the officers appointed over me, according to regulations and the Uniform Code of Military Justice. So help me God." (Title 10, US Code; Act of 5 May 1960 replacing the wording first adopted in 1789, with amendment effective 5 October 1962).

Oath I took as a Commissioned Officer

I, Oliver J. Hurt, having been appointed an officer in the Army of the United States, as indicated above in the grade of Chief Warrant Officer 4, do solemnly swear that I will support and defend the Constitution of the United States against all enemies, foreign and domestic, that I will bear true faith and allegiance to the same; that I take this obligation freely, without any mental reservations or purpose of evasion; and that I will well and faithfully discharge the duties of the office upon which I am about to enter; So help me God."

And (All Soldiers take this one)

The Soldiers Creed

I am an American Soldier. I am a warrior and a member of a team. I serve the people of the United States, and live the Army Values. I will always place the mission first. I will never accept defeat. I will never quit. I will never leave a fallen comrade. I am disciplined, physically and mentally tough, trained and proficient in my warrior tasks and drills. I always maintain my arms, my equipment and myself. I am an expert and I am a professional. I stand ready to deploy, engage, and destroy, the enemies of the United States of America in close combat. I am a guardian of freedom and the American way of life. I am an American Soldier.

LAW ENFORCEMENT/INVESTIGATIVE JARGON

BAIT QUESTION - A non-accusatory question in which the possible existence of incriminating evidence is implied for the purpose of enticing the subject to change or consider changing his/her original statements. The bait question may be based on real or fictitious evidence. An example; "Why would I find your fingerprints on the safe the document in question was taken from?" Example; "If there was a camera near the safe the document was taken from, why would you be in the video?" Notice I did not say they were there, I only asked why or if. A guilty person will not hear why or if, the innocent person will. If the person is innocent, they may say "you will not see my picture or fingerprints anywhere, I was not there. The guilty person on the other hand will try to explain why his/her prints or picture is in the video.

BODY LANGUAGE - a kind of nonverbal communication where thoughts, intentions, or feelings are expressed by physical behaviors, such as facial expressions, gestures, eye movement, touch and the use of space. Body language exists in both animals and humans, but this article focuses on interpretations of human body language. It is also known as kinesics.

CANI - Constant and never ending improvement

COIN - Counterinsurgency or can be used as Confidential Informant

FSO – Facility Security Officer. The FSO supervises and directs the security within a facility. The FSO ensures the effective implementation of the Foreign Ownership Control and Influence (FOCI) agreement between their facility and the Government. In addition to serving as the principle advisor to the Government Security Committee (GSC). The primary roles and responsibilities of an FSO are: Development of a Technology Control Plan (TCP), Electronics Communications Plan (ECP), Visitation Procedures to the facility they control, Operational Security of their facility, maintains Security Clearance Access to their facility, the Security Clearance Access Roster (SCAR), and to the various carve out programs, provides analysis and resolution of security-related matters, and a myriad of other duties related to the security of their facility.

FLEA - Federal Law Enforcement Agent

MIND VIRUS - A term used to place an idea with a Subject that has possible negative consequences, causing the person to think of hypothetical consequences to any act perceived by the person to be something they did wrong. An example of this is that if I am going to interview someone I have information on who committed some type of security breach, whatever that breach may be, up to an including espionage, I will call the Subject I am going to interview, and make the interview appointment for the following day, or I may call on an Friday, for a Monday interview giving the person a day or more to contemplate and worry why I want to interview him/her. (hypothetical consequence) Thus placing a Mind Virus causing his/her mind to think on a hypothetical consequence to their behavior or act. A

Mind Virus works to my advantage, with much success, particularly using follow on elicitation and SCAN techniques.

REID - The Reid technique is a method of questioning subjects to try to assess their credibility and to extract confessions of guilt from a suspect. The technique is widely used by law enforcement agencies however it has been criticized, as it has a long history of eliciting false confessions. For this reason, I prefer to use SCAN, however, a limited use of REID also has given me some good interview technique success.

ROI - Report of Investigation

SCAN - Scientific Content Analysis of Statements. SCAN was developed by Avinoam Sapir, an Israeli Polygrapher, who was my SCAN instructor. SCAN is considered the most effective technique available for obtaining information and detecting deception from statements of witnesses or suspects. SCAN is not a theory; it is a technique for detecting deception and obtaining information by making a series of observations. It has been proved to be a scientifically based method which produces consistent results. A SCAN analyst is able to dissect a written or verbal statement and determine whether the author of the communication is telling "the truth, the whole truth and nothing but the truth". If you are an Investigator, or employed in any profession that requires you to talk with clients, i.e. Attorney's, Insurance Investigators, etc. I highly recommend taking the SCAN course. It should be a requirement for all individuals engaged in any type of investigation process.

BSM – Bronze Star Medal. I am placing this acronym separately from the others. I will relay my experience with Award Boards in Iraq. I was medevac'd out of Iraq from 19 Jul 04 to 12 Sep 04, after developing kidney stones resulting in Stateside surgeries. The Doctors at Ft Hood, TX, advised me I had developed kidney stones from drinking Egyptian water, which contained high levels of calcium, and I was not the only Soldier who had developed kidney stones from drinking this water. (They are not pleasant; you don't want them). The only water available to us in Iraq. The Doctor at Ft Hood advised after treatment, that I stay Stateside due to being unable to clear all stones through surgery. They needed to keep a watch on the stone they were unable to retrieve during surgery. Due to my insistence, the Doctor released me back to Iraq, stating I may become ill again prior to being rotated out. (I didn't). I simply had to go back. I did not want to leave the people l served with there without me. I took them over, and I wanted to bring them safely back. If you have never been there, you will not understand my wanting to go back with my men. I considered their welfare my responsibility. So here's the point of this story.

While I was medevac'd out, the BN I was assigned held their Award Boards, Aug 04. During this period of time, all awards were to be submitted to the BN, by the Officers in Charge of their respective Units of responsibility within the BN, as the BN was getting ready to rotate back Stateside, and needed to get the awards out to BN members prior to rotation. Because I was medevac'd, I had no say or input into what Soldier deserved what award. As a Soldier, I did not perform my duty for any medal or any type of accolade. I did my duty for my Country and my Family, not for any type of honor, nor did I expect it. I am sure the men and women I served with feel the same. We did not join the military for free coffee on Veterans Day, or any other accolade that Veterans are sometimes afforded. Ask any Vet and they'll tell you they would do it all over again. That said, all the people I served with were given an Army Commendation (ARCOM) for their service in Iraq, in my absence, by Admin Staff (S1), who knew absolutely nothing of their operational actions, under AR600-

8-22, Chapter 3-15, (the BSM Regulation). Some should not have been downgraded from BSM to ARCOM. When I got back and learned of this, I immediately began writing BSM Nominations for those individuals whom not only qualified, but deserved to be recognized for their actions in a combat zone. As I was typing the first nomination, I was approached by my Commander who informed me in no uncertain terms, I was not to initiate any awards, that the awards had already been submitted, and the BN did not have time to re-evaluate them, prior to their returning stateside. I was told to immediately stop this action and not pursue any award nominations because of this. (I was told the BN did not think I would return from Stateside Medavac, and awards were issued accordingly). If I pursued, none would be looked at or forwarded for consideration. As a result, I was never able to submit any deserving Soldiers' name for BSM nomination. This has haunted me since, to the point of sleepless nights. I simply cannot sleep when I think on this. My Operations Officer, and number two of the OMT, was a Manager, not a Leader, and never stepped up to the plate in my absence. This Officer never understood you cannot manage people in combat operations, they have to be led. This Officer simply lost any leadership abilities he had during the last two months in country after an incident in which the Commander had to discipline him. Which I will not describe in this book. The small Staff I had, and my Team Leaders, and Team members, lost what little respect and trust they had in him, and further, this individual lost all credibility with me, and his actions greatly affected his integrity and character. In addition to the Commander's punitive action, I almost relieved him and placed him in a Team, however, I could not afford to have a disgruntled Officer on a Team. It's too dangerous when lives are at stake, and I am not one to pass the buck. This individual transferred to another Unit the last 30 days in Iraq. After the BN rotated Stateside in early Dec 04, I was nominated for the BSM by the BN THOPS to the incoming BN Commander. However, because the outgoing BN had not nominated me or any of the people l served with for BSM's, the nomination was declined by the new BN S1, and due to an award that was already presented. All because I was not in-country at the time the Award Boards were held.

I do not feel it was the right thing to do by the Command in which I served. I did my duty for my Country and my Family, not for any type of award or honor. However, after I was nominated, my thought was if my nomination was accepted, I would be able to write award nominations for deserving and qualified Soldiers as a result. My feeling is that if one has qualified for a particular award and is deserving and qualified of recognition, the medal should be awarded. So....there are people I served with who deserve recognition for their actions, however, have never been recognized properly for their service to our Nation. They know who they are, and this may be enough for them, but it still haunts me. I'm sure there are also other deserving Soldiers from other Units that also did not receive proper recognition. The point is, some of my Team Leaders were not properly recognized for their service. The hard work and perseverance of my Teams resulted in critical and timely reporting of vital intelligence information that maneuver commanders often relied upon to successfully engage and destroy Anti Iraqi Forces (AIF), locate weapons caches and capture key insurgent personnel. My Team Leaders were engaged in an action against an enemy of the United States. They were engaged in military operations involving conflict with an opposing foreign force, and while serving with friendly foreign forces engaged in an armed conflict against an opposing armed force in which the United States was not a belligerent party. Other than being away from my family, this is my only regret while deployed.

The Security Clearance Process

A security clearance certifies that an individual can have access to classified information or be assigned to a highly sensitive job. There are three levels of Clearances; Confidential, Secret, and Top Secret. Department of Energy (DoE) calls a Secret level clearance an "L" and a Top Secret a Q". A DoE clearance is not higher than a DoD clearance, and visa versa. The process of obtaining a clearance is not a simple one. Here's a simple water downed version of the process in case you're curious:

Following the Intelligence Reform and Terrorism Prevention Act the 2004 Defense Authorization Bill directed DoD to begin submitting almost all of it's Security Clearance Investigations to OPM, and DIS began conducting those investigations under OPM Control. Security Clearance processing does not exist within a mono-lithic structure with one agency conducting an investigation. There are dozens of federal agencies that process clearances. All agencies use the same basic procedures for granting and denying clearances, but many agencies use their own resources to make clearance decisions. Most agencies use OPM as their investigation service provider, but many agencies have statutory or delegated authority to use other investigative service providers or their own investigative personnel. As a consequence, there are significant differences in the time it takes to complete a security clearance.

To start the process, the Security Manger, called the Facility Security Officer (FSO), or in the case of an Army Subject, the S2, would notify the person of the security clearance requirement. The Personnel Security Investigation (PSI), Center of Excellence (CoE), receives a request from the FSO or S2, who sends an electronic Questionnaire of Investigation Process (eQIP), known as an SF86, to the employee. Once notified, the employee is given a number of days to gather information and submit the completed eQIP. The eQIP is an on-line form known as the Standard Form 86, which is a question-naire to capture information of a person's personal history, referred to as background. (If the employee is given 20 days to complete this task, after the 20th day, the employee will no longer have access to the on-line eQIP). After completion of the eQIP, PSI-CoE reviews the eQIP for completeness and forwards it to the Office of Personnel Management (OPM). When this occurs, OPM may request more information from the employee as necessary to complete the investigation. From this point, the completed eQIP, now called a case, is forwarded to trained and Credentialed Investigators to conduct the National Security Investigation. The Government Agency responsible for National Security Investigations is The Federal Investigative Service (FIS), and falls under the OPM umbrella. FIS is now known as the National Background Investigations Bureau (NBIB). The NBIB may in the near future merge back into the Defense Security Service (DSS). This is because there are some who feel the organization should go back into the DoD. OPM does use contractor personnel, however, the Government agency that conducts National Security Investigations, is the FIS. The investigation entails a myriad of checks; Financial, Criminal, past Employment checks, Listed and Unlisted References, Interviews, National Agency Checks, Local Agency Checks, and an Interview of the individual who requires the clearance. The investigation provides the adjudicator with actionable information. In the case of an Army clearance for example, the completed investigation is sent to the Department of Defense (DoD, Central Adjudication Facility (CAF), Ft Meade, MD, who reviews the case in accordance with National Adjudicative Guidelines, and makes a security clearance determination. My point in including this process is this; one must realize it is the CAF or requester, not OPM, who grants clearances. So what are some of the adjudicative guidelines that are looked at by trained adjudicators? Here are but a few; Allegiance to the U.S., Foreign Influence, Foreign Preference, Sexual Behavior, Personal Conduct, Financial Considerations, Alcohol Consumption, Drug Involvement, Emotional, Mental, and Personality Disorders, Criminal Conduct, Security Violations, Outside Activities, and Misuse of Information Technology Systems. Some considerations an adjudicator might make are; The nature, extent, and seriousness of the conduct, The circumstances surrounding the conduct, to include knowledgeable participation, the frequency and timeframe of the conduct, the individual's age and maturity at the time of the conduct, was the conduct voluntary, the presence of absence of rehabilitation and other permanent behavioral changes, the motivation for the conduct, the potential for pressure, coercion, exploitation, or duress, and the likelihood of continuation or recurrence.

The investigation and adjudication of a case, is conducted by highly skilled, trained, and qualified professional individuals.

Introduction

Throughout the Reserve Component there are many stories of the Soldier/Citizen. It has been my great pleasure to have served with CW4 Oliver J. Hurt, fondly known to all as OJ. His breadth of experience is only hinted at in these pages. The honor and dedication with which he served with me and others is one of many individual efforts that makes this country the strong and unique nation that it is.

The Army is made up of three components, Active (Component 1) The Army National Guard (Component 2), and the Army Reserve (Component 3). The reserve components have changed much in the time of OJ's life and military career, from drafted strategic reserve to the current all-volunteer operational force. An individual Soldier may wind up moving through all three during a life of service, and even have breaks in time in between. Reserve Component soldiers are unique in their service as they split their lives between civilian employer and military unit. Because of the training opportunities and experiences in each, they provide a unique and reliable employee to the employer, and a mature and knowledgeable Soldier to the unit. Armies fight and win best when their Soldiers are of the people.

CW4 Oliver J Hurt's stories pull the curtain back just a little on the great mix of experiences we have all had as Reservists. That is important as so few actually serve, and so many benefit. Many fellow Americans have little knowledge or understanding of the military, may these stories, vignettes, and tales open their eyes to their neighbors.

G. Lawrence Lamb III
Colonel, Military Intelligence
United States Army Reserve

CHAPTER 1

My Journey

*"For I know the plans I have for you," declares the
LORD, "plans to prosper you and not to harm you,
plans to give you hope and a future."*

—Jeremiah 29:11

I grew up in Clay Center, Kansas, where I completed some of
my elementary education, middle school, and some high school.
My mother was an elementary school teacher for forty years, and we
had moved to Junction City, Kansas, and back on two occasions as
she had obtained a teaching job there each time. We were living in
Junction City when I graduated from high school. I enjoyed growing
up in Clay Center, a mostly farm community. I was twelve years old
when I got my first job there. I worked part-time after school at the
local Wards sporting goods store and obtained a passion for knives
working there. I still have a collection of high-end knives I've collected over the years. I was paid fifty cents an hour at the sporting
goods store and bought my first knife there, a banana knife. I carried
it about a week when it mysteriously disappeared. I liked that knife,
and I enjoyed playing mumblety-peg at church camp with my friend
Bobby George, currently a retired minister. We both became pretty

good at it. When I received my next paycheck, I bought another. Banana knives were fun to play with as they have a longer blade than a normal pocketknife. At my fifty-cents-an-hour wage, paying six dollars for a knife took me over twelve hours to earn, plus tax. My second knife also disappeared. I later learned my mother had confiscated them both, thinking I would get in trouble with them. To this day, I still do not know what her thought process on this was. I was not a hooligan. As a young boy, I was always coming up with unique ways, in my opinion, to make pocket money. My father was a railroad worker, who brought home some metal packing strips one evening. He was going to use them for some project or other. The metal strip was about a half-inch wide, with a small punched hole an inch apart down the center of the strip. I learned that if you bent the metal strip every third hole, bent it in half, placed it in your mouth with one hole on top and one on the bottom, and blow—*bada bing*—you had a whistle, a loud one that you could hear for a little more than a city block. So I get a very bright idea. Make hundreds of these whistles, take them to school, and sell for twenty-five cents each. I toiled for several days until I thought I had made enough. I placed them neatly in a paper bag to take to school to sell the following day. Maybe make enough to buy a new bicycle. Overnight, they mysteriously disappeared. My mother had again done some midnight reconnaissance and confiscated them—again so I would not get in trouble. I have never figured that out. So ended my whistle business. When I was approximately fourteen years old, I got a job as a soda jerk, at Elliott's Rexall Drug Store, at fifty cents an hour. I was soon given a raise to seventy-five cents an hour and was allowed to wait on customers in the store. I did enjoy making sodas. In fact, I got damn good at it. Chocolate Cokes, lime aides of all flavors, malts, and shakes of all flavors. I personally liked root beer malts.

My childhood was a happy one. Some of my best memories are of growing up in this small town. I grew up in a loving and very strict Christian home, one filled with love but knowing there were some things our family could not afford. But we always had what we needed, and that was enough. We attended church regularly every Sunday morning including Sunday school, every Sunday evening for evening service, and every Wednesday evening for weekly service. Wesleyan Methodist Services were long and sometimes loud to make a point by the preacher. They were sometimes what you might call fire and brimstone services. Our church had strict rules one should live by. I should mention here that my grandfather was a lay minister. I have an uncle who spent fifty years behind the United Methodist Pulpit, a cousin whose spouse is a pastor, and two high school friends who are now retired ministers. My wife also has several ministers on her side of the family. I figure the more people I have pray for me, I feel the good Lord may take kindly to me. When I was about eight or nine, my Sunday school teacher gave each of us a Bible verse to learn. Mine was John 3:16. I was a typical eight-year-old more interested in playing baseball in the evenings than learning a Bible verse. Well, Sunday school rolls around, and I have to recite my Bible verse I did not learn. When I could not recite it, the Sunday school teacher spanked me in front of the other children. It was a very humiliating experience for an eight- or nine-year-old and one I have not forgotten. I learned the verse later and recited it on another Sunday. Not because of being punished for not learning the verse but because I said I would learn it. I am still that way to this day. If I say I'm going to do something; take it to the bank. A handshake with me is like obtaining my signature. My word is my bond. When I was old enough, I stopped attending Sunday school altogether and have not done so to this day. Sunday school should be a learning experience, not one of punishment if you don't learn. John 3:16 I think is one of the most powerful verses in the Bible. Put simply, if you believe in God, you will not perish. This same verse is put another way in Romans 10:9, which says: If you declare with your mouth, "Jesus is Lord," and believe in your heart God raised him from the dead, you will be saved." As I got older and involved in combat, Psalms 91 became my second favorite. Psalms 91 was used extensively during World War II by Military Chaplains. Back on point, that's not to say there was no fun involved attending church service. Boys will be boys.

I Become a Prankster

Church services became an experiment of BBs rolling upon a wooden floor, small paper-airplane flying, playing tic-tac-toe and hangman with my friend, and other assorted mischievous events. I became pretty good at making cap gun bombs. In the late fifties, early sixties, the Lone Ranger's, Gene Autry's, and Roy Rogers's cowboy shows were very popular. Roy Rogers, the Lone Ranger, and later Gene Autry came out with cap pistols. Caps came on rolled paper that, at intervals of approximately an inch, had a small patch of enclosed gun powder. When this roll of cap paper was inserted in the toy revolver, you pulled the trigger, and the hammer struck the cap filled with the small amount of gun powder, making a popping noise. It was pretty big in those days. I made cap bombs from them. I took the roll of caps and cut or tore the caps so they became individual charges. I then wrapped them around BBs and *bada bing*, you got a cap bomb when thrown. I never threw them in a church service but had fun throwing them after service. Somehow, I was never caught, which was as much fun as my church shenanigans. I have a feeling they knew who was sneaking up behind them and throwing them at their feet.

Every August of every year, our church, the Wesleyan Methodist, along with other county churches, held a good-sized revival meeting in Miltonvale, Kansas. It was held at a two-year college (now defunct) campus that was empty during summer months. It was a three-day meeting church members looked forward to. They no longer have these now. They held meetings all day long, with meals served. My grandmother always volunteered as a cook for large amounts of people during these three days at noon meal. The revival meetings were held in the evenings in a large building that had no air-conditioning or ceiling fans. The sides of the building were such that they could be raised, therefore allowing air to flow through on hot summer nights. It was not uncommon to have over one hundred fifty parishioners in attendance. When I was about 10, my friend and I were allowed to play catch outside under property lights. That particular night, we had both brought our pea shooters. Pea shooters consisted of a plastic straw and came with a bag of small peas that one shot by blowing the peas through the straws. We had each paid fifteen cents for them at the local Woolworths store, now no longer in business. Woolworths was a five-and-dime similar to a general store. On the particular night in question, we had shot our bag of peas at each other and ran out of ammunition fairly quickly. We then got the bright idea to use toilet paper from the nearby men's room, wet a small piece in a nearby drinking fountain, and shoot these at each other through the straws. Oh, oh. Then it hit us, why not sneak up in the back of the revival meeting and, from the outside, shoot these homemade spitballs for body count, then run, and hide in the dark. We made several of these shots that hit their mark, when it progressed to not using the straws to shoot the spitballs, to small wads of wet toilet paper wadded up, then thrown. They were pretty wet and deadly on target. We had hit our targets several times, when one of the men inside had had enough of our shenanigans and came outside to find the culprits. When we scalawags noticed this, we took off in the dark like Olympic track stars. We were never caught, but the guy did stop the spitball bombardment. Bless his heart.

My uncle, Philip Beals, sixteen years my senior, also attended the Wesleyan Methodist Church. When I was in high school, approximately in 1963, my uncle went to see a movie at the local theater one evening. When exiting the theater that particular summer evening, he was observed coming out of the movie by one of the church elders. Movies, makeup, nylon stockings, and so forth were prohibited by church dogma. The day after, a Saturday, my uncle—who also worked in the local drug store—and I were at work. At midmorning, four church elders walked into the store and asked to speak with my uncle. A meeting between them was held in a corner of the store, lasting about fifteen minutes. My uncle had been kicked out of the church for going to a movie. This affected me greatly as I felt going to a movie was certainly not a sin, and if it was such a sin, wasn't a church supposed to accept "sinners"? I was fifteen years old. I never attended another church service again until after I was married, some fifteen years later. Not because I did not believe in God but I felt the man-made church dogma was way out of place and was also very antiquated. Show me in the Bible where it says going to a movie is a sin. My uncle, who is a God-fearing man, did not deserve the wrath of misguided hypocritical church elders. My uncle never lost his faith however and never stopped attending church. He just began attending a church in which he was made welcome. I realize now that God never abandoned me, even though I did not attend church. There is a word in the Bible, Emanuel, meaning God is with us or God indwells us. He is always there, even though I did not attend church; I know he was there with me. Let me say at this point, that going to Church does not make you a better person. Just as staying away from church will not make you a better person. What going to Church will do, is show you how to become a better person. Some people never learn this lesson and become judgmental. Becoming a better person is up to you. I recently came across the following point: A common misunderstanding about church is that it should some-how make you a better person. It is not the act of going to church, but the encounter with God and others that changes your life for the better. Christians can sometimes be seen to be hypocrites more easily than someone who does not profess any beliefs at all, because Christian standards are defined in the Bible, whereas personal stan-dards can be changed to fit circumstances or can simply be unknown to others. The bottom line is, that all humans are hypocrites because we all fail to consistently live up to any standards of behavior that are defined. I'll stop my point here.

My uncle Phil was also a member of the Kansas Army National Guard (KANG) prior to going active duty. Every year starting from when I can remember, the KANG would march in formation every Memorial Day from the National Guard Center to the local ceme-tery, a distance of about five miles, and then march back. It was a pretty big deal for small-town folks and an even bigger deal for a young boy of 10 to see all those Army folks, walking in their khaki uniforms with rifles shouldered through the cemetery. Our family always gathered around the grave of my older brother, who died one day after birth. This is where we watched the KANG march by. My mother is also now located in this spot. It was probably at that time I became interested in going into the military, that and watching military shows on TV.

CHAPTER 2

Experiences

I experienced many things while growing up in a rural farm community, too many to write about. I will, however, mention a few.

The Outhouse

An outhouse, also known as a privy, could be one or two holes, sometimes even more. The outhouse is a small structure, separate from the main house for obvious reasons. The outhouse was basically a latrine pit with a small closet built on top of it.

When we first moved to Clay Center, Kansas, I was prefirst grade. However, remember the two-holer well. I was small, and it was a chore to use the restroom for a kid as small as I was. Going to the bathroom in the dead of winter was also a chore. We moved to a home that had indoor plumbing when I was in the first grade. I won't say too much about the outhouse but will relay a story to you.

The Spit and Whittle Club

When I was approximately twelve years of age, I drove with my family to visit our cousins in Wendell, Idaho. My uncle Roscoe, my grandmother's brother, owned a small Phillips 66 service station in Wendell, a small town in Idaho, where everyone knew everyone. My uncle had a very good sense of humor. As an example, there was a group of elderly men who liked to congregate on a wooden bench in his station, sit around a warm stove in winter, and tell war stories, smoke, drink coffee, and litter his floor with cigarette butts. My uncle Roscoe called these men the Spit and Whittle Club. On one occasion, my uncle painted this wooden bench gray, thinking it may discourage the Spit and Whittle Club from loitering too long. The following day, after painting, here they came. I think my uncle also enjoyed talking with them. He could also tell some whoppers (stories to you city folk). When the new paint did not discourage the group, he then hammered ten penny nails into the bottom of the wood, each placed an inch apart, so that the whole bench was nailed. Only the very tip of the nail poked through the top of the bench where one sit, and once seated, you could not feel them there. Then my uncle wired each nail underneath the bench to an electrical switch and painted over the top of the nails so no silver nail tips could be seen while sitting. Then one day when all the Spit and Whittle Club were seated, chewing the fat (talking to you city folk), my uncle flipped the switch, putting electric current to each of the nails. I wish I could have seen them all get up. And get up they did, spilling coffee all over the floor. It had to have been a sight to see.

Mad Mom

OK, back to the point of my story. The service station did not have indoor plumbing and had a two-holer outhouse. Just as we arrived in town on this trip, it was approximately in 1960, we stopped to use the outhouse at my uncle's service station in our 1958 four-door Ford. My mother needed to use the facilities in the worst way, so we stopped there first, as it was just inside the city limits. My mother asked directions to the outhouse, and my uncle said it was just out the back door. After my mother had been gone just long enough, my uncle looked over at my father, sister, and I and said watch this. Apparently, my uncle had rigged up a speaker under the seat of the outhouse. He picked up what looked like an old radio microphone and said, "Hey, lady, would you mind moving over to the next hole? We're trying to work down here." Well, a very short time later, my mother came running back into the service station, red-faced, and inquired of my uncle as to why he did not tell her about the workmen before she went to the outhouse. When we let her in on the joke, goodness gracious, she became madder than a wet hen in a two-story henhouse. After she calmed down, she saw the humor in the whole situation and laughed at herself. I will not forget this trip. I had several adventures with my cousins. I even tasted sulphur water from a sulphur water spring. Another story, but let me tell you about sulphur water. It's good but be prepared—hello. It's odiferous to say the least, smells like rotten eggs.

Livestock Auctions

I enjoyed going to the local livestock auction as a boy because I liked the way the auctioneer could talk so fast, that and I liked being around the local cowboys and their stories.

On one occasion, my friend Tim Ramsey and I were selected by one of the attending veterinarians to help him hold down an old sow so as to give the sow, who was scheduled for auction, a few shots. We were to hold the sow down in the pen, so the veterinarian could administer the shots. Well, that darn pig wasn't going to stay down, let alone be manhandled by a couple of teen boys. The pig turned out stronger than us, and more help had to be brought in. One of the men who volunteered for the job was an Arnold Schwarzenegger type who basically held that ornery pig down by himself. A real cowboy type. I was impressed and fondly look back on this incident. I still enjoy going to a good livestock auction, not to buy anything but now mainly for the memories and to hear the auctioneer.

The Lawn-Mowing Incident

My best friend when I was growing up in Clay Center was Tim Ramsey. Tim's father was a well-known local football coach who had passed away from surgery complications, prior to my meeting Tim. Tim's mother Eileen was a Registered Nurse who was a stay-at-home mom for Tim, his sister Mary, and their older brother Mike. Eileen was like a second mother to me, as I was over to their home as much as I was mine. Mike is now a retired Army Officer who was a combat helicopter pilot in Vietnam and an author. If you like reading about flying helicopters in combat, you'll love his book, *Memoirs of a Rotor Head*, by Patrick Ramsey. Mike to his friends. When Mike was still in high school, he enjoyed siccing the family dog, Pup, on me. I think Pup also liked to pick on me. He was a consternation and much annoying. When Ole Pup finally passed away, I was not broken up over it. Mary, I understand, is currently a children's book author, and Tim is a retired contractor. Tim and I had a lawn-mowing business in the summer of 1962 for pocket money. On one particular day, we were mowing a lawn that had pretty high grass. The elderly lady who hired us was unable to mow the lawn herself. We took turns mowing the lawn as it was a two-person job. During my turn and halfway through the job, I struck something in the grass and, as I did so, looked over at Tim who had immediately fell to the ground. I thought he was joking at first because we were always playing pranks on each other. When I realized the opposite, I ran over to him and observed I had apparently struck a small piece of wire I had not seen hidden in the grass, which had gone completely through his knee. Old Doc McVay's office was half a block away, and I helped Tim hobble to his office. I then ran the seven blocks back to Tim's home to inform his mother. I would have gotten a medal for that run had it been a competition. Tim's mother and I walked at Olympic pace back to the doctor's office and learned the wire had been removed, and Tim was all right. The wire had a curve in the middle of it. Because of this curve, it had missed Tim's kneecap and had gone through between the kneecap and knee joint. We were lucky that day. We didn't mow lawns for a while after that, but the next summer, we were back in business.

Doc McVay

One day in shop class—I believe I was in the eighth grade—while working with metal, a small sliver of metal flew into my right eye. My mother was called to the school, and I was immediately taken to Ole Doc McVay. Now Ole Doc was called such because at the time, he was probably in his eighties, and both his hands shook, but he was still in practice. When you are an eighth grader, eighty years old is ancient. It's not so ancient to me anymore. Everyone in town knew Ole Doc. He was an old country doctor who knew his business. I was taken back into an exam room by his nurse. Ole Doc walked in and said, "OK, what we got here?" I thought to myself that wasn't it obvious I had something in my eye? I didn't say anything. I was hurt and wanted the darn thing out. He took a look, turned around, and grabbed a long-handled cotton swab off a table behind him. When I realized he was going to take the sliver of metal out with that thing, shaky hands and all, I became a bit concerned. When Ole Doc got about an inch from my eye, his hand stopped shaking and became very still and straight. He got that darn sliver out, and as his hand came back from my face, his hand began shaking again. I was just glad I didn't get a shot of some kind. I still hate to get shots—needles, yuck.

I Get My First Ticket

Every year, Lynn, Kansas, has a fair called Lynn's Picnic. The city of Lynn was a driving distance from Clay Center, and on this particular day, I went to Lynn's Picnic with high school friends. Lynn had quite a rodeo along with various carnival rides at the time. While there, I observed the Pharmacist Dick Dietrick (now deceased) I worked with at the local drug store. Very intoxicated, he could hardly stand or walk and was leaving to drive home. I offered to drive him home, and he accepted as he had the good sense to know he was too intoxicated to drive. I was seventeen years old. It was just after midnight when we arrived back in Clay Center. At the time, I also worked part-time at the local Phillips 66 Service Station that had been burglarized in the recent past. We were driving past the service station when I got the bright idea to stop and check doors and windows. I was a naive kid back in those days and thought I would be doing a good thing for the business. All doors and windows were OK, and I got back in Dick's car to drive him home. As I started to drive off, I was stopped by the local police officer who had apparently observed me check the service station. After explaining to him what I was doing, along with driving Dick home, the officer searched the car. Looking back, he must have thought I had been trying to break in when he stopped the car. I personally knew this particular officer, as he went to our church, and was a good friend of my father's. He also knew me as a good kid, and I thought knew I was not there to cause trouble. I had nothing to be concerned about as I had done nothing wrong other than do a good deed by driving Dick home and had also just checked a building. During the search of the car, the officer found and confiscated a half bottle of vodka from under the driver's seat. I had no idea it was there. Apparently, Dick had placed the bottle there in Lynn. I was issued an open-bottle ticket. The officer knew the bottle was not mine. It was not my car, and I did not even drink. I tried to explain to him, and he even observed how intoxicated Dick was. He issued the ticket anyway. Dick later appeared in court for me, explained to the judge what had happened, and took full responsibility for the incident. Dick paid a fifty-dollar fine on my behalf. I often look back on this incident and wonder why I was issued the ticket. Clay Center is a small town. The officer knew me and my family and that the bottle was not mine, that I was driving a drunk home, and may have even saved the life of Dick and/ or someone else. It was a dirty thing to do, was beyond wrong, and has remained on my record since. This is the only such blemish on my record. I often thought of this incident when, as a police officer myself, I stopped cars many times for similar charges. I always made sure of the circumstances surrounding any arrest I made and made no hasty judgments. I felt I was always fair.

CHAPTER 3

Family

Hunting with My Grandfather

One Saturday afternoon, my grandfather, my uncle Phil, my uncle Bill Shields, and I went rabbit hunting in my grandfather's 1957 Ford. It was a sleek four-door hard-top car with a pretty good-sized V8 engine. I recall I was sitting in the seat behind my uncle Phil, who was driving, my uncle Bill in the passenger seat, and my grandfather beside me in the back behind the passenger seat. On one of the county dirt roads we were driving on, near Broughton, Kansas, my grandfather spotted a rabbit a fair distance across the field we were driving by. We were going about thirty miles an hour down a county dirt road, and as I looked out the open window, I saw the rabbit high tailing it in the opposite direction we were traveling. My uncle Phil began to slow the car, and my grandfather shot that darn rabbit on the move with one shot. After we stopped hunting that day, I believe we had a catch of over seven or eight rabbits. I do not like to get my hands dirty. Never have. I watched them skin the rabbits, but I simply will not skin, clean, or strip. Too messy for me. I have a lot of stories about my grandfather, who was a hardworking and humble man. Too many stories for this book. My grandfather was a farmer before retiring and moving from the county (Clay) to the big city of

Clay Center. He had hunted for food lots of times and butchered his own meat while on the farm. After moving into the city, he took a job for the county as a road mower. I recall him not retiring until he was well past seventy and only then because he had to. My grandfather was in good physical shape and could do a knee bend on one leg when he was way past seventy. When my grandfather was a young man, he helped train Charles Eckland, the light heavyweight champion wrestler of the world in 1923. Charles Eckland was a cousin three times removed. I always enjoyed my time with my grandfather and my uncles. They could tell some good stories.

My Grandmother

Both my grandparents were highly regarded in the local Wesleyan Methodist Church. They were involved in almost all church activities. My grandmother spent a lot of time at the local parsonage as a volunteer. My grandmother was Elsie Mae Beals, née Durbin. My grandmother was a hardworking farm wife who was an excellent cook and volunteered at most church meal activity. She could cook anything and make it taste good. She was also a nurse's aide at the local hospital, which is now a museum. When I stayed overnight with my grandparents, I recall getting up in the mornings and still remember the smell of coffee, bacon, sausage, and homemade pancakes or biscuits and gravy. All cooking back in those days was done with lard and bacon fat. This is unheard of nowadays. It's a wonder we are all alive and healthy. Along with this, my grandmother had made homemade blackstrap molasses syrup and homemade maple syrup. I was not fond of blackstrap molasses, but I sure liked the maple syrup. My grandmother was a babysitter for my sister and me on occasion when our mother had school activities. We were a handful. I even had my mouth washed out with soap once for saying "gosh." I'm thankful she didn't hear me on occasion in my adult life. It would have been a soap fest. When she said my first name associated with my middle name, I knew I was in trouble. I learned a lot from my grandmother who taught me such phrases as "Oliver James, for pity sakes," "for heaven's sake," "sake's alive," "merciful heavens," "for Pete's sakes," "Land O Goshen," "goodness me," "goodness gracious," "gracious me," "heavens to Betsy," "sake's alive, really!" "heavens!" and other such phrases. I have used them myself on occasion. I loved my grandmother very much. She was a wonderful Christian lady who sat a great example for her grandchildren.

Sandwich Spread

There was a sandwich spread I liked real well at my grandparents', and I always put extra on my sandwiches. It was kept on the second shelf of the refrigerator, at just my level. One summer, my grandfather butchered a hog, and my grandmother was busy in the kitchen preparing the meat for storage. My grandmother was a person who also liked to can fruits and vegetables. Their cellar was full of canned food. On this particular day, I observed my grandmother grinding on an old silver table grinder what looked like brain matter. I was about 10 years old. Out of curiosity, I asked her what she was making. Her response was that she was making that sandwich spread I liked so much out of the pig's brain. Mercy sakes, I never had another sandwich made from that spread again. Nothing went to waste after butchering. By the way, I don't eat beef tongue either. Let me say at this point that I have had my share of specialty food— chocolate-covered ants, rattlesnake. I even had a bunch of Non Commissioned Officers (NCOs) take me out for dinner in Korea in 1968 in celebration of my becoming a dog handler. It wasn't until halfway through the meal that I found out what type of cuisine I was being served. I'll let you figure that one out. But I absolutely draw the line at eating brains and Menudo or Tripe.

My grandmother's ancestry has been traced back to the pilgrim days. We always knew that in our past somewhere, we were of the Catholic faith until my grandfather's entry into our family. My uncle Phil traced this back to our several great-grandmothers. Here's how the story goes.

There was young lady named Honora O'Flynn, born in 1682 in Kerry, Ireland, and died in 1740 in Carrol County, Maryland. Honora was an Irish princess, according to Ancestry.com, who was said to be a beautiful and vivacious girl and who was kidnapped in Ireland along with ten other girls and brought to Maryland by a sea captain for barter. She was fourteen years of age. She was brought to America where she was sold for tobacco and later married our great-grandfather, who was fifty-four years of age at the time. Forty years difference. I can't imagine. Honora was said to be Catholic, and it was through this that the Catholic faith appears in our family line. I look back at this story and think what the parents of these kidnapped girls went through. I put this story in this book to explain only some of our family history, which is part of me.

I Shoot Myself (It's Not Pleasant)

I enjoyed weapons. Still do. Most in my family were hunters, and as a boy, I sometimes went hunting rabbits with them as mentioned. While in high school, I worked at a Rexall Drug Store owned by Loren Elliott. I was hired as a soda jerk, and I became quite good at mixing and making sodas. The pharmacist Dick Dietrick lived on a farm with his parents, just south of town in the county. Dick was a bachelor who for some reason took a liking to an immature high school kid. Dick would sometimes take me home with him for an afternoon on the farm, and I enjoyed talking with him and his parents. Dick's father, a traditional farmer, had a small collection of antique shotguns I enjoyed looking at. Prior to Dick becoming a pharmacist in Clay Center, he worked in a pharmacy in Wichita, Kansas. Dick had two pistols I was fond of: an Italian llama pistol and a .22-caliber six-shot Colt Fanner 50 type. The story goes that after work one evening in Wichita, Dick walked around the corner of the pharmacy to a local pool hall. The pharmacy was located in downtown Wichita, in what you would call the red light district. (I later patrolled this area as a police officer.) In the pool hall was a local gangster named George Poulos. Poulos had spent time in prison for bombing an aircraft at the local airport, a known seedy character. He had an arrest history for gambling, burglary, assault, racketeering, larceny, arson, among other felonies. He was one that could make a call to Las Vegas, Nevada, and have large sums of money sent him as needed. George was tough and dangerous but also had a good side. But only when he wanted. On the night, Dick saw him playing pool; a bet was made on the outcome of the pool game. George insisted that Dick bet against him for some reason. You simply did not argue with George, who also had an entourage of nefarious characters with him at that time. They were what you would call "bad asses," known to hurt folks as necessary. George lost, making Dick the winner of the bet. Instead of paying the bet off in cash, George gave Dick the two weapons I just described for winning the bet. On one of my visits to his farm, I had gotten Dick's permission to take the Colt out to hunt rabbits. It was a winter day, and I was dressed warmly and wearing leather driving gloves. I saw a cottontail rabbit jump out in front of me approximately fifteen feet off and stop. It looked at me with one of those deer-in-the-headlights look. I pulled the Colt very, very slowly out of the holster I was wearing and, as I did so, pulled back very slowly on the hammer so as not to make noise and scare that darn rabbit off. That was a mistake. The seam of my driving glove caught the trigger as I pulled out the weapon. *Bang*. George Poulos had filed the trigger pull so that if you simply breathed on the trigger, it fired. And it did. When I heard the shot go off before I had aimed, I knew I had shot myself. I did not feel it and had no pain. I was not happy. I pulled down my jeans and saw a small trickle of blood on my right leg, just above my right knee. I walked calmly back to the house and informed Dick of what happened. Dick naturally became pale and rushed me back to town to Ole Doc McVay. Long story short, the bullet, a .22-caliber long, was lodged one-fourth inch above my right kneecap and was, at the time, inoperable due to the proximity inside to the knee. The bullet is still in my knee, and I sometimes get checked for lead poisoning as the bullet is made of lead. I was seventeen years old. It has never bothered me and, over the years, never affected my daily three-to-five-mile runs while in the military.

I mention this incident as I later meet George Poulis professionally, as later explained in this book.

My Mother

My mother, Eva Lorene Hurt, née Beals, was a rural school teacher who taught me from the first to third grades in a one-room schoolhouse in Industry, Kansas. Mom passed away a few years back and is sorely missed. My mother's teaching salary and my father's Rock Island Railroad income just made do however. I know sometimes their income was not enough to cover daily family living expenses. We always had what we needed, and that was enough.

Mom loved teaching and loved seeing children learn. I began school in a one-room country schoolhouse in Industry, Kansas. The first through third grades were divided by a sliding curtain in the middle of the room, separating the fourth through eighth grades. At the beginning of each school day, all children recited the Pledge of Allegiance and then had a morning prayer. I recall my second-grade field trip to Abilene, Kansas, in the fall of 1956. Abilene, Kansas, is the birthplace of our thirty-fourth president, Dwight Eisenhower. Eisenhower was in Abilene on that fall day for a parade in his honor. Mami, the first lady, was on a second-story balcony platform of a local hotel as Eisenhower, known as Ike, was walking along the street with his secret service detail, shaking hands. As Ike walked past me, a kid of eight, he shook my hand as he walked by. It was a quick handshake but made a lasting impression on me. At the time, I was too young to know the significance of this. We had a few field trips, such as a train-ride trip one year, but none compared to the Abilene trip. My mother was a good teacher who genuinely cared for her students. She was a loving mother who loved all her children, grandchildren, and great-grandchildren. She set an example for all who knew her.

I Learn Several Lessons in One

It was a big deal to transfer from the third to fourth grade in that old country school. One got to sit on the other side of the curtain. Don't ask why it was a big deal. But when you got transferred, it was. Back on point. While in the fourth grade, my teacher was Ole Mrs. Lewis I don't recall her first name now, but she was a good teacher. One of the subjects taught at that time was climate, as part of science class. We were given the assignment of reading the climate chapter in our science books. Did I say I was not a good student? I wasn't and enjoyed recess more than going to class. I didn't read the assignment, and sure enough, I was called on the following day to give a description of what climate was by Ole Mrs. Lewis. I'm sure Ole Mrs. Lewis was in her thirties, but to a kid in the fourth grade, that's ancient. Anyway, I will never forget my answer to this day. Don't ask how I came up with it because I have no idea. I said climate was a small worm that liked to stay in the cracks of sidewalks. What? I don't know why I said it. It's the first thing that came to my mind. Wrong of course but, looking back, comical. Not only did I have to read the chapter about climate but had to write, "I will not lie" one hundred times. My teachers had their hands full with me. I was not ignorant. I was just a person you had to watch constantly. Here is the lesson: never lie, cheat, or steal nor tolerate anyone who does. It's just plain good advice.

My Father

My father, Irvin Oliver Hurt, known as Slim to his co-workers, was six-foot-three-inches tall and maybe weighed one hundred seventy pounds while working for the Rock Island. My father is ninety-three at the time of this writing. My father grew up an orphan who was fostered out to a farm family in Miltonvale, Kansas, until he was nineteen years of age. He later learned his birth name was Irvin Oliver Omer Fitch Hurt. Apparently, his father, James Hurt, was an International Order of Odd Fellows (IOOF) club member.

Dad was a "gandy dancer." My uncle Phil worked a year on the Rock Island Railroad on the same crew as my father. He described the work as very hard and labor intensive. My father still talks of his days as a railroader on the old Rock Island line. He can still tell some good stories. Whoopers in fact. The railroad used to soak its ties in creosote so weather would not rot them out. When a railroad spike is driven into it, it is very difficult to pull out. A metal plate was used, which was placed under the rail, and four spikes were driven into the tie through this plate. One on each corner of the plate to hold it in place. The term used for this was called tamping ties. When a gandy is used, sometimes you had to jump on the gandy rod to pull it out. Those working with gandies became known as gandy dancers. My uncle recalls that winter they were working in Cuba, Kansas. It was very cold, and the crew foreman said they could get into the railroad station to warm up if the road from Clifton onto Cuba was finished. There was no way they could do that, but they gave it the old college try and at least got warmed up in the process. My uncle Phil relayed to me that he experienced many things while working for the Rock Island. Many stories could be told about working on a track crew. Here's one. This is a story about a man known as Chief because he was an Indian. Chief rolled his own cigarettes, and he took his own sweet time in doing so. The track crew weren't supposed to have a break, but Chief would lean on his shovel and roll a cigarette and create his own break. He would take at least five minutes to smoke it while leaning on his shovel.

At the time of this particular story, the track crew was working in the Cuba, Kansas, area. Cuba was full of hardworking people, mostly of German descent. The railroad depot was about the only place for the mail to be delivered. Outside the depot was a pole for the depot station agent to hang the mail sack on. The train would not stop, but it was moving slow enough for the engineer to grab the sack of mail without stopping. One morning as the track crew drove up to the depot, there was a man hanging from the mail pole. Chief had become depressed, and it was thought that the only thing he could think of was to end his life by hanging.

My Sister and Brother, Angela Nelson, née Hurt, a year younger than I, who now has three grown children of her own, grandchildren, and great-grandchildren. I have one brother, Charles Hurt, who has one daughter and three grandchildren. Chuck is sixteen years my junior and resides in Topeka, Kansas. I am proud of all of them, and I love them all.

CHAPTER 4

Growing Up

I learned a lot from watching TV. It was not uncommon for my father and me to watch TV together in the evenings on our twenty-three-inch black-and-white TV in the midfifties and early sixties. It was pretty stylish back in the late fifties and early sixties to have a TV. There were only three to four channels you could get back then, but they were packed full of movies and Western shows I liked. My father probably watched TV with me not only because he liked to watch movies but because I also think watching TV took his mind off his workday. We watched a lot of old musicals and Western and military movies. I still like movies with Barbara Stanwyck, Bette Davis, Marlene Dietrick, Claudette Colbert, Greta Garbo, Deanna Durbin, etc. And I just have to mention Tennessee Ernie Ford, Jimmy Stewart, James Cagney, Clark Gable, Cary Grant, etc. My favorite TV show was *Sky King*. *Sky King* was a TV series that lasted thirty minutes per episode, running from approximately 1951 through 1959. I always tried not to miss a Saturday morning episode. *Sky King* flew a fabric-winged Cessna 210 named *Songbird* with his niece Penny. They lived on a ranch in Arizona and flew to rescue lost hikers, investigate criminals, and the occasional spy. I would always say at the time that someday I would like to fly airplanes. The *Whirlybirds*. The *Whirlybirds* was a TV series that lasted thirty minutes per episode from approximately

1957 through 1960. Chuck Martin and Pete Moore were fictional characters that ran a helicopter charter company called Whirlybirds Inc. They flew a Bell 47G and 47J, the same type rotor used in the old *M*A*S*H* (Mobile Army Surgical Hospital) TV series. Martin and Moore sold their services to various clients that made up the show. I always enjoyed any aviation show and thought that maybe, just maybe, I would also someday learn to fly a helicopter. *Combat*. *Combat* was a TV series that ran from approximately 1962 to 1967. It was a thirty-minute show about a squad of US soldiers fighting Germans in France in World War II, starring Vic Morrow, who was later killed in a helicopter accident, filming an episode of "Twilight Zone." I always liked the *Combat* series and thought that one day I would get a chance to serve in the military.

The *Lone Ranger* is a thirty minute TV series starring Clayton Moore as the Lone Ranger and Jay Silverheels as Tonto. The show was a typical Western one that was entertaining.

Gunsmoke is another thirty-minute Western TV series starring James Arness as Matt Dillon, the marshall of Dodge City, Kansas. His sidekick Chester Goode was played by Dennis Weaver, and there were Amanda Blake as Miss Kitty, the saloon keeper, and, of course, Milburn Stone as Doc. Most people don't know that Dennis Weaver was a naval aviator prior to his acting career. The *Flying Tigers*. The *Flying Tigers* was 1952 movie about a group of real aviators prior to World War II, starring John Wayne as commander of a squadron of P-40 pilots. The plot was about aerial combat over China. In real life. The *Flying Tigers* were not sanctioned by the US as the US had not yet entered the war at the time of their inception.

I mention these shows in particular as they became significant to me later in life, as I will explain later in this book.

I graduated high school in Junction City, Kansas, in May 1966, and after high school, I attended the Salt City Business College (now a defunct college), Hutchinson, Kansas. At the time, I was interested in becoming a computer programmer and felt a business college was where I needed to be. I enrolled in many courses: accounting, typing, bookkeeping, penmanship, and other unrecalled business-related courses. My only regret at Salt City was not taking shorthand.

Shorthand would have served me well later in life where much note taking became necessary writing reports and surveillance notes. My career interest changed as time went on, from computers to law enforcement. I had influences inching me toward a law enforcement career. I'll explain later in this book. I became a very fast typist on a manual typewriter, eighty words a minute with three mistakes per page on average. Pretty good I always felt, which served me well later in life writing investigative reports on a computer. One particular day in typing class, I became frustrated at my typing speed and number of mistakes and ripped the paper out of the machine, made a ball of the paper, and then made a perfect basket in the wastepaper bucket. Proud of myself for making the basket until unfortunately for me, the typing teacher saw this and kicked me out of her class for the hour. I was a proud kid and felt this punitive action wrong. I immediately walked into the administration office and withdrew from this college. I walked out and never looked back. Once I make a decision, it is hard to change my mind, unless you have a pretty good argument in the opposite direction. The school administration warned that I would shortly receive a draft notice if I dropped out. I decided it was time to join the military anyway and, about two weeks later, received a draft notice. I reported to the local draft board in Junction City, Kansas, in May 1968. I had just turned twenty.

CHAPTER 5

My Active-Duty Military Service

Si vis pacem, para bellum. (You want peace, then prepare for war.)

I joined the army on May 13, 1968. I did so in Kansas City, Missouri, after receiving a draft notice in the mail. In fact, my draft notice was in my rear pocket when I raised my right hand and swore to defend the constitution against all enemies, foreign and domestic. I was interested in law enforcement and wanted to make sure I got into the military police. I wanted experience, and I wanted a change. The Vietnam War was in full swing at that time, and I felt that I would probably go to Vietnam. I was also interested in aviation and thought maybe of becoming a door gunner. Fortunately for me, I did not go in that direction. The life expectancy of a helicopter door gunner in Vietnam was very short.

Draft Dodgers

At the time I joined the Army, there were some college-age males who thought it was to their selfish benefit (another way to say coward) to burn their draft cards and not serve. However, there were men who remained loyal to their country. Brave men who fought and did their duty when it was popular not to. Better men than draft dodgers and draft card burners. But that is the way it is in all conflicts. There will always be those individuals who say they stand behind their beliefs and principles but, in actuality, are cowards and hide behind an ideology, who do nothing for the freedoms given them by better men than they are. That said, conscientious objectors with religious ideology did serve their county well during World War II, as medics, some earning Bronze Star Medals and Purple Hearts and even the Medal of Honor for their bravery. What I refer to are those individuals who are actually cowards and hide behind an ideology.

The Long Bus Ride

When I received my draft notice, the local draft board arranged a Greyhound bus trip (one-way) to the Kansas City, Missouri, Military Entrance Program Station (MEPS). I thought I was going to go back home after processing and be issued a bus ticket back after my physical. I thought I would have a few days. I was not told otherwise. Boy, was I wrong. It is approximately three hours from Junction City to Kansas City by bus, and I had a front-row seat on a mostly empty bus. I recall talking to the bus driver all the way there. He was probably glad when we got to my destination. I was put up for a one-night stay at a local hotel and the next day reported for a physical. Lots of people, long lines, basic shots, and a battery of written tests. After my physical, and I might add, there were things done to me that I felt had no place in a physical. At least, things I had never experienced. I was stabbed with needles, poked, jabbed. And had a finger stuffed up my south end. Next came an interview with a doctor, if we felt we had something that would keep us out of the military. In my case, I have feet flatter than a pancake and felt this may be enough to keep me out. The doctor had me stand, and he looked at my flat feet. I recall his exact words: "Yup, ya got flat feet." He then stamped my papers with a big red approved stamp and yelled, "Next!" I was then given an opportunity to enlist voluntarily, instead of being drafted. I enlisted for three years in the Military Police, with a Military Occupational Specialty (MOS) 95B, with a secondary MOS of Infantry 11B. The 95B MOS has since changed to 31B. I was then placed in a waiting room with other enlistees to wait on a bus to Fort Leonard Wood, Missouri, where I was to report for basic training.

I Meet a Madman

We were put in a waiting room, which was quiet, except for the occasional chitchat of young kids trying to figure out what was in store for them at basic training. I knew no one there and was sitting by myself, quietly reflecting on the fact I was actually leaving home. After being in the waiting room for an unrecalled amount of time, all of a sudden, a madman came running in the back door and into the waiting room, yelling at the top of his lungs, startling all of us. He was dressed in white hat, brown shirt, with all sorts of shiny medals, and blue trousers, with a bright-red strip down the sides. With spit shined shoes. He had us count off one through, I believe, eleven of us. I recall having an odd number but do not recall my exact number. He then yelled that all even numbers were now in the Marine Corps. He then proceeded to march the evens to a Marine Corps bus, yelling that they were now maggots, other unmentionable comments, and belonged to him. Boy, did I feel sorry for them. Looking back, I often think what if I had an even number. Would the madman have accepted my Army enlistment papers I had signed in my back pocket or have torn them up? I still do not have an answer for that one. Our bus finally came, and we were off to Fort Leonard Wood for training.

Basic Training

"In no other profession are the penalties for employing unprepared or untrained personnel so appalling or so irrevocable as in the military," General of the Army Douglas MacArthur.

I arrived for basic training at Fort Leonard Wood, Missouri, in May 1968. OK, training is tough, but how tough are you? You train until you think you can train no more, and then you train some more. And I thought the United States Marine Corps (USMC) Sergeant was a madman. I got more of the same, only they were Army drill sergeants. I was a skinny kid of one hundred seventeen pounds. As I write this, I still can't believe I was that skinny. I recall the first day consisting of an Army haircut—and by that, I mean all hair was cut off—and receiving our military-issued clothing, uniforms, boots, and training gear, all stuffed into a duffle bag. I could hardly lift the duffle bag and ended up dragging it (this is called the duffle shuffle) until a drill instructor saw me and made me carry it. I think it weighed as much as me or more. After receiving our military issue, we were then marched over to our assigned barracks and made to carry our duffels on our shoulders down into the barracks basement, a dirt floor. I was never so glad to get anywhere as I could hardly carry my duffle, let alone walk down another flight of stairs. We were all made to write a letter home to our parents, advising them we were safe and under military care. We were to write the exact words the drill sergeant told us to write. I did but do not recall what he said to write now, other than remembering it was not what I would have written. We also placed our civilian clothes in a box to be shipped home. Then surprise, we were then all marched up three flights of stairs to the second floor to our assigned rooms. Carrying that duffle was quite a chore. I was assigned a room with two other recruits, three to a room. Training was not easy for a skinny kid from Kansas, but I endured. We trained in hand-to-hand combat, bayonet training, ran everywhere we went, and then ran some more. Push-ups, sit-ups, one-man carries, overhand parallel bars, rifle training with the M-14-caliber rifle, close-quarter drill and ceremony, and myriad other combat arms training. Basic training was where I shaved for the first time. Every morning, we were inspected by the drill sergeant to see if we had shaved all our "peach fuzz" off. Over time, my "peach fuzz" became whiskers, and I then had to shave daily anyway. There were a couple of times some unlucky fellow would not shave close enough to suit the drill sergeant, and they would have to dry shave in front of the formation with an old rusty-looking razor, carried in the drill Sergeant's pocket. A much-used old rusty razor I'm sure. We were marched to the Mess Facility (also known as Mess Hall) daily, now known as a Dining Facility (DFAC). Entering one by one. The first time I entered a Mess was an adventure. We all had to yell our recruit enlistment numbers out as we entered. I will never forget mine. Regular Army (RA) 68003489 was assigned to me upon my enlistment. To my surprise, I was booed by several other recruits each time I yelled my number to enter Mess. I later learned, if you were drafted, one was assigned a US number. All volunteers were RA numbers. You have to realize at the time, the Vietnam War was going on, and most were drafted, and only a few of us had actually volunteered. Draftees only had to serve two years. I do recall one unlucky fellow who swatted at a gnat while in line to eat, which was observed by a drill sergeant. It was a hot day, sweaty, standing at attention to enter to eat. Usually standing for about fifteen minutes. The poor guy was chewed out and then chewed out again, and we were all made to do push-ups in the hot sun on cement because he swatted that darn gnat. We performed push-ups until the drill sergeant became tired of watching us. We all learned not to swat gnats while at the position of Attention. I should mention that you learn to eat fast. If you don't, you will not eat. You only got about ten minutes in Mess. We learned what to fill our canteens with and what not to. Our canteens were aluminum at that time, and if one put anything other than water in an aluminum canteen, you could become sick. Our helmets at that time were "steel pots" we learned to shave out of. We did so on field exercises called FTX. In our fifth week of training while on a field exercise, we were marched into a small building crowding thirty or so men into a small area until all had gone through. Gas. Gas. Gas was the sergeant's words. "Put your gas mask on, maggots." Too late, he had already thrown in gas and had each of us recite our names and rifle serial numbers before allowing us to put on our masks and exit. Coughing, chocking, spitting, some regurgitating, trying to get one's breath was the norm outside. I got through it with a healthy respect for tear gas. Shots from the medics and, of course, our individual chat with the battalion chaplain, in my case, an Army Captain.

I Meet the Battalion Chaplain

I will never forget my first meeting with an Army Chaplain, as long as I walk this earth. As I walked into his office that hot day in summer of 1968, there was the immediate unmistakable smell of cigar smoke, a half-smoked cigar still lit in an ashtray on his desk, and half-a-fifth bottle of whiskey that I observed sitting behind him on his bookshelf with all his religious reading books. Well, I was shocked to say the least. I was brought up in a very strict religious home, and ministers were not to drink alcohol or smoke any kind of tobacco product. I do not recall the interview now, only that I found him a very nice man who seemed to genuinely care and also seemed to know what kind of hellish training we were going through. I recall not mentioning that I felt training was tough, only that he knew about the training we were receiving. I'm not a complainer, and I never ever quit—ever. I am one that will go until I keel over dead before I quit. I think he asked something about my parents and family, if I was Protestant or Catholic, and what I thought about the Army so far. I answered to the positive and was released and wished good luck from him. My Chaplain's interview lasted all about ten minutes but left a lasting impression. I began to realize chaplains/ministers were people with faults just like anyone.

Good Advice

For those who have not had the pleasure of going through basic training, I will import wisdom my uncle Phil, who is described above, told me. Never volunteer for anything. Ever. If you get to choose a bunk to sleep in, choose one on the bottom in the first-quarter section or last-quarter section of the barracks. Here's why. An example of volunteering, when we were in a hot dusty field one training day, picking up rocks and dirt out of the field to make some "pretties" as the drill sergeant called them, we piled our rocks into piles in the field we were in. We were later asked for volunteers to drive the "Captain's Cadillac." I remember what my uncle had told me, never volunteer. Several hands went up. Mine didn't. Those individuals who raised their hands then became the wheel barrel drivers to pick up the piled rocks and move them to another location. It turns out the "Captain's Cadillac" was the wheel barrel. The hand raisers probably thought they were going to get out of work by driving the Company Commander, a Captain, around as his driver. Here's why you want a lower bunk. In the first-quarter or last-quarter section of the barracks, Kitchen Police (KP) duty is not fun, especially if you have to clean out a grease pit. Smelly and odiferous to say the least. You don't want to know. Anyway, at zero dark thirty in the morning hours, individuals are picked for KP or fire duty by the drill sergeants. Guess what bunks are picked. When you walk through barracks at night in the early morning hours of darkness, you don't want to stoop over to find a body to work KP. You go to the top bunks, usually at the front or back of the barracks. Fire duty, same thing. Fire duty is OK. You just walk patrol in and outside the barracks to look for fires. There is not going to be any fires, but it is a way to make the trainees work and not sleep.

The Jimmy Dean Show. I Meet My First Celebrity.

Military training is never interrupted, ever for anything. However, there are times that a TV personality was allowed to come on base and put on a show. Jimmy Dean was a popular star and singer in the midsixties, and he had a TV show called *The Jimmy Dean Show.* Sometime around June or July 1968, Jimmy Dean was allowed to entertain the troops at Fort Leonard Wood, Missouri. Word spread pretty quick that a show was going to be put on for the troops. I don't think even the celebrities who put on United Service Organization (USO) Shows know how they can positively affect the morale of troops away from home. They can only imagine what their influence can have. It is much more positive for the troops. Even singing on the Armed Forces Radio or TV to troops they do not know leaves a lasting impression on men and women stationed away from home. I remember watching the Armed Forces TV Network and recall seeing I think they were the Burgundy Street Singers on a small black-and-white TV in Korea and remember thinking it a real treat to get to even watch TV at all. Another story in this book. Back on point, so rumor mill travels fast on a training base, and we learned that Jimmy Dean was going to be on base. We all wondered if we would get to see him. We were informed just before noon mess that we would be allowed to see that evening's performance. We were told we would be marched over from our basic training area to where the show would be held. We were all looking forward to this, if but to forget about training for a little bit. It was a busy training day as I recall, and there were lots of extra people on base that day. On this particular day, we were allowed to stand in chow line individually to enter mess rather than in Company formation. That day as I walked into the dining area from the chow line, I could see all tables were full. Plates rattling, chitchat. As I was standing there looking for a place to sit for dinner, a man in civilian clothes stood up in the middle of the room and motioned me over. As I got closer, I observed there were also females in civilian clothing at the same table. Odd, but I was in a hurry to eat, get in, get out. You normally don't see civilians in a training dining room. As I approached the table, goodness gracious, it was Jimmy Dean, among other civilians, and sitting with two very pretty actresses. I do not now recall who they were but do recall seeing them on TV shows. As I sat down, they all said hi to me and were genuinely outgoing. I was extremely shy but acknowledged them and kept eating. I did not have long to eat as trainees have to down chow pretty darn quick (PDQ). You learn to eat fast while in training. I continued eating and contemplated that I was actually eating dinner with Jimmy Dean and two very pretty actresses. The actresses were arguing about who had the largest breasts as I sat down. I was getting red-faced even listening to this argument; that's how shy I was. Now to a small-town farm kid, you never discussed such things, let alone at a dinner table. All were having a good time, including Jimmy Dean who pointed out the female with the biggest breasts in his opinion. I do not remember which one he pointed out now. You'll have to cut me some slack here because I'm a typical guy and remember the breasts over who they were. That's when the dark brownish black-haired star (I think it may have been Suzanne Pleshette. I wish could recall exactly. I do recall she had one of those husky sexy voices) looked at me (I was directly across the dining table from her) and asked, "Who do you think has the biggest breasts?" Well, I was flabbergasted. Both then pumped their chests out at me for inspection. I had never been asked this before, and I certainly did not want to disappoint the one with the smallest breasts. However, in my humble opinion, both ladies' breasts were OK with me. And I might add both were well-endowed. I do not recall my exact answer now, but I think it was some diplomatic answer not wanting to offend anyone. Everyone at the table laughed at my answer and were having fun at my expense. Now, if you were to ask me that question today, I'd probably say to whip those boys out, and I'd make a thorough visual and physical inspection. And it would probably take time to make a proper determination. But back then, I was pretty shy. I don't think I have ever had a more exciting dinner. OK, I have, but that particular dinner was unforgettable. And by the way, I got to see *The Jimmy Dean Show* that night. Jimmy Dean could tell some whoppers and could swear pretty good too. During one of the commercial breaks that evening, I recall him telling a story, using some off-colored blue language when all of a sudden, the light on the camera came on indicating back on air. Without skipping a beat, he immediately went back into a monologue he had started before the break in mid-sentence of the story he was telling his audience. The audience, of course, went wild and added to the show. I remember that I enjoyed that show very much, even from a distance.

Last Day of Basic Training

We were told our training was being cut short by several days as more men were needed for replacements in Vietnam. We were to be shipped out the following morning. I remember the Company First Sergeant standing us all in formation in front of our barracks and telling us this. Then he told us that we were all going to Vietnam, and some of us would not make it back. That he was confident in our training and ability and wished all luck. As he said this, he began becoming emotional. I have never seen an Army Sergeant (SFC/E-7) do this since. It was at that moment I realized I was probably going to Vietnam and that I may actually be a casualty, but I felt prepared either way. He then read everyone's name off and where we were being sent for further training. The First Sergeant had served in combat and knew what was going to happen, what we were going to be put through. (I can now realize his feelings as I've been there.) We could only imagine at the time. Only two or three of us were going to military police training. Everyone else was going for infantry training. Those going for military police training were being sent to Fort Gordon, Georgia.

Advanced Training

I was flown from Fort Leonard Wood with others to Fort Gordon, Georgia—my first airplane ride in August 1968. Military police training consisted of learning how to work accidents, accident reconstruction, hand-to-hand fighting, .45-caliber pistol training, Uniform Code of Military Justice (UCMJ), law enforcement operations, defense tactics, report writing, and other training unrecalled. I recall the drill sergeant's name as I write this as SSG Miranda—a small guy, maybe five feet nine inches, who seemed bigger than life. He had a unique way of wearing his drill instructor's hat. He placed the hat on his head facing downward with the bill somewhat upward. His boots were always highly spit shined. We wore the old green fatigues at the time, and we all had them laundered at the laundry across the street from the barracks. All were highly starched with a sharp crease. The saying was the crease was sharp as a razor's edge. Most days, the heavy starch was gone after an hour or less due to the humidity. Some days, we were all made to relax under the barracks on the cool dirt, just to keep us from heat injuries.

On the last day of Advanced Military Police training in November 1968, my training company was lined up in formation in front of the First Sergeant. He read off each of our names and gave us our units of assignments. Fortunately for me, I was one of only three Soldiers going to Korea. The rest of the Company were going to Military Police Units in Vietnam. Those of us being assigned Outside Continental United States (OCONUS) were marched to a large auditorium with other training companies and lined up for shots. We all got approximately twelve to eighteen shots, depending on our country of assignments. I got twelve shots. Did I say I don't like shots? I walked through a line of six medics, one on each side, with air guns. A medical air gun that shot you in the arms, both sides at the same time. It appeared as a gauntlet line as you walked through. We were warned not to move, or the air pressure in the air guns would lacerate our skin. I did not move. I saw it happen a couple of times. Poor guys. On the third set of shots, three in each arm (my sixth), the medic on my right ran out of medicine and had to reload. He put another vial in, placed the air gun in the air toward the other side of the room, and pulled the trigger. It shot all the way across the auditorium hitting the wall. I then completed my last six, again making sure I did not move. At the end of the line were medics with smelling salts as about one of three were fainting from the shots. I did not faint, but I did feel a little wobbly for a few minutes. Shots over, we went on leave. I was given fifteen days' leave and went home to Junction City. I now weighed one hundred nineteen pounds. I actually gained two pounds, maybe it was the shots. Leave over, I flew to Korea.

CHAPTER 6

Assignment to Korea

I flew to Seoul, Korea, in the end of November 1968. There were approximately two hundred of us replacements in all on the eighteen-hour plane ride over. Upon arrival, we were all placed in a large auditorium and waited in line for Gamma Globulin (GG) shots. As my time grew near, I noticed that people getting shots coming from behind the screens put in place for privacy were putting their jackets back on. At that time, all military personnel traveled in Class A Uniform. As I approached the screen, I removed my jacket and walked behind the screen, expecting shots in the arm. I was told I would be receiving an injection of Gamma Globulin, known as GG shots. This is when I learned we were getting the shots in the south end, and I was told to drop my drawers. I did as instructed, and the medic grabbed two pretty good-sized syringes, one in each hand, slapped me on my tailbone, at the same time stuck me in each buttock with the needles, and plunged the syringe in. It hurt to say the least. I describe the feeling as a thousand bee stings in each hip. This is an exaggeration, of course, but I feel aptly described the feeling. I was then loaded with others into the back of a deuce and a half (two-and-a-half-ton truck) and took a two-hour ride south to Pyeongtaek on bumpy dirt roads. It was a sight for me as all the people I saw were in traditional clothing. The ride was open-air, and we sat on wooden benches, making my shot buttocks hurt all the more. Six months later, I received another set of GG shots. I later learned the GG shots were part of a medical experiment, and only one out of three shots contained the real stuff. All others were placebos. The GG shot program was later discontinued after two years. Upon arrival to Pyeongtaek, I learned I was assigned to the Thirty-eighth Missile Battalion, Battery B, Songdo, Korea. The following day, those assigned to Songdo were trucked back north two hours to Songdo. I was assigned to Songdo for thirteen months in late November 1968 through January 1969. I was assigned as an MP Nike Hercules (Herc) guarding missiles, all pointed at North Korea. I was in the country for thirty days and promoted from E-3 to E-4. I was assigned to a location called Green, which was approximately a thirty-minute ride from our base camp. There were three sites: Green (missiles), Yellow (radar), and White (admin area), where we slept. We spent three days on assignment to Green and three days back in White. The radar folks had the same shift. Green was on top of a mountain overlooking Songdo Beach (now a resort area almost fifty years later). Between our mountain and the beach was a Special Forces Unit, who sent troops up the surrounding mountain areas during the night for security of our area. The beach was patrolled by the Republic of Korean (ROK) Army. On the beach were Claymore mines strategically placed. The beach was approximately two miles in depth. Until the tide came in, the beach was about twenty feet in length. During the day when the tide was out, the locals would go out onto the beach and dig for clams. They knew exactly where the mines were located while I was stationed there. None were blown up. Six of the eighteen missiles (Nike Hercs) were classified and could only be raised by order of the President. The missiles were a surface-to-air and surface-to-surface weapon used tactically. They were raised by order of the President (Nixon) one time while I was there. It was during an alert when North Korean fighter jets approached the South Korean peninsula. I went through several alerts in Korea. Infiltrators were coming across the border on small one- or two-man submarines, but only one time were the classified missiles raised. On one occasion, I was on one of the forward outposts, overlooking the

Yellow Sea. I observed a greenish tracer on the beach fired from my left and an orangish tracer fired back from the right. I called in on the outpost field phone to report the tracers and was told ROK was involved in a firefight with some North Korean infiltrators on the beach. I only saw a few tracers each direction, and it did not last long, but I was very alert the rest of the night. This was the only firefight I saw in Korea. Let me explain tracer rounds. When fired, a US military tracer is orange and fired every fifth round. We carried two loaded M-14 clips, seven rounds each, with tracers. The military no longer uses tracers because it gives your location away when fired. We had water trucked into our admin area three times weekly for our shower facilities. I learned how to shower in cold water on occasion when all the hot water had been used. There were a few occasions I went without a shower at all as the water truck did not make it in time. One has to remember that at the time I was stationed in Korea, the Korean War had only been over fourteen years.

The Kid

Battery B had an assortment of characters. As an example, one of our Sergeants enjoyed playing a Marvin Gaye tune, "I Heard It through the Grapevine" over and over and over—well, you get the idea. As I write this, I still hear it. One of the Private First Class (PFC) was seventeen years old, name unrecalled, too young to be assigned to a Korean outpost, known as the Kid. He was immature, inexperienced, and kind of flighty. On one occasion, I relieved him on bunker duty approximately at two o'clock in the morning at our farthest outpost. He knew I was coming to relieve him as I had just talked to him on the field phone and told him I was on the way out to him. As I approached his bunker, I heard the slide of his M-14 go click, click, indicating he had just placed a live round in the slot. I yelled to him that it was me coming to relieve him, and he challenged me for the password and countersign word. I gave him the proper password and countersign, and he advised me to proceed. When I finally walked up the path to the bunker, I was ready to physically beat him. When you talk at night, near water, your voice carries. Any enemy infiltrators know exactly where you are. I was not happy. I called him so I would not have to give the sign and countersign. Noise is noise. This is what upset me. Not so much that he locked and loaded on me. However, that didn't help. However, I realized as I approached him that he was simply a scared kid. I'm glad he heard me approach in the dark because he may have shot me. I never relieved him again. I thought he may be mentally unstable. I was a Specialist Four at the time and always requested some other Private First Class (PFC) do the honors. After a few weeks, there were not a lot of folks that wanted to work with him. I remember the day they took him out of the unit. He had consumed so much Coca-Cola in the barracks (that's all he ate or drank) that his whole body had turned as scaly as an alligator skin. The medics were called to his barracks bunk, and he was taken away to be returned home. I never saw him again. He was an excellent artist though and drew a picture of me freehand with a pencil on one occasion. I still have that drawing in my photo album.

The Case of the Blown-Up Heater

Our barracks were the old Korean War Quonset huts. Old Korean War diesel heaters were placed in the middle of the aisle on the floor between bunk beds running the length of the barracks. The heaters were painted over several times in a gray color and were well used. In order to heat them, one affixed a five-gallon can of diesel to a manual pump on the side of the heater and pumped diesel fuel into the stove, then lit it. The diesel cans were filled by a Private First Class, whom we called Diesel and Pig-Pen after the Charlie Brown character. Keeping our diesel cans filled was Diesel's only job. He looked the Pig-Pen part too. He always reeked of diesel, and his clothes were always diesel dirty. I remember on his last day as he as leaving the unit, he was clean and wearing his dress greens. I thought he was an incoming FNG until someone pointed out that he was Diesel. This is the only time I ever saw Diesel cleaned up. Anyway, when the barracks lights were on, the heaters were naturally gray colored.

76

However, when the lights were off, they were so hot they were beat red and provided night-light. One particular wintry night, one of the barracks' characters came back from the local village intoxicated. The lights were still on when he got back, and the heaters were also on but gray colored. He walked up to one of the heaters and kissed the heater pipe that ran from the heater up through the ceiling. Needless to say, he cried out in pain and looked as if he completely burned his lips off. I'm sure he sobered up quickly. The medics took him away, and he never returned. The aisle heaters were popular places to sit around on cold days to keep warm and simply tell war stories and STANS. One cold day, one of the barracks' characters got the bright idea that if he took apart a .50-Caliber machine gun round, he could make a pretty good flash if thrown on top of the heater. He proceeded to take the round apart and placed the powder in the palm of his hands. I must say here that .50-Caliber machine gun powder is actually small pellets of gunpowder and, when fired, packs quite a punch. At any rate, the barracks' character threw the pellets on the top of the hot stove, expecting a flash. Luckily, I was quite a distance from the heater when he did this because the heater immediately exploded, throwing hot diesel on all those around with a pretty loud bang. As I recall, the barracks' dummy received an Article 15 for his stupidity, and we lost one diesel stove.

My Bunker Buddy Burns His Hands

When you fire an M-60 machine gun, you should fire it in bursts as the barrel becomes very hot. Even firing in bursts, the barrel becomes extremely hot. On one occasion, we were firing the M-60 above the rice patties below our outpost on a practice mission toward the Yellow Sea. The gunner ran out of ammo and decided to change the barrel out for a cooler barrel before reloading. To do this requires you wear steel gloves so as not to burn your hands, twist the barrel off, and replace it. The gunner, being too much in a hurry, forgot to put his gloves on. I did not see him in time to warn him. He changed the barrel and realized immediately that he should have used the gloves when the skin of both hands remained on the hot barrel. Medics were called, and he was placed on light duty for several weeks until his hands healed. I recall even after being placed on regular duty, both his hands had burn scars, probably for life.

Trash Can Snake

One down day while in the admin area, I was in the barracks shining my boots, like a good Soldier should. All of a sudden, one of our houseboys shouted out. Let me say at this point that we all paid fifteen dollars a month to have our houseboys care for our clothing and shine our boots. It just so happened on this particular day, I had muddied my boots, and they needed a shine. Back on point. Apparently, one of our houseboys while emptying our trash can found a coral snake curled up in the bottom of the trash can and ran off like a wounded dog. (Coral snakes are a pretty orange and black but very poisonous.) I would have done the same. One of our Staff Sergeants (E-6) types walked up to the can, and sure enough, there was a coral snake in there. Did I say we had some crazy types, if not, let me say here that we did? I do not recall the Staff Sergeant's name now, but he was able to get a piece of thick string in the trash can and somehow make a noose around that darn snake's head. He then proceeded to pull the darn thing out and let it writher on the floor. It's a good thing the Staff Sergeant had thick soles as the snake bit at the sole of his boot. Coral snakes, when they strike, don't simply bite. They slide their teeth scratching along the bite, further injecting venom. The Staff Sergeant's boot was wet as the snake withdrew. The houseboy, including several of us, had ran to the other side of the barracks, a good safe distance off from the idiot with the snake. After the snake struck his boot, the Staff Sergeant apparently felt it was time to kill the snake, which he promptly did by stomping on the darn thing's head. He then put the dead snake back in the trash can, which the houseboy refused to empty. The Staff Sergeant finally emptied the trash can. Let me tell you, I was always checking my boots before

I put them on after that. I still don't know how that dang snake got into the trash can.

I Become a Dog Handler (MOS 95B(D))

I was in country approximately four months and offered an opportunity to become a dog handler. I became a dog handler for rest of the time I was in the country. (There are not too many Service Members (SM) in today's army that is authorized a dog handler patch as I am.) I trained with a sentry dog named Kuladof, who had his own serial number assigned, FX403. I patrolled on two-hour shifts per night walking Kuladof to each outpost (machine gun bunkers) and in between each outpost. In the winter, these patrols were cut to thirty-minute shifts. It was simply too cold for the dogs. Kuladof alerted on me twice, but I never saw any activity, so I am uncertain to this day if it was infiltration activity. To my knowledge, we were never penetrated. The dog hooch was situated on Green, meaning we had to go back to admin (White) three times weekly for food that we obtained from the mess hall. There were seven of us dog handlers, and we lived in the dog hooch alongside our kennels. We had a small black-and-white TV we watched the Armed Forces TV Network on. The only channel we got. It was the only form of entertainment we had, other than sitting around playing cards and telling war stories. Shoot That Ain't Nothing (STAN) stories were numerous and became common among us. One evening while sitting around watching this little black-and-white TV set in between patrols, a folk singing group came on. As I watched this group, two of the girls in the front row looked familiar. And then it hit me: they attended Junction City High School and was in my graduating class. While in high school, they didn't know who I was of course, maybe only in passing. I was not a popular kid in high school. I just did not stand out. But I knew them as they were popular among the kids there and way out of my circle of friends. I'm sure they won't mind me mentioning their names. They were twins, Jan and Jill Bunker. I was surprised that they had made it to a musical career. Well, when I told my buddies, the other dog handlers, they responded, "Yeah, right. You don't know them. You're telling STANS stories." Well, I wasn't. I just kind of smiled to myself and thought, *Yeah, I do know them.* I never mentioned it again. The Bunkers have had a good career in the entertainment industry. Many years later, after I had retired from the military and at a high school reunion, the forty-seventh, I mentioned this story to them, and they both seemed genuinely touched at the sentiment. Both each relayed they enjoyed working and singing on the Armed Forces Network. If you want to listen to some good music, then listen to the melodic voices of Jan Bunker and Jill Jaxx, known as the *Jan and Jill Show*. I'll give them a plug here. They have sang with some of the greats—Frank Sinatra, Tony Bennett, etc. They have appeared on TV, one show being with the Fonz in *Happy Days*, *The Carol Burnett Show*, *American Bandstand*, to name a few.

Me in Machine Gun Bunker holding an
M79 Grenade Launcher - Korea 1968

Me and Kuladof

Kuladof on the attack and Me - Korea 1968

Me in Battle Rattle Korea 1968

The USS *Pueblo*

The USS *Pueblo*, attached to Naval Intelligence, was attacked and captured in international waters on January 23, 1968. It is known today as the Pueblo Incident. On December 23, 1968, the crew of the USS *Pueblo* was released. As they were released, three F5 Phantom aircraft flew over their release site for protection as they walked across the bridge at Panmunjom between North and South Korea. As this happened, we dog handlers were watching the planes on our little TV, and then they would fly out of sight. As they flew out of sight on TV, they then flew right over our dog hooch, turned around, and flew back. As they did so, we watched them re-enter the TV screen and turn around again. It was quite a sight for about an hour. Let me explain. Panmunjom is now located in North Hwanghae Province, an abandoned village just north of the de-facto border between North and South Korea, where the 1953 Kortean Armistice Agreement that paused the Korean War was signed. The building where the Armistice was signed still stands, though it is north of the military demarcation line, which runs through the middle of the demilitarized zone. Notice I said it only paused the war. As far as North Korea is concerned, we are still at war. A bit of USS *Pueblo* history. The USS *Pueblo* was attacked in international waters and did not surrender peacefully. It was reported to have taken two North Korean subchasers, four torpedo boats, and two MiG fighters to subdue the USS *Pueblo*. The crew were not able to man the ship's guns due to restrictive Navy regulations at the time. The crew destroyed all the classified material they could, but they were simply outgunned and outnumbered. The USS *Pueblo* was sent to Wonsan while the ship's crew was taken to North Korean Prisoner-of-War (POW) camps. They were starved and tortured for eleven months by North Korea. Still, they resisted until released. In 1999, the USS *Pueblo* was moved from Wanson to Pyongyang and moored on the Taedong River, where it sits today as a museum. It is still a Commissioned US Navy Ship and the only US Ship currently in enemy hands.

Below are other incidents that I recall in Korea that are worth mentioning.

My First Monsoon

I had never seen a monsoon but had been through some pretty heavy Kansas rain. I was on patrol with Kuladof, whom I called Joe, I think maybe around September or October 1969, and it appeared it may rain. All of a sudden, a fairly good-sized wind appeared, and I looked out to the Yellow Sea, toward and beyond Songdo Beach. This was where General MacArthur landed when he invaded Korea during the Korean War, and I was looking down on this same beach. I observed heavy rain coming toward me and land. As the rain got closer, it appeared to me as a big giant wall of water coming toward me. Kuladof began whining a little. As the rain hit, the drops of rain were bigger than any rain I ever saw. It was heavy, and Kuladof and I jumped into a nearby foxhole to get out of the wind and rain, but the foxhole, which was about four-feet deep, filled up pretty quickly. We finally decided to get out of the foxhole and endure the rain, rather than drown in the foxhole. The rain lasted about fifteen to twenty minutes, but to this day, I have never seen a heavier rain.

Kuladof Bites a Two-By-Four in Half

While on patrol, you could walk your dog, by regulation, either on a short six-foot leash or a sixteen-foot leash. By the way, Kuladof weighed in at ninety-seven pounds. One particular night, I was walking Kuladof on a long leash and approached the main bunker/gate to our compound. The main gate was a makeshift plywood shack, painted green, with concertina wire strung around. Around this makeshift shack was a handrail made of two-by-fours in an X shape, also painted green. The guards were told and knew enough not to come out of the bunker when we walked by; otherwise, they would suffer the consequences. Thinking my dog was not close enough to do him harm, the guard came out of the bunker and stood behind the wooden two-by-four boards, separating a small pathway to the bunker. Kuladof, sensing he had to attack any movement, went for the guard, who immediately jumped back into the bunker. Kuladof, being mad he could not bite the guard, went for one of the two-by-four boards. I must say at this point, German shepherds have extremely strong jaw muscles, approximately a six-hundred-pound bite. Kuladof bit the two-by-four almost in half before I could pull him off. I heard it crack in two. I really liked that dog and hated to leave him with another handler when I left. I made a lot of friends in Korea, and to this day, almost fifty years later, I still keep in contact with one of my friends, Robert (Bob) Tapp.

Bob Tapp Sees His First Snow

I first met Bob in the summer of 1968 when we were both Military Police dog handlers. We became fast friends. Bob is from Orange County, California, and I know he will not mind I mention his first snow several months after our first meeting. Bob is a good man and was a great Soldier. Bob and his wife Barb are now retired and enjoying retired life. Bob and I were sitting in the dog hooch kitchen when snow began falling in the winter of 1968. The dog hooch was a single building with two rooms. One room was a room big enough for the seven of us handlers to sleep in, and one room was large enough for a small combined living room, kitchen, and make-shift arms' room. Bob had never seen snow before and was going outside often to catch snowflakes either in his mouth or in his hand. I was from Kansas, and it is not uncommon to walk through three-to-five-foot high snowdrifts in the winter, so I was not impressed. Bob, on the other hand, was. Snowfall continued to the point that it accumulated approximately two or more inches in a short period of time. Bob, who liked to surf in California, got a piece of old plywood and began surfing on the snow down a small hill near our hooch. Bob had neglected to put on anything but a T-shirt, jean shorts, and flip-flops. He was outside with summer clothing in wind and snow until he could stand the cold no longer and returned very cold, very wet, and with a very stuffy, runny nose. Bob just simply was not used to the cold weather being from sunny California. Bob had an awful head cold for about three weeks afterward. He never got tired of walking in the snow though; however, he never stayed outside for very long after that. That particular winter, we were told, was one of the coldest on record. I don't recall the temperature now but can attest to the fact it was cold because I came close to having frostbite on both feet. I came in one evening from patrol, took off my Mickey Mouse boots (rubber boots for warmth so-called because they looked like Mickey's feet), and discovered I had no feeling in either foot, and my toes were almost white. I soaked them in room-temperature water until I got feeling and color back. Bob and I keep in touch with each other almost fifty years later. I think of Bob often.

Secret Meeting in the Fall of 1968

Just before I became a dog handler, I was called to the Commander's office (CO) at White. At the time, I was a Specialist Four (SP/4), and someone with my rank never gets called to the Commander's office unless one is in some sort of trouble. I and one of my co-workers arrived at the same time. We were summoned inside the Commander's office where the Executive Officer (XO) and the First Sergeant (1SG) were. We were told we had been selected to guard a meeting of high-level civilians from the US and some Generals that were arriving by helicopter that afternoon. We were to get cleaned up, put on a clean set of fatigues, and each check out .45-caliber pistols from the arms' room. We did as told, and that afternoon, we walked into the Commander's office as ordered. From there, the Commanding Officer (a Captain) walked with us to a small building on our compound. The small building was a cement building with windows only on each end. The building could accommodate about ten to twelve people. In the building, a good-sized table had been set up with chairs, and we were told to walk in opposite direction around the building, meeting in both the front and back on each walk around. We were to do so until relieved or otherwise dismissed. We were doing this for an empty building for about fifteen or twenty minutes before the attendees arrived. The attendees were made up of about half civilians and half military. All of a sudden, a helicopter arrived and sat down next to the building. I was, of course, impressed with anything that had wings. A Four-Star General got out. All medals. He approached the building, nodded to us, and walked in. As I recall, this General flew in from Vietnam. I do not recall getting his name at the time. We did not know what the meeting was about; however, on my way around the building on my guard rounds, I could hear some things as I walked passed the windows on each end. This is the jest of what I picked up. (I can relay this now as it is unclassified.) Some unnamed Stateside civilian company had developed a rifle and was trying to sell it to the military. It was a dart rifle, soundless, recoilless, and shot like an M-16. After the meeting, all left. The General came up to us and thanked us for guarding the meeting, climbed into the rotor, and left. We were relieved of our duty by the Commanding Officer and was told never to speak of the meeting. I never did. Until approximately in the year 2000 while watching the military channel on TV, there came a program on the military channel describing the dart rifle just described. It went into some detail and, at the end of the program, advised it was never manufactured but had been developed in the late sixties. Well, I perked up and realized I may have guarded a meeting of the presentation. Our weapons are much more lethal now, with delivery systems that are astounding. I will not discuss too much weaponry.

Weapon Changeover

It was around the summer of 1968 when we turned in our M-14 rifle and was issued the new M-16 rifle. The M-14 fired a 7.62 Millimeters (.308 Winchester) round. The newer M-16 rifle fired a 5.56 Millimeters and was the standard-issue rifle during the Vietnam War. There is a pretty good difference when firing them as the M-14 has a pretty good kick to it, whereas the M-16 does not. While in basic training in Fort Leonard Wood, Missouri, I had a pretty good bruise on my right shoulder from the number of times practicing on the rifle range. I still like the M-14. It makes a good sniper-type rifle and is much easier to clean, at least for me. I relay this story because on one of my vacation trips to Oahu and the islands, I had occasion to visit old Fort DeRussy, just next to the Hale Koa Motel in Downtown Honolulu. If you get a chance, one should visit this museum. Back on point, in the museum is one of the original M-16 rifles, like the one I was issued, on display as a historical artifact. Really. Was it that long ago? Maybe so. I may have lost a little starch, but believe me, when I tell you, I still have plenty of sand.

Korean Music

The dog hooch sat just inside the Green compound, on the back side of the property. The back fence had concertina wire running along the top of the fence that was approximately eight feet high. On the other side of this fence and approximately one hundred yards back was a small village rice farm. Almost every evening, the farmers played a Korean string instrument for about one or two hours each evening. The smell of kimchi was always in the air. I can still hear and smell it. By the way, once you get around the smell of traditionally made kimchi, it's pretty tasty. I still like it when I can get it. But the smell is always with you a week after eating it. If you washed your mouth out with gasoline immediately after eating kimchi, you still would not be able to suffocate the lingering taste. I'm kidding, but it does take a while for the aftertaste to go away.

OK, back on point. We usually turned the small TV we had up loud enough to drown out that darn music, but sometimes that wasn't enough. Traditional Korean music can sound very pretty; however, some notes being played by the farmers seemed out of tune. I believe the instrument being played was a *gayageum*. The instrument sounds good if played properly. It seemed as if one song was played over and over and over. When it became too cold to play music outside, the music stopped. We were very thankful. We were young kids at that time. Our music consisted of Led Zeppelin, Jimi Hendrix, the Doors, Janis Joplin, etc. So traditional Korean music was not well liked among us younger folks. The Green compound sat on a hill approximately two miles from the small village of Songdo. Every Saturday night during the summer months, the younger local kids had a small place on the beach that they congregated at. They played "Gloria" over and over and over again on a loud speaker. I think it was the only record they had. Otherwise, the local folks pretty much kept to themselves.

Christmas Dinner in 1968

December 1968 was a very cold month in Korea. That particular memorable Christmas evening, I was assigned as gunner in a machine gun bunker, above the Main Gate Green. It had an M-60 Machine Gun pointed toward the Yellow Sea and an M-79 Grenade Launcher, along with ammunition for each, and the M-14 rifle I was carrying with ammo. I had over two hundred rounds of M-60 and was ready for anything. The bunker was thus armed as it was thought if we were attacked, it may possibly come from the sea. The bunker looked down over rice patties the locals were growing. Nothing ever happened in that manner, but the point of the story follows. There was an old diesel stove for warmth that did not produce much heat because the bunker was a mostly open bunker, and so the stove did not help. On windy days and nights, it was bitter cold but had to be manned. The Mess Hall at White had made Christmas dinner and had sent it in Mess canisters by truck. The Sergeant of the Guard (SOG) brought out a canister filled with cold meatball and spaghetti sandwiches to each of the guard posts. The sandwich tasted like a turkey dinner to me as I was a little hungry. Along with the sandwiches, the SOG had brought a small bottle of Everclear liquor and offered a jigger to me as he was doing to all outpost guards. I was cold, and I felt anything would help keep me warm. Looking back, coffee would have been better as Everclear is one hundred proof and works to freeze one's insides rather than keep you warm. This was my first Christmas away from home.

The Enlisted Men's (EM) Club and Script Money

In the sixties, there were three small entertainment centers housed in small buildings on post: in the admin area, the Enlisted Men's Club (EM) for E-4s; below, the Non Commissioned Officers' (NCO) club for E-5s through E-9s; and the Officers' Club for 0-1s to General. I was an E-4 and only had access to the EM club. On paydays, held once monthly, we lined up alphabetically in front of the paymaster and was paid in script. Script was what we called funny money and was not real currency but could be spent like US dollars on base. We could spend our script in the clubs and in the small Post Exchange (PX) we had on post. I enjoyed the EM club. It was a place to unwind and listen to music, mostly country. Sometimes the script was changed without notice to keep the Korean population from exploiting our currency with black-market issues. Most times, we knew a script change was coming. This was because the Admin cleaning staff, consisting of local Koreans, usually a few days before we knew of the change, would bring us their script they had saved working for us, asking if we would exchange to new script for them. Usually, small amounts around one hundred dollars or so, but one must remember the average income for a Korean at that time was less than four hundred dollars a year. At the time, I was not sure how they were able to get this information. As an Intelligence Officer, I now know.

CHAPTER 7

Germany

I received orders for Germany in early November 1969. I received thirty days' leave and went back home. My parents by this time had moved from Junction City to Wichita, Kansas, where my mother had gotten a teaching contract. My mother had a Masters of Education from Kansas State and taught special needs children at the elementary level there.

Transition

After leave, I reported to Fort Dix, New Jersey, for transport to Germany. I was assigned to a barracks with one other Specialist Four; all the rest of the transition barracks were E-2s and E-3s, making myself and the other E-4 in charge of the barracks. All of us were there awaiting transportation orders. This was fine with me as the person in charge gets a Noncommissioned Officers' (NCO) room to himself. There were two such rooms in this particular barracks. This was the first time I had ever been in charge of troops, responsible to see they got to mess and medical facilities as needed. At the time, all E-4s and below were responsible for Kitchen Duty (KP). When the other E-4 and I went to mess, we sat at the same table, knowing after chow we would have to report for KP on this particular day. As I sat there eating, I noticed that when an E-4 and below got up to leave and dispose of one's mess tray in the wash area, a person already on KP stopped the person leaving at the door and handed them a clean apron they obtained off the wall. I then noticed the KP change and the leaving KP then deposited their dirty apron in a used-clothes hamper near the same wall by the door. I observed the KP shifts were approximately forty-five minutes per shift change. I observed this while talking with the other E-4 and eating. After we finished, I got an excellent idea. I told the other E-4 to stay at the table, and I went to the used-clothes hamper and took out two of the dirtiest aprons I could find and then walked them back to our table tucked under my arm. We then put on the dirty aprons while sitting, and when we got up from our table, we pretended we had just bussed our table and took our trays with dirty plates to the washroom. The next two E-4s out the door were stopped by us, and we then handed them a clean apron we took off the wall and put ours back in the dirty-clothes hamper. All under the eyes of all in the Mess Hall. We had just gotten out of KP. I often think back on this and wonder why no one ever saw this exchange. I always like someone who takes the initiative. I was at Fort Dix three days before being processed to ship out.

I flew to Frankfurt, Germany, in early December 1969. I like Germany. It's a very pretty country. After landing, we were trucked to the Division Headquarters where we were assigned to units. I was assigned to the Third Infantry (Marne) Division, Third Military Police Company, Wurzburg, Germany. We were then trucked to the Frankfurt Bahnhof (train station) and trained to Wurzburg, Germany, to our unit. I remember while waiting on the train, at the train station, I needed to use the restroom. After locating one, I observed that one relieved oneself on a wall that had a waterfall coming down the wall, emptying into a trough. While conducting my business, I observed a mop cleaning in between my feet. *What the—?* I turned around to observe an older female mopping around my feet. I had never experienced this before and was a little taken aback by these turn of events. I later learned that females were hired to clean the male restrooms and were known as *pushfraus*. I was not totally shy as

I had experienced outdoor toilets in Korea. It was not uncommon in the sixties Korea to see both male and female stop in public and use the restroom as needed. Women simply pulled their kimono-type garment up and went. Morality in foreign countries is a lot different than in the US. Nevertheless, I was not expecting anyone to be mopping up after me. Further, I am not a messy person. I arrived at night in Wurzburg and was picked up by the Staff Duty Officer (SDO), taken to my unit, and was assigned a room. I was told I was to report for alcohol training the following morning at eight o'clock sharp. My first day. I did and learned the training was being conducted by the unit First Sergeant (1SG). I do not recall his name. I should mention here that while in Korea, I was introduced to the local alcohol wine drink called Soju. It is fairly strong in alcohol content and leaves one's breath highly odiferous. I was also introduced to the local beer. Let me say here that I was not a drunkard or troublemaker. I was, however, young and wanted to experience everything as long as it was legal. Back on point, the 1SG was explaining how one's reaction time decreased with each drink of alcohol. Observing me as a Flipping New Guy (FNGs we were called; I'm cleaning this up, of course), I was called in front of the class of other MPs. The 1SG told me to drink a glass of the local Würzburger Hofbräu beer. I later learned it was eighteen-percent alcohol. He held up a dollar bill and had me catch it in between my thumb and forefinger, which I easily did. As I dank another beer (German beer is served room temperature), he was explaining to the class how reaction time decreases as alcohol content in the human body increases. He again had me try to catch the dollar bill, which I easily did. He thought I would not catch it, but I surprised him. He gave me another glass of beer, at this time my third. After, he again had me try catching the dollar bill. I easily caught it. He looked at me funny and asked if I was normal and said that he was running out of beer. Then the admin NCO spoke up from the audience and told the 1SG that I had just came from Korea, not the States. Shaking his head, he told me to go sit down and join the class, saying he needed someone who had not had an OCONUS assignment. The following person missed the dollar bill first try after less than one glass of beer. I did not consume alcohol that much but realized then that one's body becomes accustomed to alcohol.

On Patrol

The Third Military Police Company Third Infantry Division was responsible for the security of one of three *Kasernes* in Wurzburg. The position I was assigned was as revolving gate duty and, once weekly, riding with a German *polizei* unit in downtown Wurzburg, clearing bars of soldiers after bar closing. An interesting job in that at each bar we closed, the local bartender, as was custom, provided the *polizei* and myself a drink before leaving for the next bar. We closed at least three to four bars nightly. You can imagine by the end of the night, we were pretty well soused. Not really, but we did feel good. We also had to fight an occasional drunk soldier, who did not wish to leave when told to do so upon bar closing. The German *polizei* had a small metal baton that, when flicked open, extended a strong spring approximately a foot-and-a-half long that had a steel ball on the end of the spring. When you got hit with that bad boy, you not only had a bruise on your front torso but on your back as well over the shoulder where the steel ball hit you. They used it quite often. The German *polizei* patrolled in Volkswagen Bugs with .45-caliber Thompson machine guns, held upright in the front between the driver and passenger. I enjoyed riding with them as there was more action in downtown Wurzburg than being on a gate. The Third "Marne" Division is a well-known and famous combat division because of their World War II tactics.

Audie Murphy

Audie Murphy, the most decorated soldier in US history, was killed in a plane crash in May 1971. The Third "Marne" Division was one of the units he served in during World War II, and a memorial formation was held with all the units on base. Well, over seven hundred soldiers and civilians and dignitaries were in attendance in an open parade field. The guest speaker was an unrecalled Sergeant Major (SGM) who had actually served with Audie Murphy in World War II. I remember as he walked to the podium, he walked past our unit. Not far from where I was standing at attention. We were all dressed in Class A Uniforms. I have never seen so many medals on one person. In addition to his SGM rank on both sleeves, he also just barely had enough room below his rank patches for the numerous overseas bars on his right sleeve and enlistment stripes on his left. He was an impressive sight and had an impressive message.

Twice weekly, two of us were also assigned street patrol near military facilities. This duty was also fun. At that time, one of our MP patrol cars was a Rambler. You don't see many of these cars today. For the simple reason, they were mechanically bad cars but rode nice. There was a car wash near our Provost Marshal's Office near the Mein River that at night became a mobile brothel. We patrolled this regularly for soldiers, as it was against regulations to participate in such activity. One night, we did catch an American soldier there acting suspicious, which was enough to give us probable cause to stop him. Come to find out, he was there pimping his wife. He was naturally arrested. I remember this incident as I thought how sad this was to begin with, but beyond this, he lacked integrity, morals, character, and had a complete lack of spousal respect. I'm sure there were others; we just did not catch them. Working an accident was also an adventure. When filling out paperwork, the accident form required seven carbon copies and the original typed with no mistakes. If you made a mistake, you had to correct all eight pages or start over. I don't like mistakes. I make them, but I don't like them. I preferred to start over; however, I did use correction fluid once or twice. Today, this is all computerized and much quicker than the three to five hours it took to fill out a report back then. On occasion, we were assigned patrol on post in a Jeep. (I'm referring to a real jeep, not a Humvee.) In the late sixties and early seventies, we were using old World War II Jeeps. They were cold in the winter, and one had to take corners slowly as they had a narrow wheel base and easily turned over. On one occasion, my partner and I were called to cover a suicide in one of the barracks. The suicide was a female spouse of one of the infantry personnel. After our investigation, my partner drove off in the Jeep and took a corner too fast in the snow. In slow motion, the Jeep turned over. My partner was later completely chewed out in order by the Squad Sergeant, the Platoon Sergeant, the 1SG, and lastly by the commanding officer. My partner learned to never drove a Jeep very fast again.

Promotion to Acting Jack E-5

Approximately six months into my seventeen-month tour, I was made Desk Sergeant at the Provost Marshal's Office. I was happy about it; however, I was still an E-4 Specialist Fourth Class (SP/4). Acting SGTs were called acting jacks at that time. I was responsible for all reports coming from five garrison cities on third shift. They were Schweinfurt, Kitzingen, Bad Kissingen, and two others I do not recall now. Most incident reports were burglaries and traffic accidents. There was the occasional fight or shooting but not on a regular basis. When an incident happened in one of the garrison cities, the city garrison Desk Sergeant would call me, and I would make an incident report (three copies)—one copy to the Brigade Commander, one copy to the Division Commander, and one copy to the post Commanding General. This allowed Command Staff knowledge of what was happening in their garrison cities before any incident became newsworthy. Most times, the duty was boring; however, I honed my report writing skills, again serving me well later in my career. These reports were distributed at the end of an eight-hour shift, at seven o'clock. I got pretty good at it but never received an actual promotion to E-5.

While assigned as a Desk Sergeant, our Battalion was always being placed on alert status, at least quarterly. All leaves were cancelled, and those folks living off post were restricted to post for at least twenty-four hours. This made it sometimes difficult for those Service Members (SM) living off post with families as they were not allowed to go home and made to stay in barracks. On one of these alerts, a fatal accident just below our Provost Marshal Office occurred. The Provost Marshal's Office was located on the second floor of the old German Army SS Panzer Division Headquarters just across the street from the Mein River. I recall the day because the Battalion Commander (CO), who was the Provost Marshal, had asked me to put his tactical gear together as he did not recall how to do it. Tactical gear, called LBE for Load-Bearing Equipment, was suspenders attached to a belt worn by the Service Member (SM) and had to be placed in certain order by regulations. LBEs consisted of ammo pouches, first-aid kit, compass, bayonet, canteen, and shovel. By the way, digging a foxhole with one of those darn shovels was a chore. The CO was having difficulty putting his LBE together. We enlisted folks wore LBEs more often and were more versed in the order of LBE makeup. If one wore the whole tactical makeup for field duty, there was what was called an ALICE pack attached to the LBE, making the complete package called All-Purpose Lightweight-Carrying Equipment (ALICE). ALICE held various articles of clothing, etc. It was approximately two o'clock on that fall of 1970 morning when as I was affixing the CO's gear when we all heard a very loud crash. We all looked down into the street from the second-story window. However, due to fog coming off the Mein River, we could not see the street. The CO and Battalion Executive Officer (XO) ran down the stairs to investigate. One of our supply folks (S4) had parked a deuce and a half, motor running and with flashing lights on, parked against the curb below our offices. A motor scooter, driven by some poor soul, had been traveling along the road in the fog and struck the back of the parked two-and-a-half-ton truck, causing his fatal accident. I recall that after the fog lifted, the German utility company washed his remains off the road and into the river. I sometimes think about this unfortunate soul who was probably simply just trying to get home.

The Swastika

While working as Desk Sergeant, described above, it could sometimes get boring until a garrison city reported in. One early morning, sitting waiting on a report to come through, I observed the bottom half of the inside door had a piece of plywood screwed into the door. The doors in this building were thick and solid heavy wood. Due to being a curious fellow, I took my pocketknife and unscrewed the plywood piece, one screw on each corner and top and bottom. The plywood piece, approximately three feet by three feet, covered an inlaid wooden swastika, black in color. It was an impressive inlay; however, I then realized why the piece of plywood covered the door. A little checking and I learned the Provost Marshal's Office was housed in the old SS Panzer Division Headquarters. Used as such during World War II. At the time, I was stationed in Wurzburg, there were still some parts of downtown Wurzburg that had bombed-out buildings from the war. A little further checking, I learned that in the basement of this building was a tunnel, the entryway of which had been blocked by cement blocks. This tunnel was large enough to drive large trucks through and move weapons and troops through by the German Army during World War II to each of the three *Kasernes* in Wurzburg. I was actually working out of a pretty famous building, famous because it was the SS Panzer Division Headquarters.

End of Three-Year Enlistment

In May 1971, I received Orders releasing me from Active Duty (AD). I arrived home that spring determined to attend college. I was living with my parents at the time in Wichita and working part-time for Pinkerton's Security as a security guard for my only income.

CHAPTER 8

The Coleman Company Arrest Incident

After leaving the military, I purchased a 1969 Austin-Healey Sprite, a pretty British racing green sports car. I drove this back and forth to Coleman Company to work, where Pinkerton's had placed me as a security guard. Coleman's employees were on strike, and my job was to guard the front gate. The picketing employees were sometimes pretty rowdy but never bothered me. I think they realized I was simply a poor college kid trying to make a living. On one occasion, the employees picked my car up, walked it past the front gate, and pointed it in the direction I drove when I left work. One of the employees opened the driver's side door and waived me in. At least, they didn't damage my car, which I kept highly polished. One day while at work, I was approached by a Wichita police detective, whom I later worked with, Richard Cole. He asked me if I had a security license. I was not told by Pinkerton's I needed one, and I had not been issued one and answered no. He then arrested me and one other guard for not having a security license, leaving the front gate wide open from any type of security. I was taken to the station and placed in a holding cell. I was never so humiliated. I stayed in the cell along with the other security guard for approximately forty-five minutes when a Pinkerton's supervisor came and bailed us out. We appeared in municipal court the following day, and the judge fined the Pinkerton's agency fifty dollars for allowing us to work without a license. Apparently, the Coleman strikers had found a way to disrupt the Coleman security process, catching me in the middle. Never mind what this did to my record. I don't think it still appears on my record.

I Meet My Best Friend and Life's Partner

I enrolled in Wichita State University (WSU) in the fall of 1971. I majored in Administration of Justice and Prelaw. I was fairly busy working part-time and attending school full-time, not as busy as I would later become. I believe we each meet people we were meant to meet, and at the time, we were meant to meet. One of my classes was journalism, a class I took as part of my elective course work. In this class was a beautiful brown-haired, brown-eyed girl I immediately took too. I admired her from afar as she seemed out of my league. I had journalism three times weekly and always looked forward to seeing her, if but to look. I was a shy guy back in those days. Our college yearbooks came out in midsemester of 1971, and I looked forward to looking her up in the yearbook to maybe obtain more information on her and to maybe even get up enough courage to call her. On the day we received our yearbooks, I was sitting on a couch outside the journalism classroom waiting for class to start. I had the college yearbook in front of me and was looking for her information in the book. I knew her name; however, I noticed there was no information beside what I thought her name was. As I sat there, I felt a presence in front of me and looked up, and oh my goodness, she is standing in front of me. I was a little shocked she had even taken notice of me. She took the yearbook out of my hands, saying the yearbook staff had erred in not including her telephone information, and wrote her home number in my yearbook next to her name, Laura Postlethwait. And she walked away after some quick small talk as class was just starting.

I was ecstatic someone this pretty even paid some type of attention to me. I was feeling good that day as I walked into class. The following evening, I called her and asked if she wanted to meet me in the student union on campus the following day, and she said yes. I was very excited when I met her between classes. We sat in a booth in the cafeteria. I learned she was a physical education major and resided north of Wichita. I was smitten and twitter patted and asked if she wanted to meet me that weekend at a local dance place, and she said yes. Well, we had several dates after that and fell in love with each other. I was a poor college student in those days and could not afford to pay attention sometimes. Because of my economic depression, she did not seem to mind going to my uncle Phil's place in the evenings and watching TV movies and eating a pizza afterward. I was invited to her home to meet her parents one evening. On the night I was invited over, her parents were on their way to an Eastern Star meeting, and we talked a few minutes, and they left. Laura's parents are good Christian folks who seemed to like me for some reason. I was invited back the following weekend, so I must have made a favorable impression. Laura's brother Mike was going to Emporia State University at the time and was home the following Saturday, the day I was invited back. When I arrived, Laura took me around the back of their home to meet her big brother. When I rounded the corner of the home, Mike and Laura's father were working on the engine of Mike's Austin-Healy in their garage. Same as mine but a purple color. Just as I approached the garage, Mike reached in and picked the motor up and away from the frame without using any type of assistance, not even a pulley, and then sitting it off to the side. Well, I was impressed at his strength. I know how heavy engines are and decided I needed to stay on his good side. I met Mike and have liked him ever since. As an MP, I had tussled with some pretty big boys closing bars in Germany, but I think Mike would equal them.

I Marry the Love of My Life

In the fall of 1972, I asked Laura to marry me, and to my surprise, she said yes. I believe two lights came together as we were meant to be. We were married on June 22, 1973, in Valley Center, Kansas. I was twenty-five years old, and Laura was twenty. At the time, we were both college students. After we married, Laura dropped out of college and found work as a Nurse Assistant. I had joined the police department, and on the day of my graduation from the police academy, Laura, who was a rainbow girl with a state position, had a conflicting meeting. However, she ran from her meeting to my graduation and made it just as I as receiving my certification. By the way, Laura was the youngest Mother Advisor rainbow girl in Kansas at the age of twenty-one. Over the years, we have hugged each other when needed, leaned on each other as necessary, and have created many memories. I am the person I am today because of her. She is the love of my life.

I Become a Father

On October 3, 1974, we were blessed with a daughter we named Janelle. A daughter needs a dad to be the standard in which she will judge all men. A saying I have always tried to live up to. We were able to bring her home early from the hospital if we promised to bring her back for blood tests two days later. We did, and I had to endure watching the nurse poke her little foot with a needle. It felt like I was being stabbed with the needle. It hurt me more than her. As Janelle grew older, she always met me at the door when I returned home from work and jumped into my arms. I miss those days. I blinked, and she was in grade school. I blinked again, and she was out of high school. It got real quiet around the house after she moved out and began college. Then she graduated college. I'm going to stop blinking. The quiet house. In the quietness of a home after they grow up and leave, you get flashbacks of yesteryear. There are scenes in one's memory of feeding them; teaching them how to use a spoon on their own, how to walk, and how to ride a bike; of signing report cards, school dances, and activities; and teaching them how to drive. And then Janelle met Justice Edge in college and married shortly after they both graduated college. I remember walking her down the aisle as if it was yesterday. I did so with a lump in my throat. Justice began work in a civil engineering firm in Texas and is now a partner in that firm. I love Justice like I would my own son. He is a good husband and father. On February 5, 2000, they were blessed with a daughter they named Emily. Then as Emily grew older, she always ran to meet me jumping into my arms when I visited, as her mother did when she was that age. Emily's too old to jump into my arms now, but I miss those days just the same. Emily became interested in acting and now has a couple of commercials out, along with a distributed antibullying campaign video as of this writing. I am very proud of them and love them all. They live on a lake in Texas, and Laura and I enjoy visiting them. We call their home our vacation home.

A Law Enforcement Career—Police Influences

It was not uncommon to drive to the Clay Center shopping district in the summer to get a Coke at the Rexall Drug Store. A real treat back in the early 1960's. The drug store is still there, but the soda fountain is now gone. The shopping district was located around the town square, in the middle of which, was the Clay County Court House. Around the town square were bench's, I recall were painted green, but there would always be some retired folks sitting on the benches reminiscing and whittlin' wood. Tobacco chewers my Father would always say. Mostly, they were known as the Spit and Whittle club. All small towns seem to have them. If I were there now, I'd probably be one of those sittin' on a bench talking with old Army buddies, that, or playin' pool in the local pool hall. I wouldn't be chewn' tobacco, though. I consider it a very nasty habit. However, as I write this, I can recall as a young boy visiting my Great Grandmother Hurt who could spit tobacco from a pretty fair distance from her rockin' chair, and hit a coffee can she kept in the corner near a door. Her chewn' tobacco was not the kind out of a plastic bag or sack. She was one of those old frontier types who chewed the real raw stuff, pieces she bit off a tobacco brick. She would sometimes miss, so you can imagine how the area around the coffee can looked. We didn't visit often, as she lived in Iola, KS. Have you ever been hugged and kissed by a tobacco chewer? When I was approximately ten years old, I was playing in our front yard with my sister when the local Police Chief rolled up and parked between our house and the neighbor's house. As a young kid, I was very impressed with the police. The Police Chief was Ernie Roll, who was known by all in our small town. He went over to talk with our neighbors a few minutes and started to walk back to his car but stopped to say hello to my sister and me. While we were talking, I asked if I could hold his gun. He of course said no but then said, "I'll let you hold one of my bullets," which he took off his gun belt and handed me. I took it and held it in my hands, admiring a real big police bullet. After a few seconds, I gave it back, and he got back into his shiny police car and drove off. This left a lasting impression on me and was a big influence in my later career choice. There were some folks in town who didn't like Ole Ernie. Clay Center in the late fifties and early sixties did not have parking meters. Every Saturday, most folks came to town off the farm, shopping for their weekly goods, and parked in front of the stores they shopped at. Woolworths department store was a popular place to shop. Once every two hours, Ole Ernie came around and marked the left rear tire of each parked car with a chalk mark. Ernie had an old broom handle stick that he cut to approximately four feet. On the end of this stick, he had taped a piece of rubber that held the chalk in place. Most folks knew about what time Ole Ernie made his chalk marking rounds. After he marked the tires, turned, and walked around the corner, they came out of the store they were shopping in, backed their car up a couple of feet, and then reparked, thus erasing the chalk mark and saving themselves a parking ticket. If the chalk mark was still there on Ole Ernie's next round, well, you got a parking ticket. Most folks could not afford the amount of money a parking ticket cost. There were always a few who got caught, but not many. Clay Center was a farming community, and sometimes the weather affected the amount of crops a family was able to sell. I also learned of a Wichita police officer during this time frame. As mentioned earlier, I worked at Elliott's Rexall Drug Store as a soda Jerk, owned by Loren Elliott. Loren has three daughters. The oldest daughter was married to Gary Caldwell, who was a Wichita police officer at the time, and I saw Gary once or twice in the store when he visited the area and did not know him personally. On one Saturday afternoon, the eldest daughter brought in Gary's police uniform shirt that had been cut in a knife fight during an arrest on the north end of Wichita. Irene, Loren's wife, was sewing the shirt up as she was telling the story of how the shirt got cut. At that time, I felt that maybe someday I could join the Wichita Police Department. Gary was not an influence; however, he was on the police department I was interested in. Irene enjoyed telling stories to us drug store employees of Gary's exploits. I mention this as I later meet Gary as an officer one time. I saw him at either an accident scene or on an ended chase he was involved in at Broadway and Kellogg, approximately in the summer or fall of 1974. I do not recall the incident now. Due to time lapse, I do not recall exact details or circumstances, only that we saw each other. I will mention one more influence.

Trooper Withem

I first knew of Trooper Withem, approximately in 1962, when he came to our high school yearly to talk about highway accidents in Clay Center, Kansas. (If you grew up in the Clay Center and surrounding area in the sixties and seventies, you will know who Trooper Withem was.) At first, he showed a black-and-white film called *Blood on the Highway* during school assemblies. Over the years, I guess technology caught up with him, and then the films became more realistic in color during high school assemblies, displaying real accident scenes. Trooper Withem was also a member of our church, the Christian Church, Clay Center, Kansas, that our family now attended. I can still see him getting out of his shiny patrol car on Sunday mornings, removing his weapon, placing it in the trunk of his car, and walking into church. His patrol car was always kept clean and washed. Trooper Withem was a man of faith and set an example for all who knew him. He became friends with my father through church activities and seemed to take a liking to me, a skinny teen of a friend. As I grew older and got my driver's license, I always remember the *Blood and Guts* film he showed and vowed not to be a statistic. I had become interested in pursuing a law enforcement career, and he helped influence that desire. Over the years and as I grew older and moved away from Clay Center, I often thought of Trooper Withem and his talks to students of all ages in the area he served. I did later become a police officer with positions in investigations, traffic investigations, and was one of the city pilots for Wichita, Kansas. I like to think Trooper Withem had some hand in my career choices. Just after I left the Wichita Police Department, as a pilot, and later as investigator for Santa Fe Railroad, I worked as a Sedgwick County, Kansas, deputy sheriff. In this position, I again ran into Trooper Withem, who had at that time retired as a Kansas highway patrol officer and was working as a court bailiff in the Sedgwick County court system. I was in court often on tickets I had given, accidents I worked, and some case investigations I helped work. One day after giving testimony, I approached Trooper Withem, and I asked him if he remembered my family or me. I think I recall him saying he remembered my family; however, more than twenty years had passed. One evening, unrecalled date, maybe around 1986, approximately at seven o'clock, I received a call of a fatal traffic accident on Eighty-Fifth Street North, just west of North Broadway. I had worked numerous serious injury and fatal accidents over the years and, on each occasion, always remembered Trooper Withem's film talks. He always said accidents don't just happen; they're caused. As I approached the accident, I observed that it was a one-car accident by a driver who had ran off the road eastbound and had struck a tree. I sometimes see accidents I have worked over the years in my sleep, those that stuck out in my mind as I do some combat situations. This was one of those accidents. This accident was no different than other fatal accidents I worked, only that I knew the driver. As I continued to work the accident, taking notes, measurements, I managed to run a tag identification in an attempt to identify the driver. The tag registration came back to Trooper Withem who had suffered a fatal heart attack, ran off the road, and struck the tree. I still recall this accident as if it were just yesterday. It was one of the hardest accidents I have ever worked, including the numerous fatal accidents I ever worked. I often look back at this accident and think Trooper Withem would have wanted me to work his last drive. So I thank Trooper Withem for a lifetime of memories in my career but also thank him for simply crossing paths with each other.

I Become a Police Officer

I applied for the Wichita Police Department (WPD) in the late spring of 1972. I weighed one hundred forty-six pounds at that time. I had gained a little weight from my tour in Germany. I took a battery of vetting tests and went through a polygraph examination and interview. On the interview panel was Richard Cole, the detective who had arrested me at Coleman's. I passed all tests and the interview process. I was then weighed in as part of the hiring process. One had to weigh one hundred fifty pounds to become a WPD police officer, and I only weighed one hundred forty-six pounds. I was told I needed to gain weight and to come back the following week for another weigh-in. My military tour in Germany had allowed me to pack on a few pounds, but not enough. I ate all the fat food I could stand. Feeling I did a good job stuffing myself and feeling heavy and bloated, I went back for the second weigh-in. I weighed one hundred forty-eight pounds at this weigh-in. The trainer who was doing the weighing told me he would give me one more chance. I was to come back the following week. I again stuffed myself, eating bananas and everything else I could think of. On the day of the weigh-in, I even stuffed some sand in my back pockets. I really wanted to be in law enforcement. I weighed one hundred forty-nine and a half pounds. I was told I would be hired and that the police training may put weight on me. I graduated police training in June 1973. A law enforcement career can be both dangerous and rewarding. Officers are well trained to be safe and aware. As a first responder, an officer provides public safety every day to those in need of assistance. The rewards are immeasurable. I had some memorable moments as a police officer described below. Let me add at this point that my stories are typical of every police officer out there in any city in the US and some more dangerous than I describe.

Psychology Examination

I was on the department for about two years when all police officers had to take a psychology test. This was to obtain an average score of all of us to use on new hires during the vetting process. After approximately three months, all officers got called to the psychologist's office for an individual evaluation. I was told by the psychologist that I should be a minister or a dentist in that order and get completely out of law enforcement. I took this with a grain of salt as I had worked too hard to get to where I was. I did consider dentistry and almost went to dental school. Chemistry courses changed my mind. I hate working chemistry. I also took the Law School Admissions Test (LSAT). My score was not high enough for one of those prestigious schools but was high enough to get me into a law school in Oklahoma. I did not go after learning my income was more than that of the municipal court prosecuting attorney, and that was not much.

I Meet George Poulos

As a beat officer, I made what I called my criminal box that I kept beside me on the front seat of my patrol car for a handy reference. It was a small gray file box I made that I had accumulated approximately two hundred mug shots in. I had the mugs cross-referenced by cars, residences, hangouts, known associates, etc., on the back of each mug card. I had some of their recent criminal history. One of the mugs I had was of George Poulos. As mentioned earlier in this book, I still had a bullet in my knee from one of his guns. I had memorized faces of some of these mugs, including Poulos'. Ones that were frequently talked about in shift meetings and ones who made the news more often. I had probably memorized approximately fifteen or so, including George's. George had a sister who lived right across the street from one of my WPD classmate friends. George's sister appeared to have a string of prostitutes she ran out of her house, and my friend had been getting tag numbers and other type of information from their vehicles and working girls' cars. He relayed this information to vice. Back on point, one evening when I was working traffic, I received an accident call on the south end of town. It was one of those accidents that caused a lot of damage, but no injuries. As I was working the accident, George Poulos pulled up in quite a hurry. At first, I did not know who he was until he stepped out of his car, and I recognized him immediately from his mug shot. He passed by me and went straight to the young women, one of whom was driving one of the cars in the accident. George was not wanted for anything, so I didn't approach him. I was annoyed however, as he was entering my accident scene. I did need to obtain information from the young women he was talking with. I later obtained her driver's license (DL) and do not recall her last name. I did not let on that I knew who George was until I released them. She was not at fault, and I had no reason to detain her. Upon leaving, George thanked me for looking after her, not revealing his name to me. As he did so, I replied, "Thanks, George." He turned around to face me and said, "You know my name?" I said, "Of course." He seemed genuinely surprised that I knew who he was, and there was also a look of "so what" on his face. I think he was probably happy the girl was not hurt. We exchanged small talk, and George was more charming than I thought he would be. He seemed impressed a young police officer knew who he was and thanked me again and left with the girl, saying, "Be careful out here, Officer." It was over an hour later that I finished working the accident, measurements, and reports, etc. I had not eaten yet and went to a small café off a main thoroughfare close to where the accident occurred. The café is no longer there, but I still recall how good their food was. I walked in and sat at a booth near the door in case I needed a fast exit, intending on finishing some paperwork and leaving shortly. When I began to place my order, the waiter and owner of the small café approached me and said there was a gentleman in the back who had just bought me a steak dinner. I looked back to thank whoever it was and decline the appreciated gesture, and there sat George and the girl. I do not recall if the girl was his daughter or a friend. I decided to leave well enough alone and accepted the dinner. Just after the dinner was brought to my booth, I got another serous accident call. I have always regretted leaving that steak.

The Brick

Let me say here that whenever I put on a police uniform, I became somewhat of a different person. You have to. My imaginary antennae went up in the back of my head. Similar to the old Martian TV series, where the antennae came up in the back of his head. I liked to have my imaginary antennae up because with my antennae up, it was like a radar all around me. I became acutely aware of my surroundings, including my six (back). Think of a clock, one through twelve. Now make that clock in your mind, horizontal, so as the twelve's position is in your front, and the six is in your rear. That is watching your six. Pilots use this mental clock while flying. You see it in the movies all the time. A pilot may say, "I got your six." Same with police officers, someone will have your six. They are looking out for you. You learn real quick when you wear a police uniform, people automatically hate you. Some people just don't like authority figures. You are no longer a person to them, only a uniform. They do not see the person or care to. You simply have to be more acutely cautious of everyone. Anyway, back on point.

The midseventies were turbulent years for Wichita, as the African American youth community were rioting over perceived wrongs done them by police. One early summer evening, approximately in 1975, I was driving west on Thirteenth Street, approaching Grove Street. The youth were out on the streets, but the atmosphere was calm. There was no rioting, and things seemed calm. I was simply there in the area to be seen. I did not have air-conditioning in my patrol car, and I had rolled my window down for air. All of a sudden, *bang*. A brick had been thrown at my car as I was driving. My speed was right at thirty miles per hour, and the brick hit at the halfway point of the brick, striking my patrol car just above my head on the corner of the window frame, missing me by mere inches. I recall feeling the wind of the brick as it hit. My point is I was lucky I was not hit as I believe it would have killed me. Somehow, I've been blessed in this manner all my career. I did not see who threw the brick, and if I had been injured or killed, there would probably have been no suspects. I would have been another statistic, another officer killed in the line of duty for no reason other than being a police officer.

Wayward Girls

One midsummer evening around six 'o clock, approximately in 1976, I received a call of a juvenile female who was causing issues with the Sisters who were running the Catholic home for wayward girls under the age of eighteen on the west side. The home was not only for homeless girls, drug addicts, alcoholics, and girls in trouble with law enforcement but was also a home for girls who had become pregnant out of wedlock. I arrived just as the evening meal was finishing and, upon arrival, was approached by one of the Sisters who had been waiting outside for me. The Sister informed me that one of the girls was throwing a fit during dinner and was out of control. The Sister told me they would like my help in calming the girl down. Just as the Sister was telling me this, a girl ran out the door we were standing by and past my patrol car where the Sister and I were talking. The sister said that's her, and she's trying to run away. I immediately gave chase. By this time, the girls in the home had congregated on the second-floor balcony yelling for the girl not to get caught and cheering that she had gotten away. I wasn't about to let one of the girls get away and was behind her only a few steps. When she zigged, I zagged and tackled her in a field across the street from the home. This is when all hell broke loose in the home. The girls started rioting, throwing chairs, food, and fighting among themselves and the Sisters. I immediately got on my portable radio and called for backup, informing dispatch the girls were rioting. Backup units arrived just as I walked up with the runner in handcuffs. This is when the Sister handed me my pistol. *What! Hello!* I was unaware that as I gave chase, my duty weapon slipped out of my holster onto the ground by the Sister's feet. I was just lucky she was the one who retrieved it as I was shocked it fell out of my holster. It could have been tragic. That's when the Sister informed me my prisoner was just fourteen years old and pregnant. She did not look pregnant and certainly in good enough health to run. I had apparently started the riot when I tackled her because all the girls knew she was pregnant. I didn't, and I'm not sure that would have made a difference in apprehending her had I known. I released the girl to the Sister after she calmed down, rather than taking her to juvenile detention. I figured the Sisters would be not only much tougher on her but also more caring. The following day, I went to police supply for a better holster. Teenage girls are some of the most serious creatures on the planet. The Sisters have their hands full.

The Cheerleader

I worked off duty for extra money at Town East Mall. The mall was owned by the Simon Brothers, and on occasion, the mall sponsored celebrities. On one occasion, the mall invited the Dallas Cowboys Cheerleaders Organization to sign autographs and pose for pictures with fans. I was assigned as an escort to Benita Briggs, a Dallas Cowboys cheerleader, and escorted her around for approximately four hours. I did not watch a lot of sports on TV, but I became a Dallas Cowboys fan for a day. During this four-hour period, I witnessed countless signatures. Long lines of autograph seekers awaited us wherever we went in the mall. While at Dillard's Department Store, one incident occurred that was kind of comical. As one individual approached for an autograph, the cheerleader coach walked in behind Briggs as the autograph seeker approached. This individual wanted a Dallas Cowboys cheerleader to sign a pair of undershorts he had just bought at Dillard's for the occasion. The cheerleading coach said, "I don't think so. Who do you think my girls are?" At that, the autograph session at Dillard's was ended with a lot of disappointed fans. If you have ever seen the movie *The Dallas Cowboys Cheerleaders*, the coach in that movie is depicted spot-on. By the way, the coach also sternly advised Briggs she was not to sign anything untoward that would be deleterious to the organization. I learned one thing: never approach a Dallas Cowboys cheerleader for an autograph to be placed on your unmentionables.

It Was Small But, Damn Sure, Looked Like a Cannon

One summer evening, approximately in 1975, I received a call of a family disturbance. Now on a family disturbance, you never went in without a backup. Ever. I always followed this rule as one could get real hurt real bad walking into a situation that could be very dangerous. As I approached the address of the call, I observed the neighborhood was a nice neighborhood with manicured lawns. I stopped a block off but was able to observe what appeared to be a husband and wife verbally arguing in the distance. I had sat there waiting on another officer for about ten minutes when the male drove off in a huff. I took this as the disturbance being over and proceeded to the residence. As I pulled up in front of the house, the female waited on the sidewalk, observing my arrival. As I walked up to her and got about three feet from her, she stuck a small silver .25-caliber automatic pistol right against my chest. That pistol, at that moment, looked as big as a cannon. I was trying to calm her along with also trying to save my life when, thank goodness, my backup arrived. Noticing the other officer, she still kept the pistol against my chest. I begin to get the feeling I may not get out the situation when my back up approached her and called her by name and said, "Don't do it. It's not worth it." At that, she relaxed and pulled the pistol away and to her side, when my backup grabbed it out of her hand. Apparently, she was still mad at her husband, and I was available. Come to find out, the female was his sister, and he had heard the address of the call across town and responded because he knew who lived there. Thank goodness for this. It wasn't until after things got calmed down that I realized my backup was one of the street Sergeant supervisors. We talked a few minutes, and he assured me he would take care of the incident and any and all associated paperwork. He did not want me to arrest his sister, and I was just happy I was still walking out alive. I sure wanted to make an assault arrest, but a sister is a sister. That was the last time I ever went into a situation by myself, even though one party had left. Lesson learned.

Police Chaplains

Police Chaplains are a very necessary and vital part of law enforcement operations. A Chaplain is a valuable resource and serves voluntarily in service to their community. I've had to use them a couple of times on accidents and suicides I have worked. No one wants to notify someone that a loved one has been involved in a fatality of any kind. This is where a Police Chaplain's service is used. As a Pilot, I enjoyed having a Chaplain fly with me on those days my partner Pilot was off. There was a Baptist Pastor who flew with me often, and I enjoyed his company and help in answering calls from ground personnel. When a Chaplain is used, it's usually a serious situation when they are called. They restore the broken, heal the hurting, and provide comfort as needed. I thought I would include a humorous story and one you may also find interesting. When I was a new officer, I had occasion to work the north end of Wichita, approximately in the fall of 1974 or 1975-ish. The particular beat I was temporarily assigned included an area on north Broadway that had several bars and a few strip clubs. One particular Friday nightshift, I was called into the Station Captain's office. One usually did not get called into the Captain's office unless you were really in trouble. Usually, a Sergeant or Lieutenant took care of any issues, but the buck stopped with the Station Captain. I was on second shift, from three o'clock to eleven o'clock, a shift that had lots of action on Friday and Saturday nights on occasion. The Captain wanted me to take one of the Chaplains on shift with me and informed me to take the Chaplain into bars with me that I checked. Let the Chaplain know what we did and what we contended with on second shift. "OK," I said, and the Chaplain met me in the hallway. I had never been assigned responsibility of a rider, let alone a Chaplain. I do not recall his name now but do recall he was a Baptist Pastor and a genuinely caring and spiritual person. Toward about eight o'clock, I checked a north end bar known to be a little rowdy at times and one known to have bar fights, knife fights, etc., on occasion. I had checked this bar several times previously and had become acquainted with the owner in passing, who on one occasion told me that I and the only other officer who checked this particular bar as often was an officer named Caldwell. I recall him asking me if I knew him, and I answered yes. I didn't relay how I knew Gary Caldwell or that I knew of Gary prior to joining the department. I only relayed that I knew Gary who by that time was no longer on the department. On this particular evening, the Chaplain and I walked in the back door near the pool tables. Just as we did, one of the pool players missed a shot. Boy, did he cuss up a blue streak. You name the cuss word, and he said it. A rant that seemed to last a long time but probably only lasted a short period of time, but several words were said that I figured the good Pastor did not often hear. I thought I could cut loose on occasion, but I believe he had me beat. His back was to us as we walked in. We begin to walk past this pool player who had obviously had a little too much to drink. As we walked by, he sensed someone behind him, not expecting a police officer as he turned toward us. He was naturally surprised to see a police officer behind him but even more surprised to see the Pastor, it turns out. The minute he saw the Pastor, he awkwardly greeted the pastor by name, and the pastor acknowledged him, and we continued our walk from the back to the front. We were only in the bar a few minutes. When a police officer checks a bar, you kind of got to be ready for anything, and you have to get used to people staring at you until you leave. You simply must have acute situational awareness. Every time I put on a police uniform, my situational awareness was very high, but when one checks a bar, situational awareness is more acute. You mainly check bars by a walkthrough to show a police presence to let people know you're there. I never had a problem in that bar that I can recall. Bars are usually dark and smoky inside, and it is a good idea to close one eye a minute or so before going in to let your eyes readjust more quickly once inside. We walked through and back out the back door, past the pool player who again acknowledged his Pastor; however, his language was not as blue. We got into the car, and I drove back out onto Broadway. The Pastor was quiet for a minute or so, as if contemplating. When he did speak, he called his parishioner by name and said, "I bet I was the last person he expected to see in there." He chuckled a little as we drove off.

Profanity Degrades

I picked up the following somewhere along the line and thought I would include it as a result of the last story. I sometimes haven't followed it as I'm pretty good at it, but I feel it has a certain truth about it. The author is credited as Martin Luther, a German friar, priest, and professor of theology, who lived from November 10, 1483, to February 18, 1546.

It is no mark of a gentleman to swear. The most worthless and vile, the refuse of mankind, the drunkard and the prostitute, swear as well as the best dressed and educated gentlemen. No particular endowments are requisite to give a finish to the art of cursing. The basest and meanest of mankind swear with as much tact and skill as the most refined; and he that wishes to degrade himself to the very lowest level of pollution and shame should learn to be a common swearer. Any man has talents enough to learn to curse God and imprecate perdition on himself and his fellow man. Profane swearing never did any man good. No man is richer or wiser or happier for it. It helps no one's education or manner. It commends no one to society. It is disgusting to the refined, abominable with whom we associate, degrading to the mind, unprofitable, needless, and injurious to society; and wantonly to profane His name, to call His vengeance down, to curse Him, and to invoke His vengeance is perhaps of all offenses, the most awful in the sight of God.

—Luther

Holiday Inn Incident

On August 11, 1976, I was working as a Traffic Investigator, answering as Traffic 13 on the radio. Assigned Traffic Investigators worked only serious and fatal accidents. It was shift change, at approximately 2:45-ish PM. I had just checked on the air as Traffic 13 and unfortunately was the first second-shift officer to do so when I got a call of a shooting at the Holiday Inn downtown. The Holiday Inn was only three blocks south of the Police Station, and I headed that way in a hurry. At that time, my thought was to confront the suspect in front of the motel, take him in custody if possible, and stop the bad guy. I was the only officer available as others had not checked on the air as available yet. I got about a half block from the Holiday Inn when the dispatcher then informed me that multiple shots had been fired from a sniper on the twenty-sixth floor and that multiple injuries and some fatalities had occurred. That is when multiple units began to check on and respond. By that time, I was almost in front of the motel and was unable to get turned around to go behind the motel because of traffic and panicking pedestrians. My thought then was I could go through the front and to the back of the motel up the stairs and then confront the suspect. I then heard multiple shots myself and decided to simply get out of my car, use it for protection, and see if I could get a good shot at the shooter. The shots stopped, probably reloading, and I got out and positioned myself as described. More shots rang out, and I could hear the rounds hitting the pavement a good distance behind me. As one can imagine, the scene I saw, directly in front of the motel, was panic, pandemonium, and horror by people on the street that someone could actually be shooting at them. When I realized the shots were not close to any person in particular, I then realized the shooter was simply shooting indiscriminately and not placing aimed shots. All of a sudden, the shots stopped, and the dispatcher came on and said the shooter had been captured and shot. All those responding officers out front of the motel were released back to duty. I then drove back behind the motel and entered through the back door of the motel. I saw several officers coming down a set of stairs, shotguns in hand. They had heard the call come out just after I had received it, ran from the police station to the back of the motel, made their way to the twenty-sixth floor, and shot the shooter in the legs. Thus, that ended the sniper incident. Those actually involved in the capture received department citations.

Officer Down

Sometime in the late fall of 1979, I answered a call in the Ninth and Grove area during second shift. The area was known as the ghetto to us officers, as the area was simply crime ridden. I do not recall the type of call or what the call was about. The point of this story is that after I made the call, it was around ten o'clock or so. I parked my patrol car on the southwest corner of Ninth and Grove. Due to the area being troublesome, I parked in an abandoned service station lot, facing Grove Street under streetlights for a better field of vision. This was not a good place to highlight myself; however, my thought was to use the streetlights as light enough to write a quick short report on the call I had just made. Due to the area I was in, I certainly did not want to turn my dome light on, making me more of a target. At that time, we were not using any type of automated system to write or call in reports, and all calls had to have a handwritten report associated with it. Across the street, just south of Grove on Ninth Street, was a liquor store. Liquor stores got robbed frequently in this area, and my parking there was twofold—to write a short report and to watch the liquor store. I was parked for approximately less than ten minutes when I observed someone walk out of the liquor store and cross the street toward me. I did not see any other individuals in the vicinity, and the traffic was light, which was unusual for this time of night in that area. The individual walked up to my window, and I rolled my window down. He said, "Excuse me, Officer, but a guy just walked out the back door of my liquor store with a shotgun." The individual further said that this person was intending to walk around the block out of my sight, then walk up behind my car, and shoot me through the driver's side window. He said, "I would move if I were you." I tried to get more of a description, but the individual turned around and left in a hurry. Apparently, he did not want to be known as a snitch. I decided not to remain parked and patrol the immediate area to look for someone carrying a shotgun. I searched for approximately fifteen minutes or so before leaving the area, thinking the liquor store owner simply did want a police car parked across the street from his store, scaring off his customers. Maybe he told me this just to get me to leave. I forgot about this incident as we were receiving personal threats in this area constantly. This is the point of my relating this story to you. In early November 1980, one of our officers, Paul Garofalo, working the same area, stopped to talk to two ladies of the evening outside and across the street from a local bar, about a block from where I had parked. As he and his partner were talking to them, an individual walked from behind Garofalo's car and shot Garofalo in the face with a shotgun and ran off. Paul Garofalo was killed instantly, and his partner received shotgun-pellet wounds in his legs. It was a tragic incident performed by a coward. I have often thought back on this incident, thinking, *Was the perpetrator the same idiot who was reported to me as wanting to shoot me that previous fall evening?* I'll never know the answer to that one. The coward who shot Garofalo was apprehended a few days later and died in prison. The interesting thing about this type of individual is that once you have them, they easily give up. They almost never fight it out as they don't want to get shot. There are the exceptions to this rule.

Comedy of Errors

Some comical things that I can recall now that happened are as follows. One summer day, I was called in to get my new car and trade my old one in. I recall the old one had a lot of miles on it and had to continually be taken to the shop for repair. I was glad to be getting a new car, but I also had to share it with two other beat officers as I was on second shift. I picked up my new patrol car and learned it had one of the newer siren systems placed in it. The siren had several tones and wailing options. I had been on the street for about two hours and received a serious accident call. I turned on the siren and proceeded code three (lights and siren). I was getting a little concerned as cars were not pulling over for me. I had a volume control on the siren and had turned it all the way up. As I proceeded through intersections, adjusting the wailing and volume, my ears were hurting. It was so loud. Cars were still not pulling over to let me through intersections, and I began to take tag numbers, intending to contact them later and inform them of state and city law about pulling over for emergency vehicles. I was at this time becoming upset as it was taking me longer than it should to get to the scene. I then heard one of the beat officers say he had arrived, so I slowed down a bit. I advised on the radio I was getting close and would be there shortly. By the time I arrived, I was fit to be tied as no one was pulling over. That's when the beat officer then asked me as I walked up to the scene why I was not responding code three. I began to then check my brand-new car and noticed my lights were not on either. I knew the system was operating properly because it was blaring me almost out of the car; it was so loud. That's when I discovered that the electrician had wired the siren into the radio speakers, thus rendering my lights also inoperable. Case solved. After working the accident, I drove back to the garage to have it rewired, ears still ringing. I destroyed my tag number notes.

Zero Dark Thirty

One fall day, I was on the west side of Wichita and received a call of a possible fatal accident on West 54, a highway that ran through the city east and west. It was after sundown and dark, and to get there faster, I took a paved north/south road that was approximately eight miles long but cut several minutes off my response time. I was going a pretty good speed, and all of a sudden, I lost all electricity, including lights on my patrol car. There were no streetlights on this road, and it became real dark real quick. I could not see a thing, including the road, so I began to tap my brakes to slow down and moved to the right so I could feel my front tires off the pavement. This way, I at least knew part of my car was on the road. I had been on this road several times, and I knew I was approaching a curve. I decided to keep my right tire just off the road and on the shoulder, thus also to help slow me down. I was finally able to bring the car to a stop in pitch-black dark. The only radio I had was my portable, and I used that to call in and say I could not make it to the accident and needed a tow. When the tow truck arrived and I had lights to see the road, I learned I was just short of the sharp curve. Had I not stopped in time, it could have ended differently. I have been lucky in several situations, including this one.

Forgetfulness

As a police officer, one liaises with bordering adjacent small-town officers. One such time, I was called to investigate an accident that occurred on the south city boundary line and the county. When I got there, a county sheriff officer was there along with an officer of an adjacent town. It was decided the accident occurred on county proper and fell under jurisdiction of the county. As the sheriff officer was working the accident, the small-town officer and I began to trade STANs (Shoot That Ain't Nothing). He relayed the following story. I have been unable to confirm the story, but believe it to be true. This happened to the officer telling the story.

One day, the officer was called to the edge of their town to escort a funeral procession to the local cemetery. The procession had several cars in it. On funeral duty, you traveled no faster than fifteen to twenty miles an hour. The officer relayed as he was driving through neighborhoods to get to the cemetery, he forgot the funeral procession was behind him. The officer said he was simply driving on patrol like always in this particular area. The officer realized he forgot about the procession when the lead hearse honked their horn at him. By that time, the officer had made several turns and had driven away from the cemetery. When he realized what he had done, he turned the procession around and finally got them to their destination. A comedy of errors. I suppose this is not the only time this sort of thing has happened.

Am I Going to Die?

Approximately in the summer to late fall of 1975 while working as a uniformed patrol on the south side, I received a call of a possible fatal car/train accident. Upon arrival, I observed that an older-model westbound pickup had been struck by a southbound train. I was the first on the scene, prior to any other responding beat officers and ambulance personnel. The train was stopped, blocking any traffic from going east or west on Harry Street, just east of West Street. There were two older folks on the grass adjacent to the curb with what appeared to be nonlife threatening injuries. I also observed a small boy, approximately eleven years old, lying on the grass in a pool of blood. He needed my attention pretty quick. When I got out of my vehicle, I immediately started for the small boy. The older female was yelling, "We've killed our grandson" over and over. As I got to the boy, I observed he was conscious and had a deep laceration on his upper lip, exposing his front teeth and also exposing some bone surrounding his front teeth. I quickly surmised he had been thrown out the front windshield upon impact with the train, cutting his face as he went through. A cut in the area he was injured will normally cause a lot of bleeding. When the boy hit the grass, where I found him, he was knocked unconscious for a few seconds. The ambulance had not yet arrived, and I realized the accident was not fatal but involved serious injury to the small boy. I kneeled down beside the boy and asked his name, taking his hand in mine to comfort him. He looked up at me with tears in his eyes and asked, "Am I going to die?" I will not forget this as long as I live, and I still get somewhat emotional relaying this incident. I looked him square in the eyes and said to him, "No, son, you're not going to die." I explained to him that he had a deep laceration on his upper lip causing him to bleed profusely and that he would have to have a few stitches but that he would be just fine. I could see the color return to his face. You never lie to anyone when asked. I was just glad I could relay this to him. And further, looking back, if I thought it was going to be fatal, I doubt I would have informed a young boy this. He needed hope. When his grandmother kept yelling that they had killed their grandson, the boy heard this and thought he was actually going to die. I went over to the grandmother and assured her that her grandson was not going to die and explained his injuries to her. This calmed her down enough to stop yelling, which was scaring the boy half to death. I was glad when the ambulance arrived. The people involved in this accident were very lucky. What one says, particularly by someone you respect and know, will be believed by them. This is why medical personnel are trained not to talk negatively about their patient under anesthesia. One's subconscious hears this and is believed by the conscious mind. I always hated to work on a fatal accident, especially if a small child was involved.

Is It Worth It?

As an assigned Traffic Investigator, my job was to work assigned serious injury and fatal accidents. I worked too many. Homicides and suicides also. Looking at death is never easy. Especially a death occurring as part of a preventable traffic accident. Usually, I called the Department Chaplain to inform folks that a loved one had been involved in a fatal accident. A job I would not want. I never had to make this call. I do recall on one occasion, having to be at the hospital to witness the identification of two children who were the victims of a fire. Their aunt made the identification. I never wanted to do that again. I'll describe one more accident.

More fatal accidents than I care to remember were alcohol related. In approximately midsummer evening of 1977, I received a call of a possible fatal accident on a street called Meridian along the Arkansas River, adjacent to the Osteopathic Hospital in Wichita. Upon arrival, I saw that a southbound little sports car had been struck head-on in the sports cars' lane of traffic by a northbound heavier vehicle, the driver of which had obviously crossed the center line. The driver of the sports car was a nineteen-year-old female, the only fatality, who had just got off work and was on her way home. The driver of the other car was a very intoxicated older male who, because of his intoxication, had taken a slight curve in the road too fast, crossed the center line, and struck the sports car almost head-on at a high rate of speed, killing the driver. I, of course, arrested the driver for driving while intoxicated (DWI), among other related charges, and took him to jail. This charge is now known as driving under influence (DUI), which not only covers alcohol intoxication but also covers drug-related offenses. I called for a Chaplain to inform the family. Now, here's the really sad part. The following day, at approximately the same time of evening, I was running radar on this same stretch of road. I was traveling southbound in about the same spot the sports car had been. A northbound vehicle came speeding my way, again going too fast to maneuver the curve in the road. I immediately turned around and gave chase. The driver stopped, and as I approached the vehicle, the intoxicated driver stepped out. The driver was the same man who had killed the teen girl the night before and almost in the same spot. I couldn't believe someone could be that stupid. I was amazed he was out of jail I arrested him again. His blood alcohol test (BAT) was over 3.0. If one has a BAT of 4.0, it is usually a fatal amount in the system. Come to find out, the individual was an alcoholic who seemed oblivious to the fact he had just killed someone the night before. I do not know the outcome of his trial. I was never called to testify. I'm positive he pled guilty and was sentenced. Driving after consuming alcohol is simply very, very stupid.

Why

"Whatsoever a man soweth, that shall he also reap" (Galatians 6:7).

People ask why God would let this happen. Why would God take a young life? My belief is that God did not cause the incident or cause a death. God gave us all freedom of choice. We are free to choose how to live, free to choose to drink alcohol, free to snort crack, free to shoot heroin, free to pull out a gun and shoot somebody. There was an accident in the midnineties involving a cement truck and a school bus, which caused the death of six innocent school children. I believe it may have occurred in Ohio, but it made national news. The cement truck driver was intoxicated and caused the accident. The question was asked why God let this happen. Why would God take the life of a young child? My thought is that God did not let this happen. God did not make the truck driver intoxicated. The truck driver caused his own intoxication by his choice, who then chose to drive drunk. God did not make the person bend his elbow to take the drink, shoot the heroin, or kill a person. The person did. God gave us all freedom of choice and the consequences of choices. Choose wisely.

News Reporters

There was always a news reporter (radio and/or TV) around on fatal or serious injury accidents, homicides, suicides, and anything newsworthy, asking questions, basically getting in your way of working the scene and getting traffic moving again. News reporting is a necessary job, but a reporter should learn to stay back so the officers working any incident could collect facts so proper reporting to the public could occur. There was one reporter I was particularly fond of, Nelson Shock. I first met Nelson when he showed up at an accident

I was working in the early seventies. I do not recall where now, as I worked so many in Wichita. Nelson was part of KFDI's Pony Express News team. I can't tell you how many times I was interviewed by Nelson over the years. Nelson was a former law enforcement officer and knew enough not to approach you when you were attempting to clear a scene. He always gave you the courtesy of remaining back while other reporters were all over you, trying to get a statement before I even knew all the facts. I later moved into a home we had just built, and Nelson and his wife Sylvia became our neighbors and personal friends around 1976. After I worked a scene, whatever the offense, I always gave Nelson the courtesy of an interview, prior to any other reporter, simply because I knew he was always factual and to the point in his reporting. Nelson always had a tape recorder slung over his back and a smile on his face. He was a friend to all, a genuinely nice and caring person, who knew most officers and called them by their first names. I liked Nelson as a neighbor. He was a professional and personal friend. One summer, approximately in 1977, Nelson and I tore down a barn together for the wood. Nelson was a hard worker and not one to sit around. No matter who you were, after he met you, he called you his friend. There were many times, I can recall as his neighbor, that Nelson was called at home in the middle of the night to cover some emergency or incoming local weather. He took pride on being the first on the scene of any incident and was a very good reporter and radio personality of KFDI radio. Approximately in the summer of 1978, Nelson was called to cover a Titan II missile incident, near Rock, Kansas. A Titan II missile had extremely toxic propellants, including the oxidizer nitrogen tetroxide. Because of this, all but the most minute of leaks of either fuel or oxidizer had to be taken seriously. Nelson, who arrived first on the scene of this incident, breathed in the oxidizer spewing in the air around the incident and became very ill and died as a result of this contact several years later. Each time I see or hear a newscast, I fondly remember my friend.

CHAPTER 9

I Become a Pilot

I suppose all those TV shows I watched as a boy with my father had an impact on me, creating the desire to accomplish my dreams. Because I wanted to learn to fly, I went to the local bank and borrowed two thousand five hundred dollars. I took a cashier's check to Wichita Mid-Continent Airport (ICT) and went directly to Beech Aircraft. I walked in and told the desk clerk I wanted to learn how to fly. The clerk informed me that there was a cost associated with their instruction and wanted to know if I could afford the hourly cost and, if so, when I wanted to start. I produced the cashier's check to show her I was serious. The clerk immediately went into the back of the aircraft hangar, and a short time later, an instructor pilot came and introduced himself to me as Pat Downy, my instructor. I completed ground school, and Pat began instructing me in a small Beech 150. This was in June 1975. After about thirteen hours, I was beginning to be a bit concerned as I had not yet soloed. Mid-Continent Airport (ICT) has two main runways and two small cross runways. During my thirteenth flight hour, I was instructed by Pat to fly touch and goes (landing and taking off). While on my third touch and go, Pat had me stop where I had landed, in the middle of the runway. As I stopped, he told me that I was scaring him and that he was getting out. This concerned me greatly. He then said to take the aircraft up and complete three touch and goes, then come back, and pick him up. That's when I realized he was soloing me. On my second touch and go, I was instructed by Air Traffic Control (ATC) that there was a heavy passenger jet coming in behind me, and I was to make a right outbound turn west until further instructed. I had never flown without an instructor beyond the airport and began to stress but followed his instruction. I never asked Pat what he thought when he saw me fly off, but I bet he was somewhat concerned. Finally, when I was a little over five miles out, I was given instructions to fly back to the airport and given a compass heading back. I landed with no problem and picked Pat up, still standing along the runway where I left him. I obtained my private pilot's license after fifty-two flight hours. I was sure proud of myself. Over the course of the following years, I rented Beechcrafts for one-hour flights here and there as I could afford. I had been on the police department for approximately two years. One of the police garage mechanics, George Mattern, had never been up in a small plane, and I agreed to take him up during a conversation in the police garage. As I did this, a nearby officer, overhearing us, said, "I want to go up too." That Saturday, I took them both up in a Beech 180 four place. The aircraft I rented had an Auto Pilot (AP), and I used this in flight. I had decided to fly to Salina, Kansas, pull a touch and go, then fly back. A flight of approximately an hour and a half or less. Because the aircraft had an AP, after I took off and was handed over from Ground Control to ICT outbound, I set the AP for the Salina Visual Omni Range (VOR). The transponder was squawking 1200, a signal that goes to the Air Traffic Control Center (ATC), letting them know I was flying on Visual Flight Rules (VFR) and not flying on instruments. As we were talking in the cockpit, George, who was sitting in the back, realized I was just sitting there watching the instruments. At about the same time he made this observation, the AP picked up a VOR signal changing the direction of the aircraft toward Salina. When the aircraft began turning without me on the controls, George became a whole lot concerned. After explaining what was happening, George calmed down a bit but was constantly watching what I was doing after that. I ended up not landing in Salina and turned back just shy of the Salina runway. As we got back to Wichita, I turned from base to final approach, and George asked if the landing was going to bounce. When one lands a plane, you want to touch down, so the tires make a little bounce. However, because George was a little concerned about hitting terra firma, I landed in such a way that even I would not have known we had touched down had I not been looking out the window. You really should feel the tires touch, but I was concerned about George. When I throttled back, George said he didn't feel a thing as we landed. I will admit it was one of my better landings though. I decided I had enough fixed wing flight hours and began hanger bumming the department's Air Section. At that time, you had to have two hundred or more flight hours to be accepted in the department's Flight Section.

Never drink fluids prior to a long flight. (Make your bladder gladder before flight)

OK.....one more fixed wing story. Sometime around 1977, a friend, also a pilot, and police officer I worked with, asked me if I was interested in taking a commercial flight to Las Vegas, NV, to fly a four place Piper back. My friend later resigned his law enforcement commission and began a career flying passengers in commercial aircraft. Back on point, Piper is a good aircraft and is easy to fly. Apparently my friend had an acquaintance, an Attorney, who had flown his Piper to Las Vegas, and had gotten weathered in the week prior. The aircraft was IFR capable, and the Attorney IFR rated, but did not want to fly back in weather. The Attorney had then taken a commercial flight back to Wichita (ICT) and needed someone to fly his aircraft back to Wichita from Las Vegas. I agreed to do this as I was needing to build my flight time. After taking a commercial flight to Las Vegas, we found the Attorney's aircraft and asked the McCarran International Airport maintenance personnel to top the fuel off.

During the fuel purchase, we spent some time at Caesars Palace, and returned a couple hours later. There is a taxi cab yarn associated with our Caesars Palace adventure, but I will refrain from telling this story. During preflight of the aircraft, we discovered a small fuel leak over the right main, (front tire). The leak was at the point where, during preflight, the aircrafts fuel level is checked. It was a minor drip, and we decided the fuel leak was not going to hinder the flight back to Wichita, and took off. Before we left Las Vegas, we both had consumed some soda and found this was a mistake just after rotating (Vr), as we both needed to use the restroom as a result while in flight. (There is no restroom on a small aircraft). My friend was Instrument qualified and we were flying IFR at approximately 9500 feet indicated toward Albuquerque (ABQ), NM, just after dark. We started to climb to 11,500 but got ATC permission in flight to alter our flight plan and descend to 9.5. We decided to cancel our IFR flight plan, as we approached Albuquerque, and take a much needed facility break. By the way, it takes awhile to climb to 9.5 in a small aircraft. We landed with no incidents in ABQ, and both of us took a much needed break. My friend finished, and left the restroom. I, on the other hand, was still going. My friend left, and purchased two 16 oz. cokes for us in the pilot's lounge. After my friend had finished drinking his coke, and I had not yet reappeared in the lobby, he returned to the restroom, to check my welfare. I was still going. I was in no need of more liquid refreshment from the coke he had just bought me. He of course made jokes about how long it was taking. I responded that he should leave because there was a possibility of collateral damage to his person. Well, I finally finished, and took my full bottle of coke to drink on the flight. We refiled our IFR flight plan and took off from ABQ toward ICT. It was just before midnight. We both took our coke bottles with us in case we needed to go again. We landed at Jabara Airport, Wichita, without any other incidents during early morning hours prior to sunrise. We never had to use our coke bottles, but I decided if I ever flew another long flight, I would refrain from consuming any type of fluids, and take a coke bottle with me just in case. Lesson learned.

I Became Air One and a Police Aviator

In 1978, the assigned Wichita Police Air Section air crew personnel were the Air Section Commander, an Airframe and Power Plant (A & P) mechanic on the day shift, and two pilots assigned to evening shift. Because I was on second-shift patrol, I would stop by the Air Section when I was not on call and the air crew were down between flights. I did this for a few months, and on one occasion, the Air Section Commander showed up. I think he knew I would be there that evening. He told me he was getting tired of me hanger bumming and decided I needed to join the Air Section. I naturally thought at first he was going to tell me to stop hanging around. I joined the Air Section as a Pilot in April 1978 and began rotor flight training on May 2, 1978.

I Solo a Helicopter

There is a saying, "Anything that screws its way into the sky flies according to unnatural principals. When your wings are leading, lagging, flapping, processing, and moving faster than your fuselage, there's something unnatural going on." Flying a helicopter may be unnatural; it is not only fun but challenging. I like that.

There is a big difference between flying a fixed wing and flying a rotor. At the time I was assigned to the Air Section, the department had two Hughes 300C Sky Knights, both light observation rotors. The department currently flies a jet-powered Hughes 500E rotor. Flying the 500E is probably like driving a Lamborghini compared to a flying a 300C, a Volkswagen. Things happen faster in a 500E. A 500E is a five bladed rotor with a Rolls Royce engine that produces 420 Shaft Horse Power (SHP). A 300C only has three blades with a Lycoming 180 Horse Power (HP). OK, back on point. On my first training flight, I was taken to a large field in the county and began learning how to hover a helicopter. I'll try to explain what it feels like. When hovering, one syncs flight controls between the collective and power, cyclic, and antitorque pedals, which control

131

the tail rotor. Taking control of a helicopter and making it do what you want it to do is a humbling experience. Learning to hover will make you sweat and may even scare you a bit. When you pull collective, the machine has a tendency to pull right due to the direction torque of the main rotor system, so you apply some left rudder and use cyclic for control. Coming to a hover is a slow-controlled maneuver. All flight controls are maneuvered in sync, coming to a stable hover. My flight instructor was the Air Section Commander, a police Lieutenant named Don Henton. Don was a seat-of-the-pants old Navy pilot who was an excellent pilot and instructor. Many times, we flew northwest of Wichita to the Wichita Speedway. The speedway had a long paved road for drag racing, which was an excellent place to practice straight in autorotations—ninety-, one-hundred-eighty-, and three-hundred-sixty-degree autorotations. An autorotation is a maneuver that simulates engine failure. When the engine quits on a rotor, it loses altitude pretty darn quick. The only thing flying the rotor on an engine failure is the wind moving up through the rotor system as you're descending. If you don't throw the collective down quickly, the drag on the rotor's airfoil stops the blades from turning. Then you're in an "oh shit" mode. Don liked to fill his coffee cup up to just about full and perform the autorotations. If you spilled his coffee, you failed. On one occasion, we were flying with the doors off, and as I completed a three-hundred-sixty auto, his coffee cup slid from the floor between us (where he usually placed it) and out my side of the aircraft in the left banking maneuver I was making. I still passed. He later told me that had the coffee spilled on the way out, I would not have passed. I never spilled his coffee by the way. I recall just before Don released me to solo, he filled his coffee cup to the brim, climbed in, placed his filled coffee cup very carefully on the floor, so as not to spill any. He then told me to pick the machine up from the ground on takeoff without spilling his coffee. I did and was released to solo.

Meantime, I was part of the flight crew on patrol over the city, and soon after I soloed in the rotor, I passed my final flight exam. I was now a certified private helicopter pilot. My dream of flying a rotor after days of watching *Whirlybirds* on TV became a reality.

Over time, I went on to obtain my Commercial Helicopter pilot's license, rotor rating. The whole process was very exciting for me, and as I write this, I can still feel the controls in my hands. I can still hear the gin of the engine and whirr of the rotor blades, hear the wind rush by, see the instruments and the ground as I fly in my memory. I miss the adrenaline flow. As I write this and I think back on my flight experience, I will relay some quick thoughts as a police pilot. I hope I have written it so you can get a feel of what it's like to fly a helicopter. I kept in good physical condition, as all police pilots must maintain a first-class flight physical. If you don't pass the physical, you don't fly. You know the FAA regulations almost by heart. We flew and adhered to the FAA Part 135 regulation. I read and studied FAA regulations along with Notice to Airman (NOTEM). I read and studied rotor crashes to keep from making the same mistakes. I kept up with law enforcement tactics, techniques, and procedures, and also law enforcement and aviation procedures and requirements. You have to be proficient and knowledgeable in both. Both pilots in the aircraft are licensed pilots; however, one is acting observer until next mission, then the roles are switched. I believe now there actually is a position called police observer, with observer training as required. The pilot, not the observer, is in command of the aircraft. All decisions are his. The Airframe and Power Plant mechanic (A & P) is critical to flight operations, and the engine is not only checked daily but also checked every one hundred hours for airworthiness inspection. Any engine failure or failure of a rotor part on mission could be disastrous. Preflight inspection of the aircraft is critical for a pilot and the maintenance of the aircraft. The preflight must be meticulous and checked properly for aircraft airworthiness. Every flight is unique because you never know what you will be called upon to perform to help ground personnel. Other agencies also use the police rotor by request. A caveat here is that if we were called upon to do something that was outside FAA regulations or the Pilot simply felt not right about the mission, we did not do it. The Pilot is always in Command of the Aircraft (PIC), no one else—ever. Never get complacent and never take anything for granted. Once I climbed into the cockpit, I became more serious and thoughtful. My thoughts turned to operation of the machine and mission, nothing else. To do otherwise is dangerous because your mind must always be on the flight, mission, and safety. Not only my life was on the line but any mistake by me as a pilot could affect the outcome of an already-serious situation on the ground. Constant monitoring of fuel and instruments. Constant monitoring of sky for other aircraft. Constant monitoring of police and air traffic communication from both Wichita tower and McConnell Air Force Base. Night flying is more intense, but once on patrol, the city looks very pretty at night. When it was time to fly, the pilot and observer climbed into the rotor and checked all instruments and controls. Once the machine was started, rotor clutch engaged and ginned to operating revolutions per minute (RPM), needles married, I rolled in power and carefully pulled up on the collective for lift at the same time and came to a hover. Let me make a very basic caveat here that is basic to the physics of the main rotor system and flight operations. I don't want to give a flight lesson here, but I find the physics of this, and still do, interesting. When a helicopter is sitting on the ground, the airfoils called blades and are not turning and are limping downward due to the weight of the blade itself. Once the engine is running and clutch of the main rotor system engaged, the blades, spinning, are straight out by centrifugal force. However, once you lift off, the blades turn upward, called a coning effect. The blades are turning faster at the hub of the main rotor system than at the end of the blade itself. The next time you observe a rotor lift off, look for this effect. I don't know why, but I find the effect fascinating. Back on point, after coming to a hover, I then hovered and maneuvered over to the helipad, a trip of approximately three hundred feet, and came to a hover. I observed the tree line in front of me and the sky checked for other aircraft, facing wind direction, noting wind speed. All instruments indicating all systems functioning properly, transponder squawking 1200, communications functioning properly (all five police radio channels and ATC channels). All clear for takeoff, and the observer notified police dispatch we were taking off and on call as Air One. As I pulled collective and rolled in power at the same time and began moving forward and up gaining altitude, (Vtocs) I relaxed a little, but only on the controls to cruise altitude. Once at cruise altitude (four hundred to six hundred feet above ground level (AGL), sometimes higher depending on mission), I generally cruised between sixty to eighty knots, unless orbiting on call, such as a burglary, officer in trouble, car chases, etc. Once airborne, man and machine must work perfectly together. You roll in power and feel one with the wind and machine. All thoughts on mission. We usually flew on one-hour flights for pilot safety and fatigue, sometimes more, again depending on mission. After an hour on mission, we returned to the heliport. Landing pad in sight, I again checked for wind speed and direction and landed at a twelve-degree slope onto the helipad into the wind. The helipad becomes what is known as a Landing Zone or LZ. You keep the LZ in the same spot on the windscreen when descending and making small corrections on all the controls as you do so, all at the same time. I began to flare around fifty feet, more or less, slowing the decent and coming to a hover, which was approximately three feet AGL. In the flare, you slowly start pulling up on the collective while adding power and left pedal to compensate for additional torque. You also start pulling back on the cyclic to stop your forward movement, raising the nose of the aircraft. Coordinate all three controls at the same time and coming to a relaxed and stable hover. Let any of the controls get away from you, and you then are in an "oh shit" mode. Bad things will start to happen. You simply have to think ahead of the helicopter and remain on top of it. After coming to a hover, I would maneuver over to the fuel station for refueling for the next flight or mission. I hope the aforementioned gives you some sense of what it's like to fly a helicopter. I didn't mention everything such as in- and out-of-ground effect, but I hope you got a hint of what it feels like to hover, take off, and land a rotor. I have many memories of flying, too many to mention here, but I will relay some of these experiences.

Ready for Flight

On Patrol at 1800 MSL

Stepping into the Cockpit

What I miss most about flying a rotor, is skimming over the trees at 80 knots plus, in light wind or fog, and low visibility, on the way to an emergency call. Pucker factor: about ten. I love adrenaline

Autorotations

While assigned as a Pilot to the Air Section, I had two real-time autorotations. When you learn how to fly, you react the way you were taught without thinking in an emergency. In an emergency, you really do not have time to think, only react and hope you were taught right. My first autorotation occurred south of the city near I-235. I was at an altitude of approximately eight hundred feet Above Ground Level (AGL), heading back toward the heliport. On a piston-powered rotor, the engine is running very hot, especially during the summer. Spark plugs can become contaminated with molten metal clogging the spark plug gap. When this happens, the engine sputters and just quits. The higher you are, the safer you are, particularly in a rotor. To give you an idea, at eight hundred feet above ground level, you have about seven seconds before you hit the ground. So you better have the rotor blades level real quick. This is done with the collective control. I threw the collective down when the engine failed and descended approximately two hundred feet when the gap cleared, and I was able to restart the engine. Some initial sputtering and then smooth revolutions per minute again. I landed at the heliport a short time later and, after a quick inspection by our A & P, was off again. The same thing happened on takeoff one other time. I was just rolling in power and pulling up on the collective, and all of a sudden, it got real quiet. I immediately threw down the collective and hit the ground with a slight thud. Luckily, I was only about two feet high when the engine quit. I was able to restart and was off again without incident. Actually, when you perform an autorotation correctly from altitude all the way to the ground, if you had a carton of eggs in the seat, you would not break any. Whenever one flies low and slow over the city at night, you are constantly looking for a place to land in case of an emergency. I never had an emergency over the city, and it was my belief that if I didn't have a safe place to land, it would not be on anyone's home. I would put the machine down, so that wouldn't happen. Even if it meant my life. It is not the person on the ground's fault I had an emergency. If it was between me or them, it was going to be me. I'm sure the current air crew feel the same.

Dropping Gas

The midseventies were tumultuous for Wichita in the summer months as described above. Several small riots occurred, and on occasion as we flew over trouble spots within Wichita for observation, we could observe a flash of light on the ground as we flew over. It was gunshots at the rotor. When I was flying, we were never hit. I think the shooter simply was unaware you had to lead the rotor with a shot; otherwise, your shot missed and fell behind due to the speed of the aircraft. One of the pilots, who had left prior to my becoming a pilot, did take what was later determined to be a 30.06-caliber round in the right intake manifold and had to land, but this is the only time I am aware that any Wichita aircrew was actually hit with small arm's fire. Sometime around summer of 1979, rioting occurred near the Twenty-First Street and Grove area, with approximately one hundred fifty juveniles involved. We were called by the Chief of Police to land on the southeast corner of Hillside and Twenty-First to contact him. We landed in the Wichita State University (WSU) parking lot, where we were contacted by then Chief LaMunyon, a good Police Commander and leader. He gave us a carton of tear gas grenades that he wanted us to drop on the rioters, so he could send in some ground troops to gain control of the riot, thus saving injuries on both sides. We took off and dropped several canisters (grenades) of tear gas among the rioters, which scattered them. This was enough for ground personnel to come in and gain control, which is exactly what they did. Let me explain a little about dropping gas from a rotor. When dropping gas, the observer pilot throws the canister of gas down and under the mainframe of the aircraft. This is so the grenade falls down, not up and out into the main rotor system. You also want the canister of gas to fall down and inward under the aircraft mainframe so that the canister does not get into the tail rotor. All kind of tricky maneuvers by both of the pilots. You also have to throw accurately so the canister of gas does not get washed into the tail rotor by the downwash of the main rotor system. I still have the grenade pulls I used this particular evening, one of which I use as a zipper pull on my flight jacket.

The Coffeepot Incident

I never saw Don Henton without a cup of coffee near. Don's coffee cup was a thick coffee cup—white on the outside but on the inside was a well-caked brown coffee mug. He never washed it, at least I never saw it. One night while on a late fall evening shift, the other pilot, Richard Dewey, and I decided to heat some coffee. The only coffeepot available was Don's. Let me describe it for you. It was a small twenty-cup coffeemaker that I think was silver in color under a coat of coffee brown. The spicket you pulled down to release the coffee was so encrusted with old coffee crud it did not pull smoothly. This is when we decided to wash the darn thing. It was so encrusted it would not clean with soap and water. We decided to soak the coffeemaker in engine cleaner that the A & P used to clean engine parts, fly our regular patrol, then after landing, see if we could clean it. It did clean after soaking in engine cleaner, and it was actually silver underneath all that crud. We were so proud that we now had a spotless clean coffeepot. We did not make coffee that evening due to not having time after having to clean the pot to make coffee. Next evening when we came in for our shift, we found Don had bought a new coffeepot and had left us a note saying he was donating his old pot to the evening crew. He went on to say in no uncertain terms that we were not to touch his coffee fixings, that it had taken him years to get his coffeepot encrusted the way he liked it, and that we had ruined it. We never touched his coffee fixings again. The moral of this story is never clean a coffeepot with engine cleaner unless you want to taste engine cleaner in your coffee for a couple of months.

Never Eat Before Flying If You Are Not Used to It. It's Not Pretty.

One fall evening, I reported for flight duty, prior to my pilot partner getting there. I began to clean and preflight the machine, checking the main rotor system, tail boom, etc. I notice the inside windshield on the passenger side was dirty, so I began to clean it. I was not sure what caused the dirt on the windshield but wanted it clean, as I did not have the first flight that night and was riding as pilot/observer operating the search light as necessary. I had to use my fingernails as some of the dirt had to be scraped away. I cleaned the windshield inside and out and finished my preflight. We took off on another patrol. The following day, I again got there earlier than my pilot partner and began to preflight. The Air Section Commander was still there, and he commented on how nice the windshield looked from the upchuck that had been there the day before. "What? Hello? You never told me someone had regurgitated while in flight. That would have been nice to know as I may have been more careful in my cleaning duties. I would at least have worn gloves. Geeez!" Apparently, Don had taken one of the records section clerks up during the previous day. (We sometimes gave flights as a reward for a job well done to ground personnel.) The clerk, who had just finished eating and had never flown before, was unprepared for a helicopter ride. Yup, up came dinner. I told Don to warn us next time. It never happened again, but from that time on, if you flew with me, I always asked, "When was the last time you ate? And have you ever flown before?" Routine flight can be as boring as boring holes in the sky; other times, you got to maneuver into some tight banks to protect ground personnel.

The Green Stamp Caper

Sometime in approximately mid to late 1980, one of our detectives, Neil Myers, had gone undercover pawning himself off as a Kansas City gangster who had obtained a bunch of green welfare stamps. Myers had made contact with two individuals who would buy the stolen stamps. Neil was very experienced and was very believable as an undercover operative. The Air Section was to provide air surveillance cover for the buy. As we were circling the buy area, it became obvious our presence was making the buyers nervous when it was mentioned the police helicopter seemed to be near. Neil was wearing a body mike that was being transmitted to our investigative channel. We gained altitude real quick, which seemed to calm things down inside. One of the buyers was George Poulos. Poulos was an experienced bad actor and was notorious for this type of activity. As we were circling high above, things became very tense inside. I should mention here that an Air Traffic Control (ATC) center is five miles in diameter and decreases in size by one mile as you go up. McConnell Air Force Base has the same ATC area. We were in between both, and in addition to monitoring what was happening on the ground, we were also monitoring aircraft from each ATC areas. George decided that instead of paying for the stamps, he was going to kill Myers and pulled a pistol. When that happened, the detectives listening to the conversation through Myers's body mike knew something had to be done real quick. They rushed into the motel room where the buy was taking place just in time to keep Myers alive and made the arrest. Poulos was again in jail. George was sentenced fifteen years to life in Lansing Prison. Believe it or not, George wrote a book while in prison and later even made an unsuccessful attempt at becoming Mayor of Wichita in 2002. Over the years, George was convicted of several felonies. He was simply tough and dangerous. But if you met him on the street, he was very charming, the opposite of his dark side. George was found dead at the age of eighty-five in his Wichita home in November 2010.

Runners

Some folks are simply plain stupid and would try to run from an officer at a traffic stop. Usually, they are initially pulled over for some minor traffic infraction and in most cases given a warning. On some occasions, the traffic stops were only courtesy stops to inform the driver their headlight was out or some such. When you get stopped, accept responsibility, take the ticket, and drive on. When a traffic stop did decide to run, I always enjoyed chasing them in the rotor though and never lost a runner, except one. On this one occasion, one of the west-side officers was involved in a chase westbound on Highway 54, also known as Kellogg Street. The run vehicle was running west past the Wichita airport on US Highway 54, which ran through two active runways. I was unable to obtain permission to cross through the ATC area due to a passenger jet landing. I lost sight of the car when I had to come to a hover between the two main runways at altitude, but the officer was able to catch the car without the assistance of the aircrew. This is the only car I lost. On another occasion, we got an early morning call at the heliport from dispatch of a runner that was driving by the heliport hanger on a street called Meridian. Meridian was so named because it is part of the thirty-eight parallel. There was no traffic on the street except the officer and runner. We ran out of the hanger to the rotor and ginned up, just as the car and the chasing officer—red lights and siren blaring—went speeding by. As I began to gain altitude, I was having to use too much power to maintain forward air speed. I realized if I gained more altitude, I simply lost speed, which would not allow me to catch the speeder. I decided to stay low to maintain speed. It was after midnight with little traffic out. The speeder turned off Meridian and up the street that went between the city and county buildings, both over ten stories high. I flew between these two buildings just above the roofs at a little over two hundred feet above, allowing me enough air speed to direct ground units in to stop the idiot before he killed someone or himself. After landing, we get a phone call from our SPIDER (Special Police Information Data Entry Retrieval) channel operator. "Damn, was that you, OJ?" Apparently, he was looking out and up through the fifth-floor window as I flew by. You just try not fly that low. It's dangerous, and you have to be aware of the environment and what you are doing at all times. Runners were fun to chase though. Especially motorcycles. I always found it amusing that I could look down at the motorcycle and see them turn around and look behind them to see if they were being chased. They never looked up and usually slowed making turns in different directions thinking they had eluded the chasing unit(s). Not realizing the chasing units had backed off after we had eyes on. All we had to do then was direct the officers to where they were. Too easy. Chase ended. One motorcycle runner I remember was a pretty good-sized crotch rocket who ran from a traffic stop on the south side. We got the call while on patrol midtown, so it didn't take long to pick up the chase. There was a lot of weaving in and out of traffic by the bike. The motorcycle driver realized he was also being chased by the Air Section and turned into the big ditch. A canal for water runoff. We never lost him; however, as we banked away circling and turned back, he attempted to hide himself and his bike under some brush. He stopped, laid the bike down, and commenced covering himself with brush. We directed the ground units in, which had by this time grown to about four units. We were radioed that the ground units still could not locate the runner, due to not being able to see him. No problem. We descended to just about twenty feet above the pile of brush and pulled pitch, blowing all the poor guy's cover off he had worked so diligently to hide under. I will admit it was a fun chase. Never run from an officer. It will end up costing you more than the ticket and sometimes your life or someone else's. It is just simply not worth it.

How to Save Yourself Some Heartache: Stop Running

I will insert this article at this point in reference to not responding to law enforcement requests.

The article is from a newspaper in New York City, New York, following the death of an individual named Eric Garner who had resisted police. The article is by an individual named Bill Bratton. I found it very "spot-on" and added my own thoughts to the article. This is the article I added to.

The simple fact, painful as it may be for some to acknowledge, is that individuals would be alive today if they had only cooperated when police tried to arrest or simply detain them.

Instead, they argue with police, refuse to put their hands behind their back, and then accuse the police of harassing them and then resist. There seems to be the precept that no one is responsible for their action(s). It's the fault of society. Really. We need to teach our children respect for authority. Police officers are not your enemy. Instilling family values and traditional ethical behavior seems to be missing from family teachings.

Police officers are not going to walk away when someone resists arrest. Police officers aren't in the harassment business. A police officer does not care if you are green, purple, brown, white, black, orange, red, or rainbow. They are going to enforce the law. That's what they are trained to do and what you pay them for.

Enforcement of "quality of life" crimes are prompted by calls from community merchants and local officials, who "definitely want more police in their neighborhoods."

The fastest way to defuse a confrontation like one ending in death is not to resist arrest.

And if folks and assorted community leaders (who seem bent on besmirching cops) truly want to prevent tragedies, they'll repeat that lesson publicly and often. Parents in particular should be teaching this to their children The Sharptons and Jacksons of the world should also be preaching this and often. People are quick to affix blame to any situation, without knowing facts, which only further complicates matters, and interferes with the judicial process. In a court of law, it is not about truth; it's about what you can prove.

Suspects have every right to fight charges against them. What they don't have is a right to fight the cops. If one does not like the way the law is written, work to change it. Burning buildings, looting, throwing rocks, bottles, etc., or shooting does not help any cause. If you want to do something constructive, work to change the law.

Bind, Torture, and Kill (BTK)

There have been books, documentaries, and a movie made on the serial killer known as BTK. I will not go into details in this book. I will only relate my involvement as one of the pilots who flew surveillance missions on this investigation. Briefly, in January 1974, a family named Otero, with exception of two sons, was found murdered in a home in Wichita. Thus began a string of murders by a serial killer known as BTK who killed ten innocent victims between 1974 and 1991. The killer was eventually caught, and that was when the public learned that a family man named Dennis Radar was the killer. During his crime spree, he sent letters describing the details of the killings to police and local news outlets, taunting investigators. The murders stopped in 1991, and many thought the killer was either dead or in prison for other crimes. Radar resumed sending letters in 2004, leading to his 2005 arrest and subsequent guilty plea. He is currently serving ten consecutive life sentences. I always felt someone who takes a life and proven guilty deserves the death penalty rather than a life sentence. The thought the poor guy has to die seems unfair to some folks. No one seems to care about his victims. The proponents against capital punishment don't seem to care that someone's past, present, and future was taken away from them. My feeling is that not only the life of the victim is taken but also the joy that life could have brought to members of their families was taken. Their past, present, and future is stolen. I watched some of Radar's trial on TV. What struck me was the callous manner in which he described how he murdered his innocent victims. I became involved in the BTK casework as part of the aircrew who was called to provide aerial surveillance on a suspect that had been developed in 1979. I was placed on a twelve-on-twelve off shift beginning at noon daily. The suspect was an individual that seemed to keep odd hours, so ground units who had constant eyes on him and called the Air Section when our suspect left his residence. We then picked up the surveillance in the air, and ground units backed off. There were many night flights, with lights out on our rotor, and some high-altitude surveillance. The suspect's vehicle was sometimes difficult to see on the streets at night, intermingled with other traffic at altitude. One of our ground units drilled a small hole on the top of the right taillight when the suspect was at home sleeping. This helped tremendously because as the suspect vehicle traveled on streets at night, we could see a bright white light shining up at us from his right taillight, making it easier to identify. On one occasion when the suspect took a date to a movie, one of the officers in the surveilling ground unit needed to relieve himself. So the suspect vehicle would not take off while one officer was gone, the other partner let air out of one of the tires. The other officer came back just as the movie was getting out. All those on the surveillance thought the suspect would change the tire and drive on. Nope. Suspect had his date change the tire; apparently, she knew how, and the suspect and surveillance entourage were off and running. What a jerk he was. The surveillance lasted approximately two months, and we went back to normal shift. On and off, we provided surveillance for BTK suspects when needed. The officers involved in his eventual capture worked hard to do so. I have been involved in many surveillance details both on the ground and in the air. A surveillance can be very boring or can be very exciting.

Celestial Illumination

One late fall evening, approximately in 1979, we received a call from dispatch at the hanger that the sheriff's office needed air assistance in surveilling a car suspected of dealing drugs. The vehicle was westbound out of the city. We ran to the machine and ginned up. We took turns flying one-hour shifts, down an hour then switching pilots and back up again. This particular shift was Richard Dewey's turn to fly. As Richard was ginning the machine, I was on the radio determining where the vehicle currently was. The car had turned north and west out of the city toward Hutchinson, Kansas. We picked up the vehicle as it was leaving the city limits. It was dusk as we took off, but still light. We followed the car into the county, and it stopped at a farm home approximately fifteen miles northwest of Wichita. I called in the location to the sheriff's office, and that's when we all of a sudden realized it had gotten very dark real quick. The rotor we were flying was a Visual Flight Rules (VFR) machine only. An observation helicopter for daylight flying or celestial illumination only. We usually flew at night and, with the city lights, never had any navigational issues. On this particular evening, we had flown out of light. We slowed the machine to fifty miles an hour to make our skids level with the ground and slow banked one hundred eighty degrees southeast toward Wichita. Thank goodness, it was not cloudy that night. As we banked toward Wichita, we saw the city lights that guided us home. After this incident, we determined that we would never fly without knowing where the surveillance would lead.

A Lost Rotor

One evening when I got to work, I learned from a day-shift pilot that an Oklahoma City, Oklahoma (OKC), rotor landed earlier. Apparently, their aircrew was asked to provide air surveillance on a drug deal that led them into Wichita from OKC. The aircrew had left OKC without much money between them as their personal belongings were left at their hanger. Our dispatcher had called our hanger and advised they needed to land for food and fuel. They were given directions to our hanger, and they landed their machine at our heliport. Our A & P checked their machine for airworthiness and fueled them back up. Their undercover operator with eyes on told them their suspect vehicle was again moving, and they were off again, after a two-hour layover. It was still light out, and luckily, their suspect car had made a drug deal in Wichita and left back to OKC during daylight hours. When this happened to the OKC crew, we determined always to take some of our personal belongs with us while on patrol.

Alcohol, Tobacco, and Firearms (ATF)

One summer day, I was called at the hanger to escort an ATF agent for a flyby of a farmhouse in the county suspected of housing illegal firearms. The ATF agent arrived, and we took off. I and the other assigned pilot weighed in at about one hundred eighty pounds each. The ATF agent, on the other hand, weighed approximately three hundred pounds, maybe a little less. I should explain that just behind the passenger on the outside of the rotor sat a gas tank that held one hundred eighty pounds of aviation fuel, making the total weight on the passenger side of the rotor approximately four hundred eighty pounds, not including that of the pilot. That's a lot of weight. I did not think to do a weight-and-balance check because my flight partner pilot weighed about what I did. So on normal patrol, a weight balance check was not necessary. The density altitude that day was high, meaning more power was needed to take off and land. I knew my mistake immediately. The rotor became very squirrelly and required every ounce of power the rotor was capable of. We finally gained enough altitude, taking longer than normal because of the weight, and I banked toward our necessary compass heading. We found the farmhouse northwest of Wichita and identified that the vehicles in the drive indeed belonged to the ATF suspect. We turned back toward the city. I knew we could not land until I bled off some of the onboard fuel, decreasing the aircraft weight enough to land. Otherwise, I would fly straight into the ground as I pulled pitch to flair out on landing. I told the ATF agent that I needed to make a few patrol calls while we were up to help justify the flight. The agent was more than willing to do this as he had never been in a law enforcement aircraft on mission. I flew on several calls and bled off most of my fuel. Approximately two and one half hours' worth. There is three hours of fuel on board. I came back to the heliport and went in very slowly, making a perfect landing. I did not tell him why we needed to burn off fuel. I never flew anyone heavy again without completing a weight-and-balance check. Lesson learned.

A Downed Aircraft

One late summer evening, approximately in 1979, the other pilot, Richard Dewey, and I received a call of a downed aircraft, northwest of Wichita, that had been stolen from a farmer's barn. Apparently, the farmer also liked collecting old aircraft and had a couple, including the one that was stolen. Richard was flying that particular mission, and as we approached the area, we learned the person who stole the aircraft had taken off with the wind on his tail and had lost control of the aircraft on takeoff. The sheriff's officer working the scene on the ground advised they had the person who busted the aircraft in custody, and we were released back to patrol. Here is the point of his story. The stolen aircraft was one of the original fabric-winged Cessna 210s flown by Sky King, one of my boyhood TV heroes. I probably saw this aircraft, known as *Songbird*, on one of the TV episodes I watched when I was a kid. You just never know how things go in a circle and come back to you.

Big City Pilots

I had some interesting emergency flights. I'll describe one. One fall day, I was called to help the Sedgwick County Air Section escort a prisoner, who had been extradited back from Denton, Texas, to Wichita. At that time, one could get out of a rotor and immediately step into and fly a fixed wing and vice versa, if you were qualified to fly both. I was. I think that one cannot currently do this as FAA rules may have changed. I flew the rotor to Jabara Airfield where I was picked up by the Sedgwick County Sheriff's Office (SCSO) in their Cessna 172, a high-wing four place. We left Jabara for a small field near Denton, Texas. The sheriff's pilot and me took turns flying as it was about a three-hour flight. We talked to each other and visualized about how the small Texas town sheriff, who had arrested our subject, would look. We realized when first meeting the sheriff, we had almost described him to a tee. We landed on a small dirt strip controlled by a Fixed Based Operator (FBO). We waited in a small outbuilding that operated as the airport control center, just outside Denton for approximately one hour. Then we both observed a car coming down the dirt road a distance off toward the FBO. As the car got closer, we could see two people inside, the driver and a prisoner in the back seat. As the car approached, dust flying, I observed that the driver's side was leaning. I figured he needed new springs on his patrol car. As the car pulled up next to the building, the driver got out. The car immediately righted itself. That's when I saw that the sheriff's deputy who got out was at least three hundred pounds, civilian clothes, cowboy boots, and gun in a Western slung holster rig, like you see in the movies, with a badge pinned to his civilian shirt. We both looked at each other and smiled at the site. We took custody of the prisoner and loaded him in the back seat of the Cessna. When we started the aircraft, the starter pull came completely out of the cockpit dash. We all got back out and called for an airframe power plant mechanic. One finally arrived and advised we would have to get it fixed back in Wichita. We started the Cessna using battery cables and were off. I was a little concerned, but our prisoner was a whole lot more concerned. We would not have taken off if we did not think it safe. Then when we were about ten miles out of Oklahoma City, Oklahoma, our windshield became full of oil with no forward visibility. That's when our prisoner had to be calmed down a little. He was given a piece of gum. We were able to clear a small hole to see out off and declared an emergency at OKC. We did not know what was causing the oil to leak. The engine seemed to be running fine with no negative reading on our instruments. We landed without incident and again called for an A & P. It was found a small seal had blown and was easily replaced. We took off after again remotely starting the engine with battery cables. We landed back at Jabara with no other incidents. After landing, the prisoner told us he was happy to be out of that dirty jail in Denton but was wishing he was still there on a couple of occasions during flight. I didn't tell him this, but I was also glad to be back. The SCSO needed to do some work on their plane. I climbed back into the rotor and took off for the city heliport.

The Lone Ranger, Clayton Moore

KAKE TV is located in Wichita. KAKE had a television show called *Kaleidoscope*, which was aired daily and filmed at Towne East

Square Mall on the east side. The show was hosted by two local news personalities/anchors. *Kaleidoscope* had several celebrities on their one-hour noontime show. I'll name a few. Ed McMahon of the *Johnny Carson Show* was a guest. Whenever the celebrity stayed overnight, they were usually put up at the Holiday Inn Downtown. When McMahon arrived, he was assigned an officer for escort and bodyguard. There is an interesting story connected to Mr. McMahon. There are two large malls in Wichita, Towne East Square and Towne West Square, both owned by the Simon Brothers Organization. East side and west side. Officers were afforded the opportunity to work off duty at one of the malls. I was one of these officers. It supplemented the small salary that officers were paid at that time. I was a pilot. Rotor pilots for civilian organizations made twice or more what we were being paid at that time. The officer assigned to Ed McMahon, himself a Marine Corps Aviator, was told to make sure Mr. McMahon made it in time to the twelve o'clock show. McMahon and officer both were waiting for the limo that was to pick them up at the motel, but the limo did not show on time. The officer decided to flag any driver down to see if they could bum a ride. Both McMahon and the officer felt it would be easy because anyone would want to meet Ed McMahon and give him a ride to the show. Unfortunately for them, the officer flagged down the first vehicle they saw. A truck being driven by a local farmer who had never heard of Ed McMahon. Both were in civilian clothes, and both thought later that the farmer simply thought they were lying to him. Another passerby recognized McMahon and gave them a ride to the show. One of the escorts I had was for the Osmonds when they were in town. The Osmonds was another celebrity group invited to be on the TV show. When the Osmonds arrived, I was assigned as escort to Jimmy Osmond, the youngest Osmond brother, while they were in town. On the day of the show, Jimmy wore a loud suit, I recall to be purple-and-white shoes and orange shirt. Jimmy had to stop off at the restroom on the way to the TV stage, and as we walked in the restroom, it became silent. Everyone stopped talking. This would normally happen when I walked into a room, and I didn't think anything of it until I noticed all the guys in the john were staring at Jimmy's choice of clothes. I don't think any of them knew who he was, only that his choice of clothing was not normal. They were just not used to seeing anyone wear clothes that loud. No one said anything to him because I was there; however, had I not been, someone would have. On another occasion, I escorted a Dallas Cowboy cheerleader around for several hours one Saturday afternoon, described above. That was good duty. Her name was Benita Briggs, and I found she was easy to talk to and a very down-to-earth type of person. On another occasion, a Saturday morning, I was called by the escort officer for Clayton Moore, one of my boyhood heroes. Moore, at that time, was prohibited of making promotions wearing his Lone Ranger mask, as it was a trademark owned by the studio. So Clayton Moore made personnel appearances in person as the Lone Ranger without the mask. Back on point. Clayton Moore's escort officer informed that the Simon Brothers Jet had not yet arrived in Wichita, and Moore needed to get to Oklahoma City, Oklahoma, for an appearance there. Moore was needing someone to fly him there. I jumped at the chance to fly one of my boyhood heroes anywhere. I rented a four place Beech for the trip. Approximately two hours before I was scheduled to fly him out, the Simon Brothers Jet arrived, and I had to cancel the flight. Mr. Moore gave his escort officer a personally autographed picture for me. I still have that autographed photo.

Weather

We never flew in weather if we could help it. Emergencies only. There were times you just had to fly though. The 300C Sky Knight is a VFR machine only, no instrument flying. I have gone up for an officer-in-trouble call who was possibly being shot at in heavy fog with forward visibility less than five hundred feet, with a cloud ceiling of about two hundred or less. That's about as crazy as I wanted to get. Kansas is known for tornadoes and high wind. On occasion, the dispatch would call us at the heliport and ask if we could fly, usually in weather. I would not fly in heavy rain, too risky in a VFR machine. That and rain can destroy the paint on the leading edge of the airfoil, causing the blades to become out of balance (described below). The dispatch many times called to see if we could go up and spot a tornado. Really, you mean you want me to fly toward tornadic wind conditions to check which direction the funnel may be moving? I don't think so. We just couldn't do it. On one occasion, I happened to be up when weather hit and was on my way back to the heliport. We were heading west and along the city boundary, near and southwest of the airport, and turning back toward the city when it hit. Checking for abandoned vehicles, etc. Routine flight, nothing happening. Light chatter traffic on the police band and ATC. It was light to medium rain, a little windy, and was riding a little bumpy in the rotor. All OK, nothing heavy. When all of a sudden, *wham*. I flew into a wind shear. "What the—really! Holy Hannah!" I'm saying this to myself and other unmentionables while rolling in power, lifting up on the collective, controlling direction with and slightly pulling back on the cyclic, and feet on the antitorque pedals. Basically regaining control of the aircraft. All this in split-second maneuvers and decision-making. A wind shear is a wind gradient difference in wind speed and direction over a relatively short distance in atmosphere. I immediately dropped from approximately eight hundred feet to about six hundred feet AGL almost instantly. If I told you the incident took more than two seconds, I'd be lying to you. Pucker factor, ten plus. I made it back to the hanger with no other incidents. There is a phenomenon you may find interesting. On occasion, I could be flying along, and it would start raining. I could drop down a foot or two, and it would not be raining. This phenomenon is known as virga. Virga is observable precipitation that falls from a cloud but evaporates before reaching the ground. If you haven't experienced it, virga can be an experience for you. There is a saying that says, "Flying is boring holes in the sky with a few seconds of sheer terror mixed in." True. I did not like to fly in weather but did on occasion when mission dictated it. In high wind, there is a possibility that an airfoil could catch wind and dip down onto the tail boom. Our machine was rated for thirty plus mile-per-hour winds, but no more. I have gone up in twenty mile-per-hour plus winds but very rarely, and that was only for officer-in-trouble calls and other emergencies.

Out-of-Balance Blades

When a rotor blade becomes out of balance, the machine shakes very badly due to the out-of-balance blade(s) and can cause damage to the machine real quick. In order to balance a blade, the A & P has to use a flashing timing light, shine it on the rotor blades, and then observe which blade is out of balance. For you mechanics, when you retime an engine, you use what's called a timing light. Balancing a rotor blade involves the same process.

A New Air Section Commander

I could bore you with more rotor stories but will stop here. The Air Section had just received a new Air Section Commander in 1981, a police Lieutenant who had a private pilot's fixed wing license. The Lieutenant had worked as the department's record section supervisor. The story circulated was that he was causing some dissension within the records section, and the Police Chief felt he needed to replace and reassign him. Due to him having a fixed wing single engine land (SEL) private pilot's license, he was assigned to the Air Section as the Commander as we had just retired the former Commander. From the start, he began creating issues, such as criticizing our landings and takeoffs, how we were doing them wrong coming into the heliport at the wrong angle, etc. At the time of this criticizing, he was not yet rotor qualified and was uncertain of how to land a rotor himself. He simply lacked experience. Looking back, I'm sure the Chief was unaware of what kind of a decision he had made placing him in charge of the section.

At the time I was initially assigned as a pilot, mandatory flight hours were in place. In order to be assigned to the Air Section, you had to have a least two hundred flight hours to qualify for consideration. One had to have at least two years on the street as a patrol officer to gain knowledge of how the city was laid out and also of police tactics and procedures. A rule that was strictly enforced because of the complexity of police flight operations. I don't know how many

155

flight hours the new Commander had, but I did not feel he was a good pilot or police officer. Safety never seemed to be on his mind. It was my thought he was an accident waiting to happen. When you fly any type of aircraft, you simply have to know what you are doing, especially a police pilot. When you are flying a police rotor, this becomes ten times more important. A police pilot will have to fly into dangerous situations. It is simply the nature of law enforcement flight operations. Because of this, safety should always be on the minds of the aircrew.

Flight Communication

The police helicopter aircrew is not only responsible for monitoring police communication but also the Wichita Air Traffic Control (ATC) Center. Police communication has five radio channels—the main channel one, police dispatch; channel two, the investigations channel; channel three, car to car; channel four, an alternate channel; and channel five, the SPIDER, described above. ATC has inbound west, inbound east, outbound west, outbound east, and ground. If one is flying on the east side of Wichita, the aircrew not only monitors the five police channels but also the ATC east channels. And on the west side, ATC west channels. All this along with any police action on the ground they are responsible for. Along with this, McConnell Air Force Base, inbound and outbound, are also monitored. It is a lot of responsibility, and safety is priority.

A Busted Rotor

On a fall evening in 1981, the Lieutenant came to the air section and wanted to fly patrol with my flight partner. At the time, my partner held a private rotor rating, with around three hundred flight hours, and the Lieutenant had just completed his rotor training as private pilot. I was the only commercially rated rotor pilot on the department at the time and was considered the Chief Pilot. I commented that they really should have more flight time before attempting to fly during the evening hours by themselves. My concern went unheeded; he was the Commander.

Two pilots, with little flight time hours between them, had just taken off at dusk but was still light. Just after they took off, I received a call from the police dispatch at the hanger that there was a report of a helicopter down. The dispatcher was wanting to know if it was ours. I informed dispatch that the crew had just taken off; it couldn't be. It had only been about five minutes since they took off. I just didn't think it could be them. About ten minutes later, the dispatch called back and informed me that it had been confirmed it was ours. I told the dispatch to call our A & P, and I immediately proceeded in my car to the accident location, hoping there were no injuries. I learned that the Lieutenant attempted to land in a confined area, at night, on a small berm approximately three feet wide along the big ditch. All Commercial Pilot maneuvers neither pilot were qualified to perform. When the Lieutenant had sat the rotor on the berm, he overshot the landing by about two feet, leaning the rotor forward over the top of the berm, causing the helicopter to fall forward and to fall toward the passenger side. As the machine tumbled over the berm, it then turned over, rotor turning, coming to a stop just shy of being turned completely over. No injuries, but they were very lucky. The Lieutenant knew better. Our A & P arrived, and we just stared at the scene knowing this was a preventable pilot-error accident. My flight partner told me afterward that he thought when they were going down, the best he could hope for was to be seriously injured. Once the rotor was stopped, my partner pilot thought he was paralyzed as he could not egress. That's when he realized his seat belts were still fastened. Both walked away. I asked my partner pilot why he allowed that type of maneuver to happen, knowing they were both inexperienced. He had more flight hours than the Lieutenant and may have been able to stop it. He told me, "He's the Flight Commander. How am I supposed to stop him?" I just couldn't believe the Lieutenant would attempt that kind of landing. He knew better. I prided myself on my safety record and became a stickler for following FAA regulations. The Commander should have been listening to his chief pilot but saw me as his subordinate. I was, but I was also his Chief Pilot. I felt I simply could not fly with someone this dangerous. I began looking for other flight jobs. I found one. I felt I just simply had to move on. I had accumulated approximately one thousand five hundred pilot in command (PIC) flight hours on police patrol. I loved being a police pilot. It was by far the best job I have ever had, other than being a father and grandfather. I loved flying over the city at night. It is a very pretty site, especially over the city on the Fourth of July. I felt I just simply had to move on. I can still hear the whirr of the rotors and gin of the engine, see the ground in front of me, see the instruments, needles married, and hear the constant radio chatter of air traffic controllers and police dispatch. I loved it. I miss being in the cockpit to this day. A few months after I left the department, the Lieutenant resigned. His decision was both good for the department and him.

By the way, married needles. There is an instrument in the cockpit that records engine RPM with rotor RPM. It's called an engine/rotor tachometer. It looks similar to a clock, only you want the hands together (married). Small hand for rotor RPM, large hand for engine RPM. On the rotor I flew, it was located just below the airspeed indicator, on the left side of the cockpit control panel. You constantly monitor all instruments on the panel while in flight. Good cockpit management is a must. Anyway, you want the two needles on the engine/rotor tachometer in sync, needles together (married) while in flight. If they split, your pucker factor goes to ten real quick. You better throw the collective down because your engine just quit. And at the altitude we flew on police patrol, you only had approximately seven seconds before you hit terra firma. So the first one or two seconds is going save your life.

Altitude

Altitude is measured from Main Sea Level (MSL). (Wichita is about one thousand four hundred feet MSL.) Indicated altitude is the reading on the altimeter when the altimeter is set to the local

Barometric Pressure (BP) at main sea level. Absolute altitude describes the distance above the ground directly below. We usually flew patrol at four hundred to eight hundred AGL (above ground level or absolute altitude). So I would be indicating about two thousand feet indicated when flying at six hundred AGL, depending on the BP.

What I miss most about flying a rotor is skimming over the trees at eighty knots plus in light wind or fog and low visibility on the way to an emergency call. Pucker factor: about ten. I love adrenaline. My advice to anyone wanting to fly is carry a light-blue card in your pocket, with a hole punched in the center of the card. When you want to fly, hold the card up to the sky and look through the hole. If the sky is not the same color blue as the card, it is not safe to fly.

My Call Sign

Here's the story of my call sign. If you thought my current nickname was from my first and middle names you would be wrong. It's actually from Orange Juice. As I was growing up, my parents called me Ollie, which is the name I used until I was in my mid-twenties. I've had several nicknames growing up, none of which stuck. At one time and in Middle School, I was called "The Tractor" after the Oliver Tractor, by my close friends. I didn't mind that name as it reminded me of hard working farm folk, which is my family background. Then in 1978, as I began flying for a living, my name changed. Whenever Air One was needed on surveillance, the surveilling detectives called for "The Starship Enterprise" on the investigation channel, meaning Air One (that was me). As my friends were promoted into the investigation section, and they needed air surveillance, they called for "Orange Juice" after my first and middle names. That turned into "The Juice", which eventually was shortened to "OJ". So, from 1978 to Present, I have been known from my flight call sign of OJ. Currently I'm called OJ or Chief, both names of which I proudly earned.

CHAPTER 10

Santa Fe Railroad

I was hired by the Santa Fe Railroad as a pilot shortly thereafter. I was assigned to the Kansas City, Missouri, terminal as a special agent/investigator and told I was hired to help develop an air section. My pitch when I initiated the process was that one could overfly over a train accident with a camera and have live action shots viewed from the accident to the head office in Chicago. It could be determined if a HAZMAT (hazardous materials) team would need to be called to the scene. The air section was not developed due to being bumped. Let me explain why HAZMAT would be needed. Most trains at that time hauled propane fuel to deliver to outlying areas. Think of one of these propane tank cars as a tea kettle. When a tea kettle gets hot, it lets off steam, thus causing the whistle sound. On a propane car, built up gases inside the car releases this gas through valves on top of the car. In a propane car, especially one that is turned over, the gases sometimes have no release. When this happens, the car goes into a BLEVE (boiling liquid expanding vapor explosion). The resulting explosion can disintegrate humans and can throw each end of the propane car itself up to two miles away from the blast. It's very loud and very explosive. I once viewed a film of a small-town Police Chief who was being filmed from a distance when a BLEVE occurred. He disintegrated right on camera. He was there one second and gone the

160

next. BLEVEs are that powerful. Back on point. I worked on third shift as a special agent investigator, checking incoming and outgoing freight. On one occasion, I got involved in a drug case on an employee and on some shootings where someone took a shot at one of the train engineers as the train passed by. I will relay a couple of interesting stories.

The Case of the Mad Rat

One night, I was assigned to check an outgoing train to ensure all seals were intact on each box car, that no break in the seal had occurred. It was pitch black that evening with no celestial illumination. At the time, we had received a bulletin that an escaped murderer may be riding the rails and coming through Kansas City. Checking seals was boring but could be dangerous if you did not watch what you were doing. On this night, I had walked half the distance of the train when I heard a loud hiss-type growl. I stopped in my tracks and pulled my weapon. I wanted to be able to leave work alive. I waited a few seconds and, hearing no other sounds, proceeded quietly. There it is again, only closer. I was hesitant to use my flashlight, giving my position away. I decided to take a chance and shined my light down the tracks. I saw that I was walking toward an overhead bridge that the tracks ran under. That's when I saw the biggest rat I have ever seen standing on its hind legs hissing at me. Big red beady eyes and all. The rat was eating grain along the tracks that passing grain cars dropped traveling under the bridge. I started to take aim to eliminate my threat, and the darn thing ran off. Well, I had just had the begeebers scared out of me. I finished checking the rest of the mile-long train with no other incidents.

The Case of the Raging Bull

There were three of us agents working as railroad special agents on the night shift. I preferred that shift because it was quiet, and if something ever did happen, third shift seemed to be where the action might be. One of our agents was a female with the brightest flame-red hair I called Flame. I had a female cousin with the same pretty flame red hair, and Flame reminded me of this cousin who died as the result of a traffic accident years before. I seemed to be the only one who got away with calling her Flame or Red. A small agent but one who would be there when you needed her. One fall evening, Flame gets a call from one of the incoming train engineers that some cattle were blocking the rails, and he was asking for assistance to help clear the rails, about five miles out. Red heads out west toward the direction of the stalled train. When she arrived, I heard her say she was exiting her vehicle to chase the cows off the track. A few minutes later, she came on the air yelling and out of breath that a bull was among the cows and was chasing her. I hear a bang in the background of her radio as she's transmitting, and she shouts into the radio that the bull had just head butted her car she was in. By this time, the situation had become somewhat comical, however; the local sheriff's office was called for assistance. The sheriff's deputy helped chase the cattle and bull off and away from the tracks. After about thirty min-utes, Red gets back on the air in a calmer voice and relayed the track had been cleared. The case of the mad bull had been solved.

The Homeless

There is always someone who seems to get all the weird calls. Red was this person. One evening just after dark, Red gets a call of a man lying next to a grain elevator, which was next to the tracks. When Red arrives, she called for backup, and I get the call to help her. When I got there, she had obtained the man's identification and had learned the individual had just been released from prison after serving time for murder. He was riding the rails, trying to find some-where to go. The problem: the man was very ill from what appeared to be flu. He not only had regurgitated on himself but had also def-ecated on himself, along with being somewhat intoxicated. He was very odiferous. Red was wanting her backup, that was me, to transport the man to Sally's (Salvation Army) home. The home was in downtown Kansas City and was where one could find shelter and warmth on cold evenings if you were homeless and needed someplace to stay. Well, I wasn't about to transport the man in my car for two very good reasons. One, the poor man was simply odiferous. I knew it would take a month of Sundays to get the odor out of my car. And two, it was not my call. If it had been, I would have transported the poor soul. We ended up transporting the poor soul to Sally's in Flame's car. The poor guy simply needed someone to care for him, needed medical help, and needed somewhere to get cleaned up and taken care of. It took right at about a month to clean the inside of her car. We were told by supervision to call the city next time. It did cost a few bucks to clean her car.

Possible Explosion

There were approximately fifty-eight sets of track in the Kansas City Rail Hump Yard. Most of the yard was used to hump trains. Humping a train is described as thus; trains were separated in the hump yard by what direction out of Kansas City they were going and then by cars. The last cars on the train were the first ones let off at any particular stop. The trains were made such that as the train arrived at a destination, the cars for that location were off-loaded and the train left to distribute other cars. Along this hump yard were several grain elevators, that grain had been brought by truck, then off-loaded onto grain cars. I received a call to check an open door on one of the grain elevators. One is always suspicious of these type calls as you just don't know what you'll find. Burglary, gangs, and whatnot. I got there and found that the last man out the door had forgot to lock the door. Further, someone had left a motor running that had now begun to blow out sparks. An open door then became a very dangerous situation, not only for me but for folks in a square-block area. Let me explain. The grain elevator was full of grain, with lots of grain dust in the air. So much so that it looked like a heavy fog inside. I should tell you at this point that grain dust is very, very explosive. Any small spark could set it off. I thought about skedaddling out of there but decided to try to shut the engine down. I was able to shut the engine down before I got the hell out of there. I next called the fire department, who wet down the grain. I was told later that I probably saved thousands of dollars of grain and life.

I worked for Santa Fe Railroad for about nine months when the railroad bumped (laid off) all employees that had no seniority to 1954. That included me, thus ending my railroad career and the Santa Fe's possible air section. I promised myself I would never put my family through another layoff. I vowed to never work for a company that had even the slightest chance for a layoff. A month or so later, the district railroad supervisor called and offered me my job back. I declined, and he then said he would like to meet with me and my wife. He and his wife flew from Chicago, Illinois, to Wichita, Kansas, to offer me my job back in person. My wife Laura and I had a nice steak dinner out of the deal, but once I make up my mind, you better have a darn good reason for me to change it. Even for a pay raise. I did appreciate Santa Fe sending one of their big cheese supervisors to talk with me though.

CHAPTER 11

Chief of Police

After a small amount of time, I applied for and was appointed Chief of Police of a small town. The day I was appointed was a proud day for me. I had taken over a small department of one executive assistant and, as I recall, a staff of four officers. It was a department in trouble. The budget did not nearly cover what was needed, and personnel strength was lacking. Further, there was no department rules, procedures, or guidelines for my officers to follow. They were working in the blind and with no written guidelines. My first order of the day was to establish some rules and guidelines for them to work by. I needed some new equipment, and I also needed to establish a reserve force to augment my personnel. I went on daily patrol during the early morning rush-hour school traffic and then back to my office writing the department's regulations. I also took over a department with some personnel issues I won't go into. I'll just say that after some accusations by other officers and some investigation on my part, I determined some accusations to be true and had to terminate one of my officers. There were other personnel issues I determined had to also be dealt with; however, I will not go into them. I simply had a department in need of guidance in the form of department regulations that were nonexistent. On the city staff was a female whom I initially liked; however, as time went on, I found her untrustworthy. Here's a couple of examples. Kansas Legislature members and State Senators could gift an organization a set of State Statutes once yearly. I personally knew a State Senator and asked if she could gift me a set. A few weeks later, the Senator dropped off a complete set of State Statutes for me at the city offices. The female I just described took the new set of statutes and gave me the old set of statues used by the city that were missing several books. She felt the police department did not need a new set of State Statutes. I needed those statues so as to verify criminal procedure. The city prosecutor had his own set and did not need new ones. I needed them worse than this city clerk. Be that as it may, I did not argue. I did not want any issues between my department and city staff. On another occasion, one of my officers had stopped to warn three children who were playing in the street to get out of the street and play in their yard so as not to get run over by a passing car. As my officer left and began turning the corner, the children went back into the street when they thought my officer was out of sight. My officer returned and was a little sterner this time but was still polite in his duties. The officer immediately learned from the children they belonged to the clerk I just mentioned as their mother. The officer was informed by the children he would be getting in trouble later. The officer then drove immediately to my office and informed me of what had happened. I told him not to worry about it as he was just doing his job and to write an incident report. I do not know what the children told their mother, but the following day, she appeared in my office demanding I discipline the officer for telling her children not to play in the street. I explained to her what had happened and that I was not going to discipline any officer for doing their job. Further, the safety of her children was my main concern. She left my office mad and in a huff. Next morning, the City Manager (CM) came to my office on behalf of the clerk. The CM was also a new hire, young and inexperienced. I informed him what had happened and that I was not going to initiate disciplinary action for the incident. The safety of the children was my concern, the concern was that the clerk wanted my officer disciplined for doing his job. I had written reports on the incident from my officers and knew the truth of the incident and was satisfied.

My explanation sufficed, and the CM went back to his office. One other concern I had with this clerk was that I had gotten approval to hire a new police officer from city council. I was looking for and needed someone with experience so I did not have to send him/her to the Law Enforcement Training Academy. One of the individuals who applied was a very experienced Los Angeles, California, Police Officer and Kansas certified. This officer was one of those present on the courthouse steps in Los Angeles when Charles Manson carved a Swastika on his forehead. This same individual was later one of Rodney King's bodyguards. This individual was also the most experienced person who applied and was my pick. The clerk was against hiring this person because he had come from an adjacent small town and had been involved in a minor political issue and resigned over it. After I was not allowed to hire this person, on the clerk's say-so, I vowed to initiate and write better vetting procedures, and I also vowed to make sure those that sat on law enforcement interview boards were law enforcement experienced for obvious reasons. The individual hired was my second pick; however, we simply needed better vetting in place. This individual I hired as my second pick turned out to be an excellent officer; however, he was sent to complete the law enforcement academy for certification, which my first pick did not have to do. Over the course of the following months, I began to be informed of rumors floating around as to my character and how I did not seem to be doing my job by some of my officers. Rumors of not being on the street patrolling enough and allowing my officers to run amuck. False rumors all, but they began making me wonder how and who were spreading the rumors. I did not think too much of the rumors at the time as I was working hard and had no reason to suspect anyone was actually believing them.

As a Police Chief, one has to make tough decisions that are sometimes not popular with subordinates or the public. A Police Chief has operational independence and works with his own personal judgment. One has to consider what's best for both the community served and staff. As Police Chief, I was responsible and accountable for the development of the annual department budget. I supervised and conducted complete and accurate investigations and prepared reports of investigation. I served as the primary representative of the department with civic organizations. I ensured that any complaints against the department or its personnel were handled effectively and in a timely manner. And I had a few. I was responsible for personnel and enforcement of department policies (which I was drafting), performance appraisals, department regulations, investigations, personnel issues, and a myriad of other actions necessary to daily operations. In a political atmosphere of small-town politics, one can become the target of unfounded rumor, innuendo of individuals with a personal agenda, and/or a simple personality conflict. I found that it is not the elected town counselors who run the city. It's the people the town counselors go to for advice who run the city. And almost one hundred percent of the time, their advice is based on their opinions and exacerbated by their inexperience. Many times also, their advice is simply armchair quarterbacking. My feeling of an armchair quarterback is one who produces nothing. They lead no one nor have they ever had to. They have never had to make quick decisions. They have no responsibilities and are accountable to none. And lastly, they suffer no personal consequences of their egregious accusations. I see them as playground bullies who want to knock someone off the top of a flag pole after one has worked hard to climb to the top. Not because the bully wants the responsibility of climbing and staying on top but simply because they have the ability to knock him off the top and feel good about doing so. My time as Chief of Police is the ugly of the good, the bad, and the ugly. There is a saying, "There are some things more painful than the truth, but I can't think of them." I do not like to admit I was terminated from a position, but here's the story.

One October morning, the City Manager (CM) walked into my office and informed me that I was being terminated as Chief for performance not to standards. He did so by handing me a termination letter signed by the city counselors. At the time the CM walked in, I was at my desk working on department regulations and was just about finished drafting the entire set of regulations. Regulations I had worked hard to complete. This would have allowed my officers some working guidelines they did not have. I had also begun an initial investigation on my Animal Control Officer (ACO) on accusations brought to me by one of my officers. I do not punish, write letters of reprimand, or terminate based on rumor, innuendo, or personality conflict. To do otherwise reflects weak and ineffective leadership. The measure of a man is not what he will do, but what he will not do. I had to have facts, which was the reason for my investigation of the ACO. I mention this because this ACO was later terminated by the city, and a new ACO was hired. One whose behavior was much worse and will not be discussed in this book, other than to say, this ACO is currently serving time in a penitentiary. Did I mention the city needed better vetting procedures? Back on point, I was shocked at my dismissal but handed my badge and city credentials to him and left. I was very disappointed and very confused. I had some personnel issues I was unable to take care of and was unable to complete a working set of guidelines for my officers. I was never approached by any city employee, including the Mayor or the CM as to unsatisfactory job performance. I had never received any unsatisfactory warning(s), job performance evaluation(s), or anything to indicate unsatisfactory work. Shortly thereafter, I attended a closed-door personnel meeting and learned my job as Chief of Police had been threatened by false rumor. Really? I answered some of the false rumors that were being spread by unknown person(s). I do not recall now what the rumors were, but I do recall they were an attempt at character assassination and affected my integrity. There was simply a massive failure of collective judgment by city counselors. I was allowed to resign rather than be terminated after explaining the rumors to be false at this meeting. I was not allowed or given an opportunity to fix what they perceived as broken. I immediately submitted my resignation. So rather than being terminated, I resigned. But the damage had been done. In later talking with the City Attorney, I was told I had an enemy on the city staff, the name of which he would not divulge. I did not know who this could be as I had an excellent working relationship with all city staff. It just simply never occurred to me that the city clerk aforementioned was this person until a few years later when I learned the clerk had been terminated for cause. Then it struck me who the rumor mill was. It just never dawned on me anyone could be that vindictive for not disciplining my officer based on the clerks perceived wrong with her children. She certainly seemed more concerned about some perceived wrong to her children than over their safety. The Clerk had no control over me so through misinformation and rumor, sought to control how others saw and perceived me, over time, and looking back, I would guess that the rumors hurt the perpetrator more than me. I took responsibility for not looking into the rumors because I was the Chief, and it was my responsibility. At the time, I felt anyone in my position, no matter who, would be the brunt of false rumors. My termination was unfair, not right, and simply political. Good people do get fired over unfair political agendas, particularly if one is doing their job and moving forward in a direction against the political flow. Looking back, I sense that maybe by attempting to promote guidelines for my officers, I may have also been challenging the status quo of having no regulations at all for the department, which the city was used to not having. This is only an afterthought. Also, looking back on this situation, I see a cascading created set of circumstances through vindictiveness by one individual with an unfortunate outcome. It just simply lacked common sense. I never contested the incident because I simply did not want to work for any employer who would believe false rumor over fact. I vowed never to work for any organization with such political overtones again. When one door closes, another will always open.

CHAPTER 12

The Defense Investigative Service

History

The Defense Investigative Service (DIS) was organized by the Department of Defense (DOD) as a National Security Investigative Agency, responsible for Personal Security Investigations (PSI) in 1972. Becoming responsible for Army, Navy, Air Force, and DOD contractors. In 1981, the first formal adjudicative guidelines were established and incorporated into DOD 5200.2-R, which is the Personal Security Investigation regulation. I won't go into more history as it is lengthy. I was hired as a special agent investigator in August 1987. I had been trying for three years to join this organization and, in August 1987, was offered my choice of three areas in Continental US (CONUS). I elected to work at the location offering the lowest cost of living. I began work on August 11, 1987, and have not stopped since. I volunteered for any Temporary Duty (TDY) assignment that became available to learn how other areas of the country worked and learned and honed my investigative skill along the way. I read every investigative book on interview techniques I could find and volunteered for every investigative school I could. Supervisors, currently called Supervisory Agent in Charge (SACs), across the country were calling my SAC requesting me personally for a TDY assignment to their area. Meantime, DIS became known as the Defense Security Service (DSS) in approximately 1996. This name change occurred because DIS at the time had all the industrial security assets, polygraphers, polygraph school, and some national security treaties. The word *security* fit more into the charter than the word *investigative*. DSS then became the Federal Investigative Services (FIS), under Office of Personnel Management (OPM), in March 2005. This occurred for numerous reasons I won't go into in this book. More politics than not. The Federal Investigative Services (FIS) conducts investigations for over one hundred federal agencies—approximately ninety-five percent of the total background investigations governmentwide—including more than six hundred thousand security clearance investigations and four hundred thousand suitability investigations each year. In January 2016, the National Background Investigations Bureau (NBIB) was created under the DOD umbrella but reports to OPM. FIS is currently in the process of standing up as the NBIB in 2017. The DoD umbrella covers only the IT portion of the organization. (Are you confused yet?) DOD assumed responsibility for the design, development, security, and operation of the background investigations program. This change occurred to provide a strong national security focus and to concentrate solely on its mission to provide effective, efficient, and secure National Security Investigations for the federal government. At the time of my writing this, there is the possibility of NBIB merging back into DoD, under the DSS umbrella. It is felt DoD should take over their own security clearance process, and allow DoD to manage personnel security, physical security, law enforcement and other insider threat programs. I have nothing but good to say about working as a National Security Investigator. It is an excellent career with exciting investigative challenges. There are some things that should happen in my opinion and my only minor observations. I have many suggestions that should not be taken as criticism. Some suggestions follow: I would suggest taking a closer look at going outside the agency for any position other than the director or hiring of new agents. I could write another book on this subject but will stop here. There are some managers who have never served in the military and therefore do not know what type of occupational training a particular military occupational field has. I see this as an impediment to developing a system to better utilize the skills of assets already in place.

I have observed that investigators who are trained in only one investigative questioning technique tend to be less adaptable to some confrontational interviews than those trained in multiple techniques. Those trained in multiple techniques learn to readily adjust to unexpected responses from a source. A lack of multiple skill sets may actually fail to catch a false statement using basic techniques. So I would add more advanced investigative questioning techniques to the training curriculum, with refresher training more often.

OK, one more observation: remote locations. When employees are located in the same large geographic location or large metropolitan areas, employees have the advantage of national objectives, such as the development of new programs unavailable to those in remote areas. There are more training opportunities in larger metro areas. When working distances, remote employees can sometimes be forgotten in the scheme of national operations. Out of sight, out of mind. With increased globalization, remote locations are necessary. However, I would suggest an effort to expand opportunities to remote areas in overall objectives, particularly on newer developed programs. There is a myriad of talent in the remote areas that is untapped by national leadership. I'll stop my observations rant here.

Personal Security Investigation (PSI)

Cleared personnel are primary targets of foreign intelligence services. They are the keepers of our nation's secrets and often are working outside Continental US (CONUS) exposing them to vulnerable positions.

The Personal Security Investigation or PSI is a process designed to provide assurance that personnel are reliable, trustworthy, and loyal to the United States and not vulnerable to foreign manipulation or coercion. A PSI is a National Security Investigation and is a very deep and very penetrating look into an individual's personal history to determine vulnerability to influence. The PSI also looks at the terrorism aspect during the investigation. A National Security Investigation does not predict the future behavior of an applicant. The security investigation is only part of a broad security program. After a security clearance is granted, any breach of security after the PSI or behavior indicating a security risk must be reported through other security programs, such as the Facility Security Officer (FSO) of the organization the subject is employed. In the case of a military subject, it would be up to the Security Manager or S2 of the Subject's unit of assignment. The PSI is a significant deterrent to counterintelligence, terrorist activities, and insider threats that keeps our government safe. A PSI is initiated when an individual is determined to require access to information deemed to be classified information by the government. A PSI is not a background investigation. The difference is that a Background Investigation (BI) is conducted to confirm or verify information. If the government wanted a simple BI, a private security company could be used or a simple check at the local police department would suffice. It is simply more professional to inform a source that they are part of a National Security Investigation and is more informative to the source as to the nature of the investigation. In our world, part of the process is referred to as an interview of the Subject of the investigation. A PSI is not an interrogation, which refers to a custodial type process. In a criminal investigation, a crime has been committed. There is always some type of evidence left at the scene, trace evidence, fingerprints, saliva, blood, hair, and other seen and unseen physical evidence. Once an arrest has been made, an interrogation is performed on the suspect by a trained professional. A PSI, on the other hand, is an interview to determine if a crime may have taken place, through an elicitation process. The investigator does not know a crime has occurred, however. If someone is selling information, it's up to a PSI investigator to determine this through the interview and investigative process. A PSI is performed by highly trained investigators familiar with how Foreign Intelligence Services work. Their investigations are thorough, professional, complete, and concise. The FIS Academy in Boyers, Pennsylvania, is certified through the Federal Law Enforcement Training Center (FLETC).

I will write a small effort to give you an idea of how an investigator works.

A Day in the Life of a National Security Investigator

I work as a National Security Investigator, and I conduct investigations on those individuals who have applied for a security clearance. This includes Department of Defense (DOD) personnel, both military and civilian, and other agencies whose personnel require access to classified national defense information. The National Security Investigator plays an absolutely essential role in protecting national security and the security of our homeland. Whether an investigative assistant, program analyst, contracting specialist, investigator, or a supervisory agent in charge, each is a vital part of the team that ensures that the federal government has a "suitable workforce that protects national security and is worthy of public trust." By constantly maintaining the highest personal and professional standards, it ensures that the Federal Investigative Service is meeting expectations and protecting our national security.

The majority of cases I investigate are easily investigated single-issue cases or a case with no issues; however, some cases contain multiple complex issues. These cases involve applicants with unresolved issues, such as delinquent debts, criminal records, pedophilia, drug use, current alcohol use/abuse, foreign preference or nationality concerns, and deliberate falsification. Occasionally, I conduct investigations of a counterintelligence nature as assigned.

My office is located within a secure area, facility, and building. The offices are specifically designed for interviews of an individual. Personnel are required to clear an area facility gate, locate the building our offices are situated in, and then clear the locked door to our outer offices. Once inside, I go directly to my office. Some interviews are conducted in our offices, out of the remote necessity of the area we work. Some are conducted elsewhere as necessary.

After turning on my computer, I go into password-protected databases in order to "gen" them up for use during the day. I then review a list of cases assigned to me personally to determine what needs to be completed on each case for that day. I then return any phone calls from messages left for me on cases I am working. I marry any messages or e-mails to the case before returning any phone messages. I then check my daily e-mails, which is vital to the Federal Investigative Service. It is a lifeline to all other agents, adjudicators, and reviewers. All information is passed via e-mail or database messages from all hands meetings to another agent trying to schedule a meeting with me.

After returning phone calls and answering e-mails, I open the cases assigned to me. As an example, if I open a new case on an individual, I review the SF-86, the electronic questionnaire for investigations. What adverse information did the applicant disclose? Not disclose? I document this on a scoping sheet of my making. I determine what the investigative scope is, dates of investigatory scope, where I need to conduct the investigation, employments, neighborhoods, record checks, law checks, reference interviews, etc., and what are the issues, listed or unlisted. I then review any investigative reports associated with the case. What was not mentioned or disclosed by the applicant? What do I need to resolve an issue or investigate to a proper conclusion? Can I mitigate any issue appropriately according to federal guidelines? And OPM policy? I take these and other questions into account before I schedule the actual interview of the Subject or Source reference of the investigation.

Training

Learning to be a National Security Investigator responsible for national security personnel security investigations takes close to five years before one is comfortable in your abilities, and often more. The normal progression of training includes what was formerly known as

Basic Agents Course (BIC) but is now formally known as the Federal Background Investigation Training Program (FBITP), which is a Federal Law Enforcement Training Center (FLETC)-certified course, a year of probation, and a yearly ride along with a Special Agent in Charge (SAC). Along with this, the investigator must continually read and keep up with agency policies and the investigators' manual. During the training period, a mentor may initially be assigned, so you can ride along with him/her to see what it's like in the field. I also constantly read books dedicated to intelligence, counterintelligence, interview techniques, espionage, treason, terrorism, and other periodicals relating to my profession. I also keep track of the current Military Equipment Task List (METL) put out yearly by the Defense Security Service (DSS). This is to maintain a current vulnerability threat to personnel I investigate. You also have to have a working knowledge of Executive Orders, DOD Directives, Regulations, and Regional Operating Instructions. You must know the indicators of terrorism and the indicators that support terrorism. I will not list these as they are simply too long a list. Along with this, we maintain a monthly area staff meeting to inform area agents about relative issues and an opportunity to question management about other matters. Much of our training is informal and comes in small doses from other experienced co-workers and supervisors. Agents solicit opinions from their co-workers about complex case issues they are working on.

The Interview

Based on this snapshot of the case, I choose one of a few or several investigative options. How do I want to approach the interview? Will my office space do, or will I need different space? Is the office the right color, such as "truthful blue"? Does the office have windows? Where do I seat the subject I am interviewing? What investigative techniques do I need to use during the interview? SCAN, Reid, i.e., elicitation techniques, etc.? You have to elicit detailed personal security information as a basis for investigative leads to stand alone for review of an adjudicator. To do this and to resolve issues, I keep neurolinguistics in mind during my interviews, along with body language, to determine if I need to pursue further questioning to resolve an issue. As an investigator, I have to be able to use each and do so within seconds of an observation during an interview and to transition smoothly among several techniques. I am militarily trained in counterintelligence, as are other agents, so I do use what I have learned in my investigatory process and training. I also keep up with any changes to these techniques because I am also a trained instructor (both from the military and NSA). Do I need to place the Subject in a questioning vice? And turn the screws with each question? Or can I simply ask a direct question and expect a truthful reply without a deception? These are learned by control questioning. One has to recognize deception during questioning and exploit the deception or deliberate omission. I always base any further questioning on the subject's response to any previous question I ask on an unresolved issue. You have to be a good listener, which is key to any interview, think on your feet, and determine if an elicitation technique should be used or simply drive on with the response given. My attitude determines the environmental direction the questioning takes on any type of interview. So I always approach any Subject or reference I question with a good attitude. Even if I have had a bad day that particular day, the reference will never know this. I have done this for over thirty years as an investigator. This creates a favorable interview environment and determines a favorable outcome of any questioning. Work habits and questioning technique vary greatly with each agent, and this is because of the agent's level of expertise and experience. It is generally accepted that any agent with over five years' investigative experience is at their accepted level of expertise; however, this depends on the agent's level of investigative training. What type of cases the agent has been assigned, etc.? Has the agent kept up with his/her profession by continual reading? Taken courses on his/her own, etc.? As an example, some agents are militarily trained, such as in counterintelligence or other areas of expertise, and attain an earlier expertise level in that area, and some agents are simply BIC trained. Some agents with over five year's investigative experience, on the other hand, struggle with the complexity of a case, directly affecting the closing timeline. This is due to not being trained in a particular area of expertise required on the complex case.

After my workday is over, I can't help but look back on a complex investigation and question myself. I always keep in mind I am not a background investigator. I am a professional trained and certified federal investigator and perform National Security Investigations directly affecting national security. (If the government wanted a background investigation, the requestor could go to the local police department, a private investigator, or to a private security firm.) Am I interviewing the person stealing secrets? Committing espionage? Did I do all I could to resolve an issue? Did I cover all interrogatories on each issue? Should I have used a different investigative technique to clarify a complex issue? Should I have tried more elicitation techniques? Bait questions, mind viruses? I sometimes question my day's line of questioning. Should I have asked the questions differently or should I have dug deeper? Did I turn my computer off? Did I turn the office coffee machine off? Did I miss any telephone messages? Could I have simply done things better or more efficient? There are a myriad of other things a special agent does and performs during an investigation; however, it is done as a matter of fact in the performance of an ongoing investigation, again depending on the investigator's experience level. The Japanese have a saying—I cannot pronounce, however, in English. It means "Constant and Never-Ending Improvement" (CANI). This is what I strive for every day. It simply makes me a better investigator.

After the investigation is complete, I write a Report of Investigation (ROI). The final product should be a clear and concise ROI. An official record is being produced. The accepted philosophy is that if one cannot write a good ROI, the investigator should not have conducted the investigation in the first place. This is because the ROI must stand alone for review and adjudication. The ROI must be accurate, complete, and relevant. Has the report been written to cause mental processing of the information easier? Has use of ample white space been used effectively? Has proper syntax been used? Has proper and effective punctuation been used? Is sentence structure used properly? Does the ROI reflect all issues identified in the investigatory process? These questions and more must be asked by the investigator. The ROI must be the best written report you can produce based on your investigatory process.

Then I go home, sleep, and get up and do it again the following day.

The Personal Security Investigator (PSI)

My other thought is that the Personal Security Investigator is a determinant to National Security. The investigator is a tool used by National Security to determine who may be selling secrets, involved in criminal, terrorist activity, sabotage, treason, or incitement to rebellion, and a myriad other activities making one vulnerable. There are those who would dispute this thought. But my belief is that while other means may critically influence the process, after whatever devastation may be inflicted on the American public by espionage and other activity, one must establish, or must present as an inevitable prospect the person who conducts an investigation. This is the PSI investigator. The Federal Investigative Services employs a brotherhood of serious professional investigators, and we are good at what we do.

Counterintelligence (CI) Selection

In 1997, I was selected as one of the Southwestern Region Counterintelligence Point of Contacts (POC). This appointment was based on my certified training in counterintelligence. I became responsible for briefing region personnel on how to recognize a counterintelligence issue, what triggered a CI issue, how to weave intelligence in the PSI product, and how to investigate it and report it. I briefed on what intelligence questions were to be asked, how to ask questions, and conduct the interview process. If a CI issue was suspected, I reviewed the completed case and forwarded the case to the CI Section in Washington, DC. The PSI is not an intelligence investigation; however, it is the first line of defense for detection of an issue that may require a strategic CI investigation by a chartered intelligence agency. At the same time I was the CI POC, I was also an adjunct instructor at the Defense Security Service (DSS) Academy, Linthicum, Maryland. I taught interview techniques and mentored agents going through training. I was confident in my abilities and enjoyed being an instructor and mentor. In order to understand the investigative process of the cases I wrote about below, one must have some basic knowledge of how a foreign intelligence agency works. I will not include any Potential Espionage Indicators (PEI) or follow-on questions. There are too many to include.

You have to be knowledgeable of who is targeting the United States. Below are only a few.

In addition to the intelligence services of friendly as well as unfriendly countries, sources of the threat to classified and other protected information include:

foreign governments—both friendly and unfriendly
foreign and multinational corporations
foreign government–sponsored educational and scientific institutions
freelance agents (some of whom are unemployed former intelligence
   officers)
computer hackers
terrorist organizations
revolutionary groups
extremist ethnic or religious organizations
drug syndicates
organized crime

What Type of Information Are Our Adversaries Trying to Collect?

Everything that will help another country, organization, corporation, research institute, or individual achieve its political, military, economic, or scientific goals. It is important to realize that the scope of foreign intelligence interest in the United States is virtually unlimited. The most critical areas include future military and political intentions, military capabilities and vulnerabilities, economic and commercial policies, and foreign policy initiatives. Increasingly, however, technology ranks high in foreign collection priorities.

How Is HUMINT (Human Intelligence) Collected?

In theory, intelligence collection is a carefully planned process that follows these steps:

Identify what information to be collected.
Where this information is located.
Who has access to the information? (Usually, someone already in possession of a clearance)
Contrive a means to meet and assess individuals with access to the desired information.
Identify a susceptible individual and then recruit that person.
Maintain some means of secure contact with the source and receive a steady flow of valuable information.

There is a spotting, assessing, and recruiting of potential targets by a Control Officer; however, I will not go into this process.

CHAPTER 13

Cases

The interview, being noncustodial, is a nonadversarial or non-confrontational conversation. However, the interview can actually be confrontational if the person being interviewed has committed an illegal act, whether it is known or unknown by the interviewer/investigator. The person being interviewed perceives the interviewer/investigator as the enemy. This is because the interviewer is someone who could cost the person his job, his family, his embarrassment or shame, and his security clearance or someone who could eventually send him/her to jail. As a National Security Investigator, I have no arrest authority by agency charter; however, I do inform law enforcement authority when I find a crime has been committed and provide them with the information I have collected. I use the word confession in the below cases, but as an interviewer, I really don't want a confession. I want the truth. In the search for truth, I keep an open mind and use objective methodology.

Due to the nature of a PSI investigation, I will not relay some methodology or names. I will only mention a few cases you may find interesting; names and locations will also not be mentioned. I have investigated numerous of these type cases, and the below are only samplings.

Foreign Contact

When one has foreign contact, it does not mean one is selling the Nation's secrets. On the other hand, if one holds a Top Secret security clearance and has access to classified information, one must determine through a National Security Investigation if the information one has access to is protected. The following case was relayed to me through an intelligence agency that conducted a strategic intelligence investigation but was unable to find anything that their agency could charge the individual with. (As a retired Army CI Agent, I maintain contact with intelligence agencies and agents I worked with.) I was personally contacted as to their findings because the intelligence agency felt that the individual's vulnerability and suitability was in question, which would affect the individual's security clearance and classified access. After review, I referred the case to our Counterintelligence Section in Washington, DC. I never saw the case opened to me and thought the case had been adjudicated.

The Case

Approximately a little over one year later, I got the case for investigation. The investigation was for Top Secret (TS) access, requiring a Single-Scope Background Investigation (SSBI). The term SSBI will actually become an antiquated term in the near future, as all investigations are going into a Tiered Investigatory System. I will not explain Tiered investigations because the explanation would be lengthy and is considered FOUO and SBU, and involve operational capabilities. For the purposes of explanation, I will refer to a TS investigation as an SSBI. There are many types of Personal Security Investigations (PSI), but the SSBI is a complete investigation to determine vulnerability for TS access. The SSBI requires a subject to complete a form known as a Standard Form (SF) 86. This form requires some time to complete as it requests personal history information, known as Personal Identifying Information (PII). PII is considered For Official

Use Only (FOUO), Sensitive But Unclassified (SBU) information that is protected under the Privacy Act of 1974.

When the case was opened to me, I found that a Federal Law Enforcement Agency (FLEA) had executed an arrest warrant on a foreign national who was residing illegally in the local area. The foreign national was arrested on previously convicted felony drug charges and connection to a drug cartel and connection to arms' dealers. The foreign national was also a known arms' dealer. The suspect's personal property was confiscated, which revealed photographs of a compromising nature with an unknown person. One of the photographs was a picture of this person in a company work uniform, leading the FLEA to my Subject.

The FLEA had questioned my Subject to determine a connection with the foreign national. My Subject denied any connection to any foreign national or affiliations to any criminal activity, during FLEA questioning and was released. My Subject was told by FLEA to report to their supervision that a FLEA had questioned the Subject. This was because the Subject held a Government position and was required to do so. During questioning of the foreign national, the FLEA also learned an affair occurred between the married foreign national and my Subject who was also married. This created vulnerability and other issues on the part of my Subject. The foreign national disclosed to FLEA that my Subject had given the foreign national access to a restricted area for business purposes and had also attended social gatherings with the foreign national, where other foreign nationals were in attendance, some of whom were known drug dealers and arms' dealers. The foreign national was also a small business owner who was trying for government contracts and informed FLEA that my Subject was helping the foreign national to obtain government contract work. This would allow an uncleared illegal alien onto Government property and possibly allowing access to restricted and classified areas.

I began my investigation with many questions that needed to be answered. Was National Security compromised in a restricted area? Had classified information been compromised? And what information? How many foreign nationals did the individual have

185

contact with? What kind of activity had my Subject been involved: drugs, arms, additional foreign contact? Too many questions had to be explored and answered. I began by interviewing co-workers, supervisors, and listed and unlisted SF-86 references. Most of these references relayed unacceptable work behavior and work ethic and violation of employment regulations and rules. The Subject's supervisor expressed concern over the Subject's suitability and reliability. Further, by Government regulations, the Subject was required to report contact with a FLEA, which was not reported by the Subject. Investigation disclosed the Subject had previously submitted an SF-86 for adjudication, and there was no foreign national association divulged. This investigation was adjudicated earlier as normal with no discrepancies by another government agency, which I thought was unusual. Apparently, the Subject failed to truthfully answer some questions on this SF-86, and further, the investigation failed to find this. The Subject omitted some answers to circumvent the investigative process to avoid detection of issues. References indicated the Subject had bragged to co-workers and friends about attending large parties out of town, known to be held in an expensive home. The Subject was reported to have ownership of several expensive vehicles that the Subject could not afford on the Subject's known salary. Indicating suspicious affluence. The Subject associated at work with co-workers who were known to have mental issues and boyfriend/girlfriend problems. Thus affecting my Subject's stability. The Subject is someone who cannot keep a confidence, which would indicate the Subject may divulge classified information in normal conversation. A check of medical records regarding the Subject's psychological and emotional health indicated work-related stress, and the doctor's notes indicated the Subject was seeing an unknown psychologist, not disclosed by the Subject on security paperwork. There were many undisclosed discrepant issues on the Subject's paperwork. The Subject failed to disclose on security paperwork any association with a foreign national. It was my job to get the Subject to acknowledge association with a foreign national, ascertain the nature of the relationship, and determine why the foreign national was not disclosed, along with other obvious discrepancies. Had my Subject been involved in: drugs, arms, additional foreign contact? Had Subject been engaged in espionage or sabotage against the U.S. Did Subject have knowledge of this type of activity? Had Subject been approached by foreign intelligence? or had Subject sold classified information or materials to unauthorized person(s)? Did Subject have any knowledge of this type of activity? Had Subject had contact with any representatives of a foreign government? I had to identify any information gaps, analyze information I had collected, and determine questioning technique and direction of investigation.

Then you will know the truth, and the truth shall set you free......John 8:32 (NIV)

Questioning of the Subject

The Subject was advised that full cooperation and participation would help in timely adjudication and truthfulness would be of absolute significance during the interview process. The Subject initially denied any contact with a foreign national or having an affair outside marriage. (If the Subject was unwilling to admit any foreign contact or affair, it placed the Subject in a position of vulnerability.) There was the possibility that the Subject was susceptible to being blackmailed, pressured, or coerced into acting against the best interest of the US. I will not divulge some investigative interview techniques; however, the Subject later recanted earlier statements and confessed to knowing a foreign contact and of having an affair. The Subject denied knowing the foreign national was dealing drugs or arms. There were many deceptive indicators exhibited by the Subject during interview. One of which I will mention. When someone lacks the use of pronouns in a statement, such as "I," they are usually deceptive. Some control questions must be asked, but analyzing the lack of pronouns has proved ninety-seven percent accurate. When asked why I should believe you, the Subject attempted to explain why I should. This question alone would make any innocent person mad or upset, not try to explain why. The Subject denied providing any restricted or classified information to anyone and attempted to explain away any perception of affluence. The Subject initially denied all accusations but later confessed to most. The Subject was not taking any responsibility for any misconduct. The Subject did not confess to all questions but did confess foreign national association and nature of the relationship. Those that were not confessed to, all had deceptive indicators, either through body language, Scientific Content and Analysis of Statements (SCAN), Neurolinguistics, Elicitation, and other obvious untruthful statements/behavior. SCAN is a technique used to detect deception in statements, both verbal and written. The Subject completed a sworn and signed statement and, one day later, wanted to change the original statement, which the Subject was allowed to do. Both statements were kept for adjudication. The Subject also agreed to a polygraph examination. An interesting observation on a polygraph examination question will be addressed in the below case. This Subject was no different in the response to the question, "how do you think you will do?" The case was again forwarded to the counterintelligence section for analysis.

Here Is an Investigator's Tip

Would you like to know how to determine if someone is being deceptive to you ninety-seven percent of the time (statistically)? Here's how.

Scientific Content Analysis of Statements (SCAN) is an analysis that follows a two-step process. First, investigators determine what is typical of a truthful statement, referred to as the norm. Then you look for any deviation from this norm. Truthful statements differ from fabricated ones in both content and quality. Investigators examine words, independent of case facts, to detect deception.

Pronouns

Pronouns are parts of speech that take the place of nouns. Common examples of personal pronouns include I, me, you, he, she, we, they, and it. In a statement analysis, either verbal or written, particular attention should be given to the personal pronouns I and we, and all possessive pronouns, such as my, our, your, his, her, etc. By the way, the age, gender, or language of subject. does not make a difference.

It should be noted that truthful people give statements using the pronoun I, which is first-person singular. Any deviation from this norm deserves close scrutiny, for it could be an indication that the person is not totally committed to the facts in their statement and, therefore, not telling the whole truth.

Example

You are trying to determine if the person you are interviewing took a classified document from a facility without authorization. Here is a very basic and simple description. You ask this person what s/he did during the day from beginning to end the document went missing. The person then says or writes, "I woke up at six o'clock, and I took a shower, and then I went to work. When I got to work, set up the coffeepot, checked e-mail, and then I went to a meeting."

This person probably took the document when s/he first got to work because the person did not own the statement. S/he said "set up the coffeepot" and "checked e-mail." S/he did not say I set up my coffeepot, etc. The person did not own their statement, leaving out personal pronouns. However, it probably is not fact. You must ask further questions to determine truth; however, a good start to focus furthering questioning is at the point subject set the coffeepot up. There is also a way to determine probable time of day or time of incident from a statement, both verbal and written, but I will not go into this technique. It's too lengthy to explain.

Let me explain how simple this technique is in a real life scenario. A few years ago a local Police Department asked me to see if I could determine the perpetrator of a $3,000.00 Larceny from a church using SCAN statement analysis. Person(s) unknown had taken money from a church Pastors office during a Sunday service. The Detective working the case had three suspects determined to be in the area during the time the money went missing. One, a young female, just turned 18, two, the Church janitor, and the third, a man witnesses reported in the area of the Larceny during the church service. At issue was the young female, who had previously injured her head, and the detective did not want to perform a polygraph on the suspects because of this head injury. The Detective was wanting to know if I could help. I informed the Detective to have each of the suspects write a statement explaining in detail what each did upon arrival at the church on the day in question, to the end of the day when each left. The Detective called all suspects, one at a time, into his office and each wrote their statements, which he later had me review. After analyzing each statement, one just simply glared guilty. All statements but one had proper pronoun use. There were other verbiage conflicts, which I will not go into, however, the lack of pronouns gave it away. The Janitor simply lacked proper pronoun usage not owning his actions. I provided a list of questions to the Detective that should be asked during interrogation, that would bring the suspects guilty feelings to the surface during questioning. In fact, prior to the Detective's questioning the janitor, this individual informed the Pastor a large sum of money had been deposited into a personal bank account which had been obtained as a gift from a relative. The janitor informed the Pastor if anyone checked this account, it would explain the deposit. The janitor was already feeling guilty and trying to cover guilt feelings. After reading the janitor's statement, I was even able to inform the Detective when the Larceny may have occurred during the church service, and provided an approximate time of occurrence. I will not explain how this is done, as it is too lengthy to explain. The above example is only one reason an investigator should have the suspect of a criminal nature, or of an intelligence nature, no matter what language it is written, write his/her own statement. The Larceny was solved using this pronoun technique. It is that effective.

The above are examples of how SCAN can help you determine the truth. Bait Questions and Mind Viruses work well with this technique. I prefer to analyze written statements, however, SCAN works equally as well verbally during an interview or interrogation.

Mirroring

Mirroring is a technique I have used with some success, and I mention it because I used it in a limited manner with the first case mentioned above. Let me explain what mirroring is. Mirroring is the subconscious replication of another person's nonverbal signals. Mirroring is the behavior in which one person subconsciously imitates the gesture, speech pattern, or attitude of another. I use this technique mainly as a rapport-building concept at the beginning and during my interviews. Mirroring generally takes place subconsciously as individuals react to gestures by the interviewer, such as folding one's arms, then unfolding. The subject will see this subconsciously and react with the same gesture. Mirroring is common in conversation as the listeners will typically smile or frown along with the speaker, as well as imitate body posture or attitude about the topic. Individuals may be more willing to empathize with and accept people whom they believe hold similar interests and beliefs, and thus mirroring the person with whom one is speaking may establish connections between the individuals involved. This technique is similar in nature to elicitation in that it has to be fluid, smooth, and matter-of-fact. And accomplished by an experienced investigator. A word of caution: never let the subject of investigation see you attempting to mirror. If observed by the subject, you might as well end your interview because any questions asked after that will not be answered naturally, and the subject will know you are simply inexperienced, and information obtained will not be volunteered.

I have also used what I call negative mirroring. Here's an example. Many years ago during an interview of a midlevel Army Officer, who was obviously in a hurry and noncommittal to any questions I asked during the interview, the Officer constantly looked at the watch worn. The Subject simply did not want to be there and was in a hurry. The Subject had a company to Command and had no time for the interview we both had agreed upon a time for. This is when I looked at the Subject in the eyes and asked a question but, at the same time, nonchalantly took my watch off and placed it in the top drawer of my desk. All observed by the Subject. This simple act told Subject subconsciously, without saying it, that I was not interested in time during the interview process but also told the Subject we would finish when we finished. The Subject immediately slowed down and took time in answering my questions, which made the interview go faster. The Subject subconsciously got the idea. A good real-life example of mirroring was relayed to me by a Naval Lower Half Admiral during an interview I conducted many years ago. I had asked this Naval Officer if he had noticed anything unusual during a recent OCONUS (Outside Continental United States) trip to an unnamed country. His response was classic foreign counterintelligence usage of mirroring. Unfortunately, for the foreign intelligence officer using this technique, is the fact that this Naval Officer was also trained in this technique, himself being a trained intelligence officer. Mirroring is simply not a good idea to use on someone from another known intelligence background, which was known by each party involved, unless you are very adept at it. This alone is a definite no-no and simply unprofessional. However, on the other hand, mirroring can be used by foreign intelligence as a blatant in-your-face technique. In this particular case, it was used during a counterpart meet-and-greet dinner from each country. Each time this Naval Officer mentioned something he enjoyed, his counterpart also enjoyed the same thing. When a particular food was mentioned that was liked, the counterpart liked it also. When the Naval Officer caught on, which was quickly, he was able to turn the tables and use it against his counterpart. During this same OCONUS travel by this Source and in another country on the same business issue, the retired Naval Officer had not mentioned the fact he was a retired Admiral. His paperwork only reflected his status as an engineer among a group of engineers.

On the way up to their rooms in the motel they were staying, one of the engineers in the group asked the elevator operator a question. Without hesitation, the elevator operator looked over at the Naval Officer and said, "Admiral, you can answer that question better than I." The Naval Officer had not mentioned he had ever been in the military or connected to the military in any way. The moral: don't trust your elevator operator to be an elevator operator. This was an in-your-face blatant act by foreign intelligence to inform this Source he knew who he was. By the way, never stay in an assigned motel room. But the issue of an assigned motel room is another story, which is too lengthy to place in this book.

Mano a Mano with a Retired Federal Agent

I have conducted numerous investigations and have conducted thousands of interviews on both Sources and Subjects of investigations. Over time, one hones his skill level with investigative techniques such as SCAN, mentioned above, body language, Elicitation techniques, and Reid. Reid Interview and Interrogation techniques were developed by an individual named John Reid and is widely used by law enforcement investigators in criminal investigations as an interrogation tool. A Personal Security Investigation (PSI) is non-custodial in nature; however, there are some useful Reid interview techniques that can be used in a PSI. I personally prefer SCAN and Elicitation techniques and the use of body language during most of my interviews. Again, in a criminal investigation, the investigator knows a crime has been committed. During a PSI investigation, the investigator does not know his Subject has committed a crime. To me, when you are attempting to find out if a crime has been committed (espionage), it is much more challenging to find it.

I received an open investigation on an SSBI on a contract investigator applicant, who was a retired FLEA. This case was a little more challenging due to the experience level of the applicant. The applicant was wanting to conduct PSI investigations as a retirement contractor job. Our agency hires contractors to help with the large workload throughout the US, and this person was interested in doing this. Some history on the case: a Confidential Informant (COIN) had come forward and relayed the Subject had been involved in criminal conduct prior to retirement. (I will not divulge this conduct.) Further, the Subject had sought psychological counseling prior to retirement and had gone outside the Subject's agency to keep the agency worked for from finding out. The Subject failed to truthfully answer some questions on the SF-86. The Subject omitted some answers to circumvent the investigative process to avoid detection of issues. If the agency the Subject worked for had known of the Subject's behavior, the Subject would have been terminated, and criminal charges would be filed. Let me say here that the acronym COIN can also stand for Counter-Insurgency; however, I am using the acronym as an informant.

Subject Interview

I will go into a little more interview depth questioning detail on this investigation to provide a better understanding of the questioning process. The Subject was not responding well to either direct or indirect questioning. The Subject was denying all accusations he was questioned and presented with. Of course, the Subject was unaware of the information our COIN had presented in a signed and sworn statement.

Direct Questions versus Indirect Questions

I will illustrate this by relaying the following. In the late sixties, a waitress on the south side of Chicago was killed just outside the small café she worked at. Several suspects were quickly developed and interrogated. One of the questions asked by the detective in charge of the investigation during the interrogation was "Did you go to the café to eat on the day of the murder?" This was asked by the detective to determine if any of the suspects were in the café on the day of the murder and to establish if they were in the vicinity at the time of the murder. None confessed. Time elapsed, and the case got cold. Approximately eighteen years later, a younger detective made an arrest on this murder after developing a suspect connected to another murder. When the detective obtained a confession, the old detective who had lead the initial investigation asked to speak to the perpetrator and was given permission. Upon questioning the perpetrator, the old detective asked, "Why didn't you tell me you went to the café to eat when I asked you?" The perpetrator said, "I did not go to the café to eat. I went to the café to kill her. You did not ask me that." Sometimes a direct question should be asked.

The applicant I was investigating was an experienced investigator with over twenty years of criminal investigative experience. This applicant was also an experienced counterintelligence agent, and I will not go into this history. This applicant was also very familiar with the very questioning techniques in which I was using. Every question I asked, the Subject was obviously familiar with the technique used. I then began using a combination of Elicitation techniques. These techniques can be used very successfully on academics, law enforcement, and engineers, etc. This is because most are either egotistical or will want to relay to you how intelligent they are. These traits can be used against them.

Elicitation Questioning Technique

Elicitation is one of the most difficult and sophisticated interrogation/interview techniques. It requires careful planning, discretion, and skillful application. Elicitation will appear to be normal social or professional conversation, and it is highly effective. You may never realize you were the target of elicitation or provided meaningful info. Only the skilled and experienced interviewer can employ this method with success. The elicitor must be resourceful, use initiative and imagination, and be unusually perceptive. He must be persistent without being obnoxious and remain in complete control of the conversation at all times. Elicitation is the most difficult interview/interrogation technique to learn or teach.

Elicitation is the use of conversation to extract information from people without letting them know they are giving information to you. It is a discreet way to obtain information without the Subject knowing what information you are seeking. It's subtle and very useful. You simply have to be proficient at it. Questioning must flow smoothly. However, it takes experience to pull off correctly. Once a Subject senses what is happening, you might as well stop the interview.

There are many elicitation techniques, too numerous to mention. And most are used simultaneously, so I will not mention them in this book. However, I'll relay to you why it works. An experienced investigator understands certain human or cultural predispositions and uses techniques to exploit those. Natural tendencies that may be exploited include:

a desire to be polite and helpful to strangers, a new acquaintance, or an interviewer

a desire to appear well-informed, especially about one's profession

a desire to feel appreciated and believe they are contributing to something important

a tendency to expand on a topic when given praise or encouragement; to show off

a tendency to gossip (this tendency is someone who may not be able to keep a confidence)

a tendency to correct others

a tendency to underestimate the value of the information being sought or given, especially if one is unfamiliar with how else that information could be used

a tendency to believe others are honest; a disinclination to be suspicious of others

a tendency to answer truthfully when asked an "honest" question

a desire to convert someone to their opinion

Here's an investigative tip for you: do not draw special attention to yourself or your professional affiliation. There are several methods to deflect an elicitation attempt on you if you are fortunate enough to recognize it. I will mention a few. However, if executed properly, you will never know you were the target of an elicitation and will never know what information you gave up.

You can deflect the attempt by referring to other sources, such as public sources, websites, or simple press releases.

You can ignore the question you think improper or deflect the question with one of your own.

You can give a nondescript answer, such as I don't know or simply tell the elicitor you stay out of such discussions or simply say you cannot discuss it. A word of caution, someone who tells you "I don't know" or "I forgot" usually does remember. Ask more questions. Subject is stalling for time. OK…one more tip: A word of caution on the use of the word discuss by a Source. The word discuss has the connotation of an issue, problem, or where one has to argue or debate someone else into something. Verses saying talk. Example; If you ask your supervisor a question, and the supervisor tells you s/he will "discuss" the issue with higher, should tell you that the supervisor feels the question will possibly be an issue with his/her supervisor and some convincing will have to occur in the conversation. There's a problem associated with the question, or there will be a debate over the question. Or the supervisor feels the question or suggestion will go nowhere. Versus the supervisor telling you s/he will talk to their higher. The word "talk" meaning non-issue. If a Source relays to the investigator that s/he discussed the missing document with his security officer or supervisor, you can bet there was some convincing needed, or debate, by Source to explain the missing document. If, on the only hand, Source said s/he talked with their security officer, you can surmise there was no issue associated with the missing document, or there was no compromise of information. Ask more questions. OK…I better stop here. I'm not teaching, but writing a book.

Back on point, my Subject continued with denials. I decided it was time to offer a polygraph examination. My interview had gone on long enough. I had observed some deceptive indicators and behavior;

however, the Subject was not going to confess, and I could not conduct an interrogation because a National Security Investigation is noncriminal. I asked, "Should it be necessary to confirm what you told me today, are you willing to undergo a polygraph examination?" The Subject responded, "Yes, I have nothing to hide." Most inexperienced investigators might stop there and put a report together. I continued and asked, "How do you think you will do on the polygraph examination?" The Subject's immediate response was "I think I will do OK." I had him, and the Subject knew it. I saw it in the Subject's eyes. Let me explain. A truthful person would answer, "I am telling the truth. I'll pass" or some similar statement. Anyone who responds with "I think," "I should," "I could," "I probably will pass," "If I don't pass, there's something wrong with your machine" is deceptive. No one "thinks" they will pass or say "I should" pass if they are innocent. An innocent person will be confident he will pass and answer, "I'll pass. I want to take a polygraph." I asked for a signed sworn statement, and the Subject wrote a one-sentence paragraph denying all accusations. This in and of itself is odd, given an experienced criminal investigator with over twenty years' investigative experience. The Subject did not get a contract job.

Kill Them with Kindness

I was assigned a case in the early nineties, which involved a Subject who had been accused of incest by his daughters who had reported this to their middle-school teacher. The middle-school teacher then promptly reported this to social services. Let me point out that whenever a Security Questionnaire is filled out, the individual is also required to sign a Release of Information, which allows the Government to conduct a National Agency Check (NAC) record search, including Federal, State and Local checks of both criminal (Privacy Act 1974) and financial (Privacy Act 1978) history. An investigation is not conducted or opened without this signed release. During the NAC search on the Subject, it was determined that a social services case had been opened and an investigation initiated by the social service agency for sexual abuse of a family member.

The Subject required access to classified information and did not list the required fact he had been under investigation on his Security Questionnaire, making him vulnerable to coercion and/or exploitation. Prior to interviewing the Subject, I reviewed the social service investigation and became aware of the accusations and statements made by the Subject's three juvenile daughters, two of which were preteen. One daughter had aborted a pregnancy by her father (the Subject). Another daughter had the Subject's child and had placed the child for adoption, and one daughter had not yet been impregnated. During the social services investigation, the Subject's spouse had been interviewed by a social services investigator. The subject's spouse, a registered foreign national alien, admitted to the social services investigator that she was aware of the incest and actually supported it. The spouse had relayed to the social services investigator that she was born in a foreign country that condoned this type of father/daughter conduct. Let me interject here and say when someone from a foreign country moves to the US, they then fall under US law and should fully assimilate into US culture. After researching the case and conducting interviews of supervisors, co-workers, and listed and unlisted references, I scheduled an interview of the Subject. I made it a point to contact the Subject on a Friday for a Monday interview. This technique allowed the Subject to contemplate on any hypothetical consequences to any perceived act the Subject felt guilty of. Thus, making it easier for me during the interview process to obtain the truth. At the time of this case, I used this technique not having a name for it. In later years, other agencies began using the term "Mind Virus" for this technique, which I have described in this book. Here is the point of my including this investigation. Whenever you interview someone who you feel is human detritus, you do not want your own feelings known to the Subject or to influence your interview in any way. To me, the Subject was a repugnant and offensive individual. You have to put aside personal beliefs and biases. Treat all persons as you would want to be treated. Kill them with kindness. Had I gone into this interview in an aggressive manner or one of anger and disrespect, I would not have gotten anywhere. After I showed the Subject some kindness and respect, I was able to get the Subject to tell the truth of his relationships with his daughters. The Subject was born and raised in the US and knew right from wrong based on his moral foundation, making him feel guilty as the result of his actions and behavior. The Subject was expecting a rough interrogation, rather than a nice guy conducting an interview. I was not concerned my kindness may be seen as weakness or lack of confidence by the Subject. I was confident in my abilities; this tells the Subject I was confident enough in my interview skill set that I do not have to resort to aggressive techniques. I have never used techniques that would be considered aggressive. I don't need to because I am confident in my abilities and skill sets. Honey will catch more flies so to speak. The Subject was not expecting me to be nice to him, which made me more likable to him. Being nonaggressive may have even made him feel somewhat indebted to me. We need to hang on to goodness and virtue. When someone does something unspeakable to someone, you do something about it because you can.

Addict

OK, one more. I received an open investigation on an individual who required classified access to the SECRET level. After review of the individual's paperwork, I did not observe anything out of the norm. It was a late July day, and temperatures were hovering around one hundred degrees when I called the Subject in for a scheduled interview. The Subject occupied a professional position and one who was responsible for lives on occasion. The Subject arrived at my office in dark clothing, buttoned to the top button. The individual's shirt was long sleeve and buttoned at the wrists. Further, the individual had brown cloth gloves on each hand. Odd? On a hot day? This immediately put me in mind of a drug user. I was proven right. I requested he remove his gloves, and the individual complied. That's when my original suspicions of drug use proved correct. On both hands, between each knuckle, were needle marks, known as "tracks." I immediately asked about drug use, and the Subject admitted to using drugs. The Subject raised each shirtsleeve to exposed needle tracks and needle scars on each arm. The

Subject admitted to a heroin habit at two thousand dollars per week. Come to find out, the Subject's spouse was a dealer making approximately eighteen thousand dollars per week in drug profits, thus not only supplying the Subject but perpetuating the Subject's heroin habit. It should be noted that the Subject's Government salary was not near enough to cover his drug habit. The Subject was denied access during the adjudication process and later terminated. This case was referred to a Federal Drug Task Force. As a result a local drug ring was arrested and eliminated because of my interview.

Investigation Experience

Experience will always trump youth and immaturity, and by immaturity, I also mean inexperience. It takes time to develop and hone investigative skill sets. The point is you need experience to determine deception on complex interviews. Five years of investigative experience is sometimes not enough on complex issues. You need to learn how to beat the grass to startle the snakes.

Enhanced Tactical Interrogation Techniques

I have never used enhanced interrogation techniques. As a strategic intelligence officer, I have never been trained in tactical interrogation techniques, other than being in an opposing-force scenario. Do I believe in approved tactical enhanced interrogation techniques? Yes. Interviewing someone in a nonadversarial, noncustodial interview is much different than a tactical interrogation of an enemy who hates you and everything you stand for or represent. Enemy combatants have been trained in tactical resistance. These techniques work and have saved countless lives. Notice I say approved tactical enhanced interrogation techniques. Unapproved enhanced techniques are considered torture. It is against the Geneva Convention to torture prisoners. We play by the rules; they don't. And that is what separates us from evil. I'll stop with that.

CHAPTER 14

US Army Reserves

In 1983, a friend whom I had met as a co-worker was a US Army Reserves (USAR) Army Captain. He knew I was a college graduate and wanted to know if I was interested in becoming an Army Officer by joining the USAR. I decided to do so after being told that due to my education, there was a USAR program that would allow me to become an officer by appointment. I was presented with paperwork that would allow me to obtain a set of tracks (Army Captain). That was in September 1983. In November 1983, the USAR did away with this program, one month after I joined. I was stuck as a Specialist Fourth Class (E-4). That seemed OK with me as I was not doing manual labor and did not mind the work. However, ambition took hold, and I began moving up in rank, becoming a Specialist Fifth Class (E-5). At that time, the Army had enlisted technical ranks from Specialist Fourth Class to Specialist Eighth Class. This technical program was eliminated in the mideighties. To explain the technical Specialist's ranks, the ranks were not to reduce a specialist's privileges but to augment the prestige of Non Commissioned Officers (NCO). An NCO's primary role was enlisted leadership, and specialists received pay commensurate with their specialist rank. I had made Specialist Fifth Class when the program was eliminated. To make a long story short, I gained in rank to a Sergeant First Class (SFC E-7).

Upon moving out of State, I decided to go into intelligence and went through the basic intelligence course. My first assignment as an army Special Agent, Military Intelligence and Counterintelligence, was with the First Military Intelligence Center, Phoenix, Arizona.

Open Source Intelligence (OSINT)

One of my assignments at the First Military Intelligence Center was working with Open Source Intelligence (OSINT). Before I obtained my Commission, I was assigned as Team Leader, Sergeant First Class (SFC) of a team assigned to gather OSINT information on an unnamed country. Once a month, my team gathered at the public library in Phoenix, Arizona, to gather all OSINT we could find on this country. At the time, our Unit was attached yearly to an OCONUS Intelligence Battalion, and we were gathering OSINT as part of this mission. Over a period of six months, our team looked at periodicals, magazines, books, newspapers, computer articles, pictures, editorials, TV, radio, audiovisual, etc. All information obtained from this effort was made into a Target Country Assessment. By the time we had completed the assignment, we learned a myriad of information. This OSINT turned classified once made into a Target Assessment. One would be surprised at what information you can obtain if you know how. The OCONUS Intelligence Battalion may still use some of the information we collected as OSINT.

Military Intelligence

After much hard work, I applied for the Warrant Officer Program, was accepted, trained, and became an officer and gentleman by act of Congress. I already was a gentleman, but Congress made it so. I became a Military Intelligence Officer, specializing in Counterintelligence in mid-1995, Warrant Officer Candidate School (WOCS) is not easy. I will just say this about training. Do you want it bad enough to earn it? How tough do you think you are? If you want the position bad enough to earn it, you will make it. I won't go into the training I received. I'll start with my assignment as a Counterintelligence Instructor in a Unit (5-104th Military Intelligence Battalion) at Fort Huachuca, Arizona. I began by being assigned as an instructor with a group of highly qualified Senior Chief Warrant (CWO) Officers. Warrant Officers at that time were assigned as the instructors, with the Non Commissioned Officers (NCO) as assistant instructors, and being in charge of getting our students to/from class and also making sure paperwork and student documentation was properly filled out and in order. Eventually, I was assigned as a remote Officer Instructor with another warrant, a Chief Warrant Officer 4 Dr. Rick Fuhrman, whom we called Dr. Rick. Dr. Rick was a PhD Psychologist and also a Polygrapher. He was a good knowledgeable instructor. We were assigned to instruct the Utah National Guard (UNG) in Salt Lake City (SLC). We traveled there once monthly as MITT instructors for approximately a year. We graduated several new Counterintelligence Agents. I must mention here that most of the people I helped train in Utah served with me in International Zone (IZ). I trained them well. I watched them make history in Iraq and was very proud of their accomplishments. Over time, I was assigned as an Officer in Charge (OIC) of Counterintelligence Instructors at the unit in Fort Huachuca. I not only taught the courses I wanted to teach but was also responsible for managing the entire course. I will explain some courses we taught, but I think you might also be interested in the selection process to become an army counterintelligence (CI) agent. A Strategic Intelligence assignment. One must apply to become a CI agent from a feeder Military Occupational Specialty (MOS) in one of the Intelligence specialties. I will briefly describe the selection process to submit a packet to become an Army Counterintelligence Agent. The person must be able to meet the physical demands through a medical exam, and have a good physical profile, normal color vision, a good score on an intelligence test, be able to obtain and hold a TS/SCI, demonstrate clear enunciation and comprehension of English and grammer skills. The person can never have been a member of the Peace Corp, and have a clean law enforcement record. The person must be a U.S. Citizen, and immediate family must be U.S. Citizens. No immediate family can reside in a country with known mental coercion. The individual must be a minimum of 21 years of age, and have an enlisted rank between E-4 to SGM, and hold a career field in the 35 Series (Intelligence) field. The selection process requires three recommendations by the individual's command structure. The individual must have demonstrated neatness, posture, stature and Physique, a good physiognomy, and demeanor. After the individual is scrutinized by his/her command, and completed a lengthy interview process, the person submits an applicant packet to the Department of the Army (DoA), who again scrutinizes the individual, his/her military training and evaluations. With all of the above, DoA looks at the individual through a looking glass for character and moral values. Can this person undergo the required training? Is this person intelligent enough? (Once selected, one goes through an interview process with a CI agent, some report writing samples, Command recommendations, a thorough and comprehensive background investigation, and other processes.)

The CI Agent who conducts the interview of the applicant then makes a report to the Army, and the applicant is considered along with numerous other applicants. Once selected, the applicant then waits for a class date. The selection process is lengthy and once selected for training, you know you are among the best. The CI course is not an easy one and some are washed out. I will not go into describing the training process, however, I will tell you about some classes I have taught, which will give you an idea of the type of training an Army Counterintelligence Agent receives.

Some courses I have taught and/or was course manager of were security programs, use of interpreters, CI jurisdiction, national security crimes, military intelligence law, questioning techniques, intelligence contingency funds (both classified and unclassified), source interviews, report writing, terrorism, counterterrorism, espionage, counterespionage, information collection, evidence collection, dead drops, elicitation, spotting, assessing and recruiting, personal meets, surveillance, countersurveillance (tails: how to detect them and how to lose them), surveillance detection routes, communication, tradecraft, nonofficial cover (NOC) (described below), backstops and when and how to use them, link diagrams, association matrices, and time event charts. There are other classified classes I taught, but you get an idea of some of the courses CI agents go through. The course teaches agents basic how-to strategic counterintelligence, which is how to collect, analyze, and use information. Army CI Agents must be taught properly and thoroughly. Strategic counterintelligence investigations are difficult, because they are often conducted clandestinely and have an enormous burden of proof. Depending on the type of investigation required, there are certain steps, agreements and concurrence's Army CI must go through to even begin an intelligence investigation. A CI investigation on an individual who provides intelligence (U.S. Secrets) to other countries verbally, further exacerbates and makes for a more complex and protracted strategic intelligence investigation. I became quite good at teaching interview techniques and surveillance techniques. I enjoyed giving students the benefit of my knowledge and experience.

Non Official Cover (NOC)

I will not talk too much on this issue, only to give an idea of what NOC is. NOC is not taught as part of the current strategic CI curriculum but was taught when I was initially assigned as an instructor.

When under NOC, operatives assume covert roles without ties to the government for which they work. Such operatives are typically abbreviated in lingo as an NOC (pronounced "knock"). Non Official Cover is contrasted with Official Cover where an operative assumes a position at an otherwise benign role. This provides the operative with official diplomatic immunity, thus protecting them from the steep punishments normally meted out to captured operatives.

Operatives under NOC do not have this "safety net," and if captured or charged, they are subject to severe criminal punishments, up to and including execution. This is where an operatives "backstop" comes in. Backstopping an NOC is a complicated process and very important to the life of the NOC. I will not go into backstopping as it would take another book. Backstopping, put simply, is when an operative would want a driver's license issued under his/her assumed name, as a very simple example. Operatives under NOC are also usually trained to deny any connection with their government, thus preserving plausible deniability but also denying them any hope of diplomatic legal assistance or official acknowledgment of their service.

I Don't Like to Talk to You

In one of my advanced interview techniques classes in Fort Devens, Massachusetts, I asked one of my students during class to tell me a little about himself, as I did some other students. After class, I approached this student and asked how he liked the course, and during this conversation, I informed him a little more about himself he had not revealed to me or his classmates in class to give him an idea of what the questioning techniques course could do. I told him things about himself he thought he had not revealed. Then he said, "Damn, Chief, I don't like to talk to you because you know what I'm thinking." I smiled inwardly and said, "No, I'm just listening to what you tell me. Use what I teach you, and you can do the same." I did not realize until that moment what type of impact my instruction was having on the people I taught. I enjoyed teaching these advanced interview technique courses. It never ceased to amaze me the ingenuity of some of my students. At the end of the Elicitation Technique class, I always gave a twenty-four-hour assignment of going out and using their new interview skills to bring me back a date of birth or social security number or both from a complete stranger. There were usually two or three that brought them back. They were the individuals I surmised that would be good interviewers/interrogators in their respective units.

I had been the Officer in Charge (OIC) of the Counterintelligence Instructor Section for approximately one year and then was appointed the S2, a busy job and part of the Battalion Staff. The S2 is responsible for the security and intelligence of the Battalion, in my case numbering one hundred sixty Service Members. During the summer training session, this number swelled to sometimes just under three hundred. I was also used as an instructor and course manager as necessary. I had a staff of four and enjoyed this position. I held this position until the time of my retirement.

Staff Functions

I'll explain briefly what the Staff Function of a Battalion is, as I was the Battalion S2 and part of the Command Staff, referenced above. The Command Staff consists of more seasoned and Senior Officers who oversee staff sections of groups organized by the needs of the Battalion. This hierarchy places decision-making and reporting under the auspices of the most experienced personnel and maximizes information flow of pertinent information sent out of the command overall, clarifying matters overall. This frees up the most senior members of the command at each level for decision-making and issuing direction for further research or information gathering (perhaps requiring men to put their lives at risk to gather additional intelligence). Operations staff officers also are tasked with battle planning both for offensive and defensive conditions and issuing contingency plans for handling situations anticipated during the foreseeable future.

S1	personnel and/or manpower
S2	intelligence and security
S3	operations
S4	logistics and supply
S5	plans
S6	signal and communications
S7	training
S8	finance
S9	civil-military cooperation (civil affairs)

In hoc signo, vinces.
(By this sign, thou shalt conquer.)

CHAPTER 15

I Go to War

"We do not see what's behind evil. We do see the results of evil."

In November 2003, I was told by my unit that I was being activated as an instructor to Fort Huachuca for two years, beginning approximately in late January 2004. In mid-December 2003, I went on Christmas leave, and upon my return in early January 2004, I immediately made a medical appointment for an over-forty physical in Fort Bliss, Texas, for my two-year activation to Fort Huachuca. Laura went with me to this physical, which I passed. On the way home from the physical, I received a cell phone call from someone identifying herself as a Major from the 368th MI BN Personal Office (S1) in California, asking me where I was. I thought it was someone from my Unit at first, playing a prank on me. I learned real quick it was not a prank. Apparently, while I was on leave, the 368th Military Intelligence Brigade had cherry-picked me off the instructor detail for a one-year tour in Iraq (IZ). I had not been given the courtesy of notification for this change of orders. I was asked if I could be in Fort Hood, Texas, the following day. Of course, I couldn't, and orders were cut for January 13, 2004. I arrived in Fort Hood, Texas, on that date, where I learned the 368th Military Intelligence Brigade had assigned me to their Unit for train up to Iraq. Part of the train-up process is filling out of personal wills and other such paperwork. It is a humbling experience filling out this paperwork for your family, knowing you may not come back.

Fort Hood, Texas, Train Up

"Blessed be the Lord, My Rock, who trains my hands for war, and my fingers for battle" (Psalm 144:1).

I underwent tactical training at Fort Hood from January 13, 2004, to February 7, 2004. The Captain in Charge of our deploying Unit was certainly not a leader. He was later relieved of his Command in Afghanistan (AFG). There were fifty-four of us, which were split into two groups, one going to Iraq and one going to Bagram, Afghanistan. The Captain explained he had handpicked those going to AFG because he was assigned to Command this group. This group was to be an intelligence group specifically collecting intelligence on and for capturing Bin Laden. A more important mission in his mind. The other group, the one I was in, was going to Baghdad to be under Operational Control (OPCON) to the 502nd Intelligence Battalion in TAC HUMINT operations. To give you an example of the toxic leadership from the start, the Captain stood all in formation and had the temerity to inform all that the NCO Corps would be running most of the operations, and the Warrant Officers assigned would be used in a support role to operations. Thus subordinating Chief Warrants to NCO Operations. Really? I don't think so. This reflected a complete lack of knowledge, understanding of rank structure, and abilities of both enlisted and officer ranks. Myself and others were surprised someone in Command would actually think this way. Well, this immediately alienated all Warrant Officers assigned. I should mention that most Warrant Officers (WO) assigned were experienced Staff-Level Officers, Chief Warrant Officers (CW/3) and above. In October 2003, the Warrant Officer branch was changed making a Warrant Officer 1 equal to a First Lieutenant (1LT/0-1). A CW/2 is equal to a Captain (0-3). A CW/3 is equal to a Major (0-4). A CW/4 is equal to a Lieutenant Colonel (LTC/0-5), and a CW/5 is equal to a Colonel (COL/0-6). The WO remains a technical specialty rank in any particular MOS. A WO was made part of the branch of his/her Military Occupational Specialty (MOS), meaning if you were an Infantry WO, you wore the Infantry Officer Insignia. If you were an Intelligence Officer, you wore the Intelligence Officer Insignia. Prior to this, all WOs wore the WO Insignia. By doing this, the WO then became eligible for Command at the level of their rank. The ranking of a WO was made clear to the Captain who was in Command of our small company when manifesting the troop aircraft on our departure to Kuwait. A military aircraft is loaded by rank. At the time, I was a CWO/3, and all CWO/3s were loaded before our Captain, who was a little surprised at this. He was very egotistical.

We Arrived in Kuwait

In early February 2004, we flew to Kuwait. I spent seven days in Kuwait waiting for ammo and other supplies to take down range. We were assigned tents to sleep in, as I recall, fifteen per tent. Our shower facilities were mobile home-type facilities with showers. Restrooms were of the port-a-potty type. Kuwait is a pretty country but mostly desert where we were. It was at this time I saw my first big camel herds, being shepherded by camel herders. Dust storms. I have been through some Kansas dust storms, but nothing compared to the ones we had in Kuwait. We experienced a couple of large sandstorms while in Kuwait, and I also learned to shower in cold water again. I had learned to shower in cold water in the late sixties in Korea, but one gets used to one's comforts. In the small in-processing building on our compound was the biggest spider I have ever seen under glass. *Huge* is the only way to describe it. I thought it a fake at first. I later learned it was a camel spider that was common to that area. While in Kuwait, we spent time on weapons' ranges, firing the .50-caliber Machine Gun (MG), .60-caliber MG, and Squad Automatic Weapon (SAWs). The SAW, designated the M-249, is an MG that fires a 7.62-millimeter round. All very lethal weapons.

While in Kuwait, I signed for Night Vision Equipment (NVE), which I turned over to my Non Commissioned Officer in Charge

(NCOIC) on the Tactical HUMINT Team I had been placed in charge of. NVEs, also known as Night Optical Goggles (NOG's), are interesting to use and turns the night into day for you when used. We were in Kuwait for seven days awaiting transportation and ammunition. After finally getting ammo, we were off. All Officers carry nine-millimeter pistols in a war zone, and we were issued fourteen rounds and one extra clip per Officer. I thought this odd as we were going into a War Zone. With only fourteen rounds? When I got into Iraq, I was able to finagle seven more rounds, but that's all I had the whole time I was there. All enlisted were issued fourteen rounds of M-16 rounds for their M-16 rifles. The day before we left, the Brigade Chaplain held a church service. There was about one hundred twenty of us in attendance. At the beginning of the service, the Chaplain's Assistant marched from the back of the tent to the front of the tent up the middle isle playing "Amazing Grace" on the bagpipes. I recall feeling very lonely at the time, knowing the following day, we were actually going to War. The following morning, we were off and running. I should explain that when one lands and takes off in a C130 Transport Aircraft in a War Zone, it is almost straight down and/or straight up to keep from getting shot down. It is quite a ride. Kind of like a power takeoff in a rotor, only much faster.

CHAPTER 16

Iraq

We landed at the Baghdad International Airport (BIAP) on February 7, 2004.

Upon arrival, I was assigned to B Company of 502nd Military Intelligence Battalion as a Team Leader responsible for collecting HUMINT information in the Baghdad area from developed sources, Camp Victory. Just after landing, we were all assigned living quarters and told all those assigned to B Company of 502nd Military Intelligence Battalion to report to the main room in the old Republican Guard Headquarters. All members of B Company were in attendance. This is when we were given a Rules of Engagement (ROE) card to carry and given guidelines on enemy engagement by the Battalion Commander. That is when this question was asked, "Does anyone here know what scoring a round is?" No one raised his hand. Silence. OK, I knew. I raised my hand and relayed what scoring a round was. It is against international law and probably needed to be brought up, but it's a sure bet scoring would not have happened with this group as no one but me knew what it was. This was covered in our rules of engagement (ROE) card but not explained. The difference between the American military and our enemy is this: we play by the rules of International Warfare. They don't. The American military is the most lethal force on the face of the earth, but we are also the most compassionate. Here is a scoring description for you.

Scoring a Round

During the Vietnam War, there was what was known as scoring a round by field troops. It was reportedly used: however, I do not know this to be the case. The practice of scoring predates the Vietnam War by over a hundred years and is against International Law. Scoring was done by taking an M-16 round and cutting an X in the top of the bullet with a knife. Scored deep enough, the bullet split into four separate parts or expanded upon impact. Scoring slows the bullet down, and more of its kinetic energy is transferred to the intended target, creating a larger wound for lethality. The Hague Convention of 1899, Declaration III, prohibits the use of expanding bullets in international warfare.

I had four men on my assigned team, including me. My first team mission, day three in country, was as security detail on another team's source mission into an area known as "assignation alley," so named because it was frequently hit by sniper, mortar, and rocket fire. My team accompanied a source meet to a small hut in the middle of a large field. I remained outside with my team on security detail of the source meet. At this meet, there were two children playing in the dirt outside the hut, which sat in the middle of a large dirt field the size of a football field or larger. The concern was the cement block fence surrounding the field. The fence was approximately five feet or more in height and could easily conceal an attack. The children's mother made each of us a hot jigger of Iraqi tea, which her daughter brought out to our parked jeeps. It was a sweet tea and tasted good.

After the meet, we headed back to Camp Victory. Before I could put my team to work developing sources, I was contacted by the Commander of the Company I was assigned and asked if I would take over as the Officer in Charge (OIC) of the Company Operation Management Team (OMT) 52. The Lieutenant that had been placed in charge of the OMT had it so messed up that he had the

Commander confused as to what the OMT mission was. The 502nd Military Intelligence Battalion was not a TAC HUMINT Battalion and had no operational TAC HUMINT experience. I was glad I was asked to take over as OIC of an OMT because at the time I was having knee problems from daily jogs and runs. My knee somehow got better over a month or so. It may have been the heat we operated in making my joints feel better. I don't know. It's one of those life's mysteries. The Company I was assigned needed some OMT organization and leadership. The Lieutenant was not cutting it. He simply had no experience in HUMINT operations and had no operational leadership experience. He was transferred to a team near Al-Kūt, where he remained for the rest of the tour, and I took over as OIC of the OMT in his Chain of Command (C2). It is a very humbling feeling knowing your decisions affect the lives of the men and women who depend on you. I try not to think on this very often.

The OMT was located in building 66C, Camp Victory, Iraq. The OMT room was a secure room, restricted to those who had a need to access. My OMT staff consisted of six personnel: myself as OIC, a CW2 I assigned as my Operations Chief, an SFC I assigned as my NCOIC, a Sergeant I assigned as my reports/night-shift NCOIC, a Specialist (SPC) I assigned as my Computer Technician, and an SPC I assigned as my Imagery Analyst. The OMT staff was comprised from the 368th Military Intelligence Battalion, Detachment 16, Phoenix, Arizona; the 415th Military Intelligence Battalion, Louisiana Army National Guard (LAANG); one member of 294th Military Intelligence Detachment (Counterintelligence), Guam Army National Guard (GUARNG), and two members organic to the 502nd Military Intelligence Battalion.

My Teams

OMT 52 began with five Tactical HUMINT Teams (THT): THT 515, THT 516, THT 517, THT 518, and THT 525. In early April 2004, THT 515 was sent to Karbala, and THT 525 was sent to Al-Kūt to help in operations of C Company and later permanently assigned. OMT 52 then consisted of three teams: THT 516, a Strategic Debriefing/Foreign Military Intelligence Coordinating Authority (FORMICA) team; THT 517, a walk-in team; and THT 518, an Iraqi Military Intelligence Report (IMIR) Team. These teams were located at the Green Zone, now known as the International Zone. In July 2004, OMT 52 gained three new teams: THT 530, THT 531, and THT 532. In August, THT 532 was transferred to A Company, and THT 531 was temporarily transferred to the First Team (first Cavalry) for operational purposes. In September, THT 510, who was attached to the 16th Military Police Brigade, was reassigned to B Company OMT 52 and then attached to the 89th Military Police Brigade in October 2004, becoming THT 524. OMT 52, at end of tour, had three teams operating in the IZ (THT 516, 517, and 518), two mobile teams (THT 530 and 531) operating in the greater Baghdad area, east of the Tigris River, and one team (THT 524) assigned to the 42nd Military Police Brigade but reporting through OMT 52. At end of tour, I had Operational Command of twenty-six THT personnel and a staff of six. My OMT reported to the Battalion Tactical Human Operation Section (THOPS). I wish I could give you the names of all the members of my teams, but the list would be too much for this book. My Team Leaders: THT 516 Sergeant First Class Jorge Huerta, THT 517 Chief Warrant Officer 2 Christopher Miasnik, THT 518 First Lieutenant Kristine Gilpin and Staff Sergeant Juan Tirado, THT 524 Direct Support to 42nd Military Police Sergeant First Class Robert Lownes, THT 530 Master Sergeant Keith Jenkins, and THT 531 Sergeant First Class Timothy Travis. All my team leaders were excellent, knowledgeable, and professional leaders and were very tactically and technically proficient. I would like to list all the THT team people I served with, but they would be numerous. I am very proud of them all and honored to have served with them.

The Loss and Sacrifice of a True Hero

I will not talk much on the sacrifice of our heroes. I certainly have served with them, and I have walked beside them. I will mention one, however, who was assigned to my THT 531. My caveat to this is that all the men and women I served with; I considered heroes in Operation Iraqi Freedom (OIF) II. There were three THT teams assigned to me six months into my tour called two point fivers or OIF II.5. This is because individuals assigned to these teams came in six months after OIF II and stayed six months into the OIF III tour. These teams were able to cover areas during rotations back to the States between OIF II and OIF III. One of the brave members of THT 531 was Roberto Arizola Jr., known to all as simply Sergeant Arizola or Robert. I recall Sergeant Arizola, a Border Patrol Agent, who was from Laredo, Texas, sitting with me and telling me about his family, how proud he was of them, the knife they had sent him as a gift, which he proudly showed me when we had talked individually. I talked individually with my soldiers as I did with Robert on several occasions, sat, and ate dinner with him in the DFAC. Robert was an excellent soldier, brave, knowledgeable, tactically proficient, and an excellent squad leader and THT member. THT II.5 folks came in the country in June 2004 and stayed up to June 2005 during the OIF III rotation. When the 502nd Military Intelligence Battalion rotated, the 250th Military Intelligence Battalion then took over, and all OIF II.5s were assigned to them. Approximately four months after I rotated back Stateside in 2005, I learned Robert had been killed just seven days prior to his rotation back home. I received this information via the SECRET Internet Protocol Router Network (SIPRNet) from one of the individuals in the THOPS that I had served with who had remained with the II.5s until June 2005. Sergeant Arizola was killed in action while on Tactical Control (TC) on a THT mission in Baghdad on June 8, 2005, when an improvised explosive device detonated near his jeep. I currently have a picture of Robert on my desk. It was an honor and privilege to have served with him. I think often of Robert and miss him much, and I treasure the time I knew him. I do not like to think back on this and will write no more as it is an emotional subject for me.

Tactical HUMINT Operations (THOPS)

The THOPS received reports from the BN OMTs and disseminated these reports to higher. I will not go into too much THOPs, but to say the THOPS chief was my buddy Chief Warrant Officer 3 Russ Hamilton. Russ and I were both SFCs (E-7) together in the 368th Military Intelligence Battalion in Phoenix. We were in the same Warrant Officer course together, graduating on the same day only three minutes apart, in alphabetical order. Meaning, he had three minutes' time and grade on me, and he has never let me forget he has time and grade on me. We knew each other but worked in different sections within the Phoenix unit. We were roommates the entire year in Iraq and became lifelong friends. Russ and I have similar backgrounds as he is a retired Arizona State Trooper and an excellent and knowledgeable Counterintelligence Agent.

You may find this interesting. My Iraqi Military Intelligence Regime Team, consisting of highly motivated agents, developed two high-level Iraqi Military Officers, who each had four Lieutenants reporting intelligence information to them, who each had eight sources on the street reporting to them. In addition, this team held monthly meetings with Kurdish, Sunni, and Shia area tribal leaders. All my teams developed good information; however, this team developed a lot of good actionable intelligence due to their mission.

My OMT established over twenty-seven source dossiers with tracker, a Collection Plan, an Evaluation Tracker, a Reports Master Control Log (Draft Intelligence Information Reports (DIIR), *Satellite Pour L'observation de la Terra* or satellite for observation of earth (SPOTs), Basic Source Data Sheets (BSD), a Source Roster, a Daily Activity Report (DAR), a Convoy Tracker, Daily Intelligence Summary (INTSUM), and a Daily Situation Report (SITREP). In addition, the OMT established, a Mission Book, a Mission Checklist, and an OMT SOP.

Some accomplishments of my teams:

THT 517 developed over two hundred twenty-eight actionable intelligence reports. THT 517 was the International Zone (IZ) walk-in team, and due to their hard work, the theater rewards program paid out to an informant for a weapons and chemical cache in August 2004. This team was influential in the confiscation of one hundred barrels of precursor materials for chemical weapons and the confiscation of weapons cache of over two hundred seventy weapons. This team was also influential in the apprehension of an Iraqi Intelligence General, black list number 149. Following are other accomplishments of THT 517: participated with four hundred Multinational Force (MNF)/Iraqi National Guard (ING) personnel in a special operations raid that netted twenty-five detainees that may have led Coalition Forces to a missing KBR worker, apprehension of a taxi driver that led to the bombers of the Green Zone Café and Haji Mart, apprehension of three members of a kidnapping ring in south Baghdad, apprehension of a Vehicle-Born Improvised Explosive Device (VBIED) maker, and discovery of two VBIED factories that also included enough materials to make one hundred Improvised Explosive Device (IED). This THT worked diligently for six months trying to track Al-Zarqawi and collected numerous Anti-Iraq Force (AIF) DVDs, including beheadings, which were forwarded to Document Exploitation (DOCEX). This teams' sources led to numerous interventions against unfulfilled lethal threats against Coalition/Multinational Forces. Let me say at this point, watching a beheading is not pleasant. I will not describe it for you. Our enemy is very ruthless, very lethal, and has no remorse about killing Christians.

THT 518

THT 518 successfully transitioned from an Iraqi Military Intelligence Regime mission to a TAC HUMINT mission in September 2004. THT 518 wrote over seven hundred Iraqi Military Intelligence Regime reports of actionable intelligence for the Chain of Command (C2) special projects. Soon after the transition, THT

518 paid a source though the theater rewards program for a weapons cache. THT 518 developed a source that was able to recover equipment taken from a convoy that was attacked by insurgents in May 2004 and executed their mission with a great deal of success.

THT 524

THT 524 was assigned to my OMT for reporting purposes only but was actually working with the Military Police on missions in the Baghdad and surrounding area, outside my operational control.

THT 524 was the only THT in the Battalion that developed a level three source and the only team to establish a high-ranking Iraqi Cabinet Source. THT 524s reporting directly affected counteroffensives by maneuver commanders. The THT was repeatedly tasked for special missions by the Composite Training Unit Exercise (C2X), resulting in the capture of numerous high-value targets, including Combined Joint Task Force 7 (CJTF-7) black list number three, one of the only top ten targets detained during OIF II. THT 524 also completed numerous special missions including several raids with the Iraqi Special Forces, resulting in over five hundred arrests, providing real-time information flow. The THT coordinated with Task Force (TF) 626, resulting in the detention of four individuals personally responsible for the beheading of US contractor Nicholas Berg and direct reconnaissance of targets, resulting in the capture of two dump-truck sized VBIEDs destined for the United State Embassy in Iraq. Reporting from various sources resulted in numerous raids, crippling two terrorist groups who had been in control of the cities of Al-Adhamiya and Al-Karkh. THT 524 ran numerous high-level sources, including top echelon members of the Iraqi Security Forces, the Iraqi Interim Government, and the Iraqi intelligence community, resulting in such a high flow of national level intelligence that a team from the Joint Intelligence Deployment Command (JIDC) was assigned to THT 524 to expedite the flow of the information gathered by the team. The successes of the team while tasked to the military police resulted in new doctrine being written by the US Army Intelligence Center (USAIC) at Fort Huachuca, Arizona, including this task organization into the Military Police concept of operations.

While conducting their day-to-day operations, the team came under attack numerous times, including several IEDs, three VBIEDs, dozens of Rocket-Propelled Grenades (RPGs), and innumerable small-arms attacks. The team responded aggressively to these threats, with the team gunner receiving confirmed kills and an unknown number of additional unconfirmed kills. The operational tempo for the THT was extremely high, including several twenty-four-to-forty-eight-hour continuous missions and months running operations outside the wire seven days per week. THT 524 executed their mission flawlessly and with a great degree of success.

THT 530

THT 530 was assigned to the OMT in July 2004. The THT, new to the OMT, was in the process of developing intelligence and sources at the time of the Replace in Place (RIP). One of the THT's sources, a Category-One (CAT I) interpreter, provided actionable intelligence on Muqtada's militia. Due to threats on him and his family, the source moved and became unavailable.

THT 531

THT 531, also new to the OMT from July 2004, along with some OMT 52 staff, went on an approved raid with the 1st Brigade Combat Team, First Team, resulting in the detention of some of the Abu Saraf gang.

I am proud of my teams' accomplishments. I was not successful because of me. I was successful because of the men and women I served with, and they never failed to do their duty. I had confidence in their ability, courage, and devotion to duty. The OMT was responsible for developing Priority Intelligence Requirements (PIR). Source missions were the result of PIRs that came through THOPS. THOPS got PIRs through Command and determined what OMT was responsible for each PIR. The mission logistics were controlled by the Company. I was responsible for the operations of OMT missions, both strategic and tactical. The success or failure of a mission rested with me. What routes were taken? What were the alternate routes? What were the vehicles to be used and were they in good order? Did the convoy tracker indicate all necessary information and communications? The source, who is it? How was the source developed? What information was going to be collected? Did it meet the requirements of the PIR? And was the collected information worth the lives of my team members? Was there enough ammo? Were the men prepared? How long was the anticipated meet? Did the Security Team have all the information necessary to protect the source meet? No mission, no matter how well prepared you are, will never go exactly as planned. Was the team fluid enough to meet any threat? And a myriad of other unforeseen questions. Examples of PIRs are as follows. What sheiks control what areas of the country? Who is making IEDs? What tribe controls IED shops? Who are the snipers? Who is providing weapons and to whom? What countries are involved? And others. My teams developed sources to answer these PIRs. In all, my OMT wrote over seven hundred actionable reports, over one hundred fifteen of which went to National Agencies. Let me give you an example of a report. A team develops a source who develops the location of an IED shop. In a home located just outside Sadr City. Across the street from this home is an elementary school. Next to this house is a small medical clinic. You better have your coordinates right because if you send a striker team in there and they take out the elementary school and not the IED factory, innocent lives are lost. You simply have to get it right. Accurate report writing with coordinates is a must, no mistakes. I began to review all reports my teams submitted. Not only for accuracy but for content I could use operationally.

My Admin Non Commissioned Officer

I found my time was limited with the Operational Tempo (OPTEMPO) I had and the dynamics of the environment. I needed to develop the skills of one of my Non Commissioned Officers (NCOs). After looking at personnel files, I found that one of my NCOs, a Sergeant (E-5) had a Master's Degree and was performing tasks I knew was not challenging enough for her. (We later promoted her to Staff Sergeant (SSG) (E-6). I knew this as this particular NCO was constantly complaining about the job held. I appointed her my records NCOIC and gave her more responsibility than she had and also made her accountable. She had some difficulty initially because the unit she came from did not make her responsible for anything, and she was not used to being accountable. That was the problem. After some training and help from the THOPS Section, she became quite good at reviewing reports. After a short period of time, I only reviewed reports periodically. She reviewed all reports for accuracy. If she found a mistake, she contacted me and the Team Leader for corrections. She became very good at it. So good she trained three incoming OMT Staffs just before rotation back home. I had the honor of reenlisting her in front of the Battalion while we were in California on our way home. I understand this NCO has now been promoted into a First Sergeant position of an Intelligence Company.

CHAPTER 17

Leadership

I will insert my thoughts and philosophy on leadership at this point. To be a leader in a combat environment, you have to have good judgment, you have to be experienced, and you have to surround yourself with experienced people and staff. Every moment matters. Each decision will define you. No matter whether you are in a combat environment, corporate environment, or in any leadership position, you have to show strength and commitment to your decisions. You have to show courage, and you have to show good judgment. You earn respect, not demand it. You are their leader, and they look to you for leadership, and they began to trust your leadership to provide guidance. It is a very lonely feeling to look an individual in the eyes and send them outside the wire on a mission, knowing they may not return. Your decisions must be correct. Developing a source tactically is a very dangerous thing to do. It takes will and courage, and this is why selection into counterintelligence, and subsequent training, is so very important by all involved from leaders to operations. Not only does developing a source put a team in danger but if the source is discovered, s/he is killed. We never had a source discovered; however, there was communication traffic between intelligence offices where we learned some sources had been discovered and killed by their own people.

There is a difference between developing a source in a tactical arena versus spotting, assessing, and recruiting a source in a strategic environment. I will only talk about a tactical environment in this book. Strategic source development is a whole other book. A TAC HUMINT leader of OMT teams must have good judgment. The person must have experience and be confident in their teams' abilities. You must learn to trust their instincts and knowledge. There are those whose books I have read, such as that of Secretary Robert Gates, under the Obama Administration. In his book, he mentions how bad he felt sending men into combat. That he is still bothered by it to this day. I know he is. So am I. When the Battalion sent down Priority Intelligence Requirements, they knew a team would have to leave the wire to contact or develop a source for the information. I know it bothered them. Here's the difference. I had to look them in the eyes and send them outside the wire on missions. I always tried to be the last person they saw when leaving the wire and the first one they saw when they returned. I briefed and debriefed. I never lost a man. Before I sent a team out, I always, always checked with the S2 for developing situations outside the wire. I checked my real-time information for sniper activity, improvised explosive device placements, what routes they were taking, what alternate routes they had planned, whether they have their communication plan in order, how to call for the Quick Reaction Force (QRF) from Command if needed, how to call for medical help, what kind of source and what kind of information were they collecting, etc. Because we did not have an assigned security force, when one team left for a source meet, I had to use one of my down teams for security backup on the same convoy. This limited the amount of time my teams had for source development because of having to run security details. When leaving the wire, I ensured my teams had all information available to them. Because I was responsible for them and their mission. I was responsible for their very lives. It was a very lonely feeling. I just simply could not make a leadership mistake. It changed me personally. I can't describe it better than that. They received a convoy brief by me on what to do in emergency situations, etc., before they left the wire and a debrief upon their return. When I asked someone to do something, they knew it was not a request. I never had to ask twice, and I never had a mission where I did not have a volunteer. My teams consisted of a good group of soldiers, and I am proud of each one of them and their accomplishments. There were very different leadership styles in the Battalion. Some more experienced than others. The Battalion had one of its top Leaders who felt yelling at subordinates was a way to get things done. It was a constant. Even the Battalion Chaplain spoke to this in one of his sermons.

A leader who has to yell or shout at his/her subordinates attempts to mask his/her inability to lead. It's toxic leadership at its worst. A toxic leader can denigrate morale, degrade communication, and, in a combat environment, increase the level of stress already present. (There was only one occasion where I raised my voice to one of my inexperienced Officers. This particular Officer became one of my best Team Leaders by the time we rotated and was instrumental in a large contingency fund payout to an informant for some very useful actionable intelligence.) The only other time I recall raising my voice was when the Company First Sergeant entered my OMT and attempted to task one of my people I had on assignment writing a needed report, without checking with me first. When confronted, the First Sergeant addressed me in a condescending manner and simply forgot who he was talking to. You simply can't make all the people happy all the time. However, this type of continued toxic leadership is hostile, unprofessional, and abusive. Some Leaders believe a successful leader is one of power. That is not a leader. A leader is someone who thinks of being someone of value. A leader does not create followers; a Leader creates more leaders. A leader is a person who can adapt principles to circumstances. A bad leader can destroy a good staff, causing good employees to lose all motivation. As a leader, you have to make your decisions based on your experience and the information you have, because the consequences are your responsibility and lives can be lost in a tactical environment. Indecision can destroy a Command. My leadership philosophy is one of always being on the offensive. I do not like to take a defensive posture.

As a leader, one of the most powerful things you can do is demonstrate that you are willing to listen. Realize what you don't know and seek it out. Encourage your staff to take the initiative to identify problems and give them the freedom to find solutions. Never tell people how to do things. Tell them what to do, and they will surprise you with their ingenuity. In the environment we were in, there was simply no room for leadership indecision or mistakes. Lives were at stake. However, if you make a mistake, be responsible enough to change your direction. Be fluid. Your ego is not your amigo. Do not let your job, or your position, get in the way of good judgment or common sense. I am very proud to have had the honor and privilege of leading men in combat operations.

Leaders, as motivators have followers and managers have subordinates. There is a difference between being a leader and being a manager. Leaders should communicate their vision of the direction they see their work going more often to the rank and file. If not, the organization dies; morale sinks. This is part of the communication process. Leaders should lead and remain focused to their vision and allow their subordinates to manage the staff. Successful leadership requires more than just assigning tasks to the team. It calls for a leader who can inspire team members to achieve their full potential. People want to be guided by a person they respect, someone who has a clear sense of direction. To be that person, there are certain things that subordinates should not wonder about, such as follows. Is my leader experienced? Does s/he know what they are trying to convey? Can I trust him/her? A leader must be a subconscious motivator to success.

There are too many people who think the way upward in their careers is to set the boss's hair on fire with lurid stories about the depredations or encroachments by their peers. Subordinates are quick to describe a weakness in the organization, but this is only whining as a professional discourse if no solution is also offered. (Note if a subordinate makes a suggestion or observation, pass it up. Don't assume higher would not be interested in the observation or suggestion. Too many times a good suggestion is never followed up on simply because the first level manager felt it not pertinent to operations.) Stories are fabricated or exaggerated and unfortunately some believed by staff without checking facts. The only way to defuse this kind of internecine feuding is to get to know and trust one another. Internecine feuding turns into gossip. Gossiping conceals a person's incompetence as a thinker and points equivocations toward an innocent victim to manipulate others into believing conclusions with no regard to truth or reality. Gossip is full of evasions and obfuscations of actual truth.

Good communication from senior leaders down creates an atmosphere of transparency within an organization; however, a leader should be ever mindful that communication is only a part of the transparent process. If a leader, senior leader or not, tells his/her subordinates s/he has an open-door policy but, when contacted, tells the individual to go through their first-line leader, the "open-door policy" really is not there. It's just lip service. If there is an issue or problem, the individual should seek to first contact their lower-level supervisor who should try to solve the issue at the lowest level, prior to going up the chain; however, the individual should also be told by their immediate supervisor they can go up the chain of command (C2) if they feel the issue is not solved. Otherwise, a good open-door policy does not create transparency.

As a leader, you need to remember that the rules, regulations, and policies also apply to you. If you think otherwise, your integrity is in jeopardy. Do not be afraid to fail and be confident in your ability. Own your decisions and be accountable for them. Fully develop your ability and apply this to enhancing the lives and careers of the people you work with. As a leader and mentor, your subordinates should be seeking you and looking for your counsel, advice, and guidance. Think about what you are going to say before you say it. You are their leader. They are going to listen to you. If you have to remind your subordinates you are in charge, you're not. There are some subordinates, who because of inexperience, want to skip the learning process and go directly into a leadership role. Unfortunately, these types of promotions happen all too often. Remember that incompetence is difficult to disguise from those you serve. There is a thought by Dr. Joseph Murphy (who is described in this book) which is; "There are many people who do not understand the process, only perceive the results, and they call it Chance". Some want the position without having to work for it, not realizing nothing will ever simply be given them. They try to circumvent the process. You simply have to understand the process before being given more responsibility. One must try harder, become stronger, understand the process, and be confident in your skill sets. This is what makes a competent leader.

Leaders should work with their assigned staff so that all are conscious of a vital current uniting them as one team without distinction of rank. This is especially true of first-line supervision teams. This way, each team member knows their job and assigned tasks. They know their tasks are equally important to the team and organization. They know, however, who makes the decisions, and they know any decision will be a decisive one based on experience, one based on available information and one that will be executed as a team. We all answer to someone.

So is there any one leader I have tried to emulate? Not really. Every leader I have worked with is part of me and my leadership style, both military and civilian. I have studied leadership in numerous schools and course work. Personally, I like General George Patton, although there were some excellent leaders throughout history including the American Revolutionary and civil wars. I like the way General Patton promoted in the field on occasion. You may find this technique interesting and one that I read about as told by his Adjutant, Colonel Porter Williamson. Patton selected leaders on accomplishment, not on affection. Those that were up for promotion were told to dig a trench eight feet long, three feet wide, and six inches deep, just on the other side of a barn wall. It made no difference if the promotion was Enlisted or Officer. The wall usually had a window or a knot hole, thus allowing General Patton and his Adjutant to watch the trench digging. Most men with this task would first sit around awhile arguing why such a shallow trench is to be dug. It's not deep enough for a gun emplacement they would argue. Some would argue the trench should be dug with power equipment. During the complaining, one of the men would finally say, "Let's get the trench dug and get out of here. Who cares what the SOB wants to do with the trench?" That's the one Patton would promote. Patton would never pick a man who slobbered all over him with kind words. Patton would say too many Commanders pick dummies to serve on their staff. (I personally found this to be a very true statement.) Such dummies don't know how to do anything but say yes. Such men are not leaders. (I have personally seen this happen.) Pick the one who can get the job done. This is the type of leadership I like and try to emulate.

CHAPTER 18

Operations

I found that General George Patton's saying "Compared to war, all other forms of human endeavor shrink to insignificance" to be true. If you haven't been there, you simply will not understand this statement.

So the question always asked of me is "did you ever have to kill anyone?" My answer is no. I was not there to kill anyone. I was there to collect intelligence. However, the intelligence gathered by my teams resulted in enemy elimination. I hope with extreme prejudice. Do I feel responsible for enemy life? Certainly not. We do not murder our enemy. We kill them before they kill us. We stay alive for our country and let our enemy die for theirs. General Norman Schwarzkopf was asked if he didn't think there was room for forgiveness toward the people who harbored and abetted the terrorists who penetrated the September 11 attacks on America. His answer (which I totally agree with) was "I believe that forgiving them is God's function. Our job is to arrange the meeting." Let me interject one more tactical thought: we as a nation should stop projecting what we are going to do and when we are going to do it. Our National tactical decisions, along with our intelligence community, should remain in the shadows. Enough said.

ISIS and Al-Qaeda

I was asked what my thoughts were on eliminating ISIS (Islamic State of Iraq and Syria) and Al-Qaeda. My answer may be a lengthy one, but I think there is much to this question. Here is my response. You declare war, then you kill them, and then you go back and kill their goat. Harsh. Yes. But so is beheading innocent men, women, and children only because of their beliefs. This is murder, plain and simple. There is no joy in killing our enemy, but they are the ones who forced our hand. My THT Teams brought in videos of beheadings obtained through our protected sources for intelligence purposes. Let me tell you, it is not a pleasant thing to watch. These videos were collected as evidence and turned over to Document Exploitation (DOCEX). We did so in an effort to glean any type of intelligence we could. I will not describe to you the act of beheading. I do not like to think back on it. I will say this though, it does not make any difference if you are male, female, adult, or child. If you are deemed an infidel, an apostate (Christian), you are beheaded. Age or gender makes no difference. Can you imagine a preteen—say six, seven, or eight—hands tied behind them, made to kneel, and being beheaded by an adult, whom as a child you grow to trust to protect you? Or to behead a parent? It takes a lot of hate, in my opinion, to perpetrate this horrendous act, particularly on a child. Life to a U.S. Citizen, who is raised with any type of moral foundation, cannot comprehend the horrendous and egregious act of a beheading or of setting a living human being on fire and watch the life being taken from them. I simply cannot describe this to you. So those of you who read and disagree with my response and have not experienced this will probably never understand my belief of elimination of the threat. But that's OK. I will add that if you haven't been there, my advice is to listen to your intelligence professionals rather than an agenda. Take politics out of it and ponder it awhile. Doing otherwise lacks common sense and is dangerous. The meaning of life to an ISIS member is a whole lot different than what life means to us. They don't care if you're republican, democrat, conservative, liberal, Catholic, Jew, or Christian. If you are not of the Muslim faith, you're an apostate. Not worthy of life. They are afraid of our freedom. They do not think we are willing to die for our freedom we are so very blessed to have.

Let me ask you a question. What other country does not have American blood spilt on it, to protect other's freedoms and way of life? This statement also includes those countries who have asked for U.S. help and involvement. My opinion is that someone fighting for their freedom, will always win over someone only fighting for their rights. The Civil War is a great example of this. Let me give you a political example of American blood on foreign soil. In the 60s Dean Rusk JFKs Sec Def was in France when DeGaulle decided to pull out of NATO. DeGaulle said he wanted all US Military out of France as soon as possible. Rusks response.. "does that include the ones buried here?" DeGaulle....no response. The U.S. did pull our military out, but the point was made loud and clear.)

ISIS fighters simply lack morals and have no meaning of life. They are in a holy war against all infidels. They are at war with the West, with us, with you. This is their purpose in life. Unfortunately, many in the US do not feel a war footing. ISIS does not take prisoners without conversion to Islam, professing *Shahada*, and then they kill them. And oh, by the way, they also rape male prisoners. They rape innocent children and turn them into sex slaves and kill their parents in front of them. Even forcing a six-year-old female into marriage to an ISIS member. Is this harsh? I think so. The culture is different you may argue. You would be correct because Sharia Law is different and is in direct contrast to our Constitution, creating a culture clash. Is taking a six-year-old female as a wife and consummating a marriage OK with you? Really? It's a perversion and a skewed interpretation of the Quran. Let's negotiate a peaceful solution of appeasement, you might argue. Let me ask you a question. When did appeasement ever work, even on a personal level? We all know the answer to that one. We as Americans should not be sticking our head in the sand and hope the issue of ISIS goes away. It won't. ISIS is evil in its purest form. Niccolo Machiavelli, a sixteenth-century, Italian Diplomat and Political Theorist wrote, "There is no avoiding war; it can only be postponed to the advantage of others." ISIS is one of the most brutal enemies the US has faced in modern times. We (the United States) seem to be ignoring ISIS as the evil enemy it is. The US has the most lethal military force on the face of the earth. We need to use it before it's too late, and we begin to have these atrocities in our county. It's already started. Machiavelli's quote is as true today as it was in the sixteenth century. Sun Tzu, a Chinese military General, Strategist, and Philosopher who lived between 544 and 496 BC, wrote in his book, *The Art of War*, "Thus, what is of supreme importance in war is to attack the enemy's strategy." Sun Tzu also said, "Strategy without tactics is the slowest route to victory. Tactics without strategy is the noise before defeat." It is my opinion the U.S., at this point, is not attacking ISIS strategy. This is perceived as weakness by our enemy and is inimical to the US. ISIS is not content on restoration of the caliphate, the purest form of Islamic jurisprudence. ISIS hopes to bring about the apocalypse. I have walked in valley of the shadow of death, and as someone who has been there, I can say Al-Qaeda and ISIS are vicious and unconscionable. ISIS wants us on their soil to fight them. So be it. This is where they must be defeated. They simply do not understand the lethality and resolve of the American Military might. We need to use it in full force. Islam is a peaceful religion, you might say. Really. Remember this, the first name of ISIS is Islamic State. Some are peaceful, and those that are need to step up and condemn those that aren't. ISIS will kill their own people; any Muslim they deem too westernized, such as listening to music. Really? We in the U.S. already have part of the Muslim population not only disrespecting our Flag, but also protesting the flying of our Colors representing freedom, our forefathers, and yes, even our generation, fought so hard to keep. Why, you might ask, does radical Islam hate us so much? The answer is a simple one and not a mystery. Read the Quran, which is the sacred writings accepted by Muslims as revelations made to Muhammad by Allah through the angel Gabriel. Islam teaches that apostates (anyone who rejects Islam, which includes Christians) are to be killed. And in specificity, the Quran states, "Fight the heads of disbelief" (9:11 and 12), which can only mean that war should be waged against apostasy. I recently read an article from a speech by Andrew C. McCarthy, a Senior Fellow at the National Review Institute, to the Heritage Foundation. Part of his speech was that "An inconvenient point is that Islam is not a religion of peace. There are ways of interpreting Islam that could make it something other than a call to war. But even the following benign constructions do not make it a call to peace; "Fight those who believe not in Allah." and "Fight and slay the pagans wherever ye find them, and seize them, beleaguer them, and lie in wait for them in every stratagem of war," are not peaceful injunctions, no matter how one contextualizes".) In my opinion, this is a very true statement. They will not negotiate, and they will not negotiate, and they will not reason. They are illogical in their religious view and zeal for jihad. They hold no values and are against everything we are. ISIS simply must be contained and destroyed. Display no mercy as this is taken as weakness. Understanding and complacency is foolish at this point. You do not fight evil with tolerance. An intelligent thinking human being simply cannot come to any other conclusion. How many more people have to die before we wake up? When is enough enough? We are far beyond any diplomatic solution; they don't want one. It's time to do something. The enemy of Freedom should now experience the power of Freedom. One must be pitiless in the implacable pursuit and elimination of ISIS. The only way to stop this "holy war" is to develop a strategy: name, identify, and eliminate the threat. We need to eradicate the jihadist and Islamic extremists associated with Islam. To quote Winston Churchill "We defeat them if we resolve to see them for what they are". You pull out the weed, replant with a good seed, and then educate. Let me make one caveat: my above thoughts are guided by my years of involvement in the intelligence community and my strategic and tactical experience. Let me provide you with one global statistic. I could provide more, but this should do. According to US intelligence, there are 1.2 billion people of the Muslim faith in the world. Of that, there is an estimated sixteen to twenty-five percent of the Muslim faith that are radicalized. With this, you might say, "Yes, but there are seventy-five percent that are peaceful. Why should we worry?" Let me throw this out at you. That sixteen to twenty-five percent represent one hundred eighty to three hundred million people of the Muslim faith that are radicalized and dedicated to the destruction of Western civilization. That number is as large as the population of the United States. Think about that for a minute. This should give you pause or, at the very least, concern you. It's the radicals that behead and the radicals who kill and massacre. That's why it should give you concern. All you have to do is look at history to know why this holy war must be stopped. My advice: listen to and trust the perspicacious analysis of your Intelligence Professionals. It's dangerous to do otherwise. I will stop my rant here.

Spouse Support

Let me say at this point that when a Soldier is deployed, so is his/her spouse. All spouses are part of the deployment, even though they are not physically present during our deployments. They nevertheless are in harm's way in that they have to mentally endure not knowing from one day to the next if a telegram will arrive. A telephone ring can be just as loud as any mortar or rocket. Decisions of different areas of responsibility and myriad of other things a family must endure and address. Don't think for a minute the spouse has not endured the same hardships as a deployed spouse. The spouse is the power behind the Soldier. The spouse doesn't want any type of recognition. All they want is for their loved one to come home. They are as much a hero as their deployed spouse.

Team Communication

When I took over as OMT OIC, one of the first things I did was determine how the communication between my Teams and my OMT office was set up. I found that each jeep was outfitted with a Single-Channel Ground and Airborne Radio System (SINGARS). SINGARS is a Combat Net Radio System, along with a SINGARS base station in my office.

Some History

SINGARS replaced the older tactical air-to-ground radios (AN/PRC 77) radio, which was a single-frequency radio. The AN/PRC 77, pronounced Pric 7, was a heavy radio that we used in the field in the sixties and seventies. Let me mention a little about the AN/PRC-6, a Walkie-Talkie used by the Army in the late Korean War era through the Vietnam War. Raytheon developed the RT-196/PRC-6 following World War II as a "handy-talkie." The AN/PRC-6 operates using wide-band FM on a single crystal-controlled frequency in the 47 to 55.4 megahertz low-band VHF band. The range is about one mile but much less in a jungle setting. When on a field exercise, called an FTX, we used the PRC 7 but called it the PRC 6. I never used a PRC 6 walkie-talkie on an FTX, but most folks referred to the PRC 7 as the PRC 6, which was erroneous. I hated to be named the radioman for a field exercise because having that Pric 7 on my back was just plain heavy.

Back on point, SINGARS are secure radio nets; however, when sending my Teams out, I found that the SINGARS's range was only about two miles. I needed better communication as source meets were much farther than that. I needed to be able talk to my teams in the field in case I needed to advise them of enemy activity in their scheduled meet area, and worse, my teams needed to be able to call for the quick reaction force (QRF) or field medics if needed. The other issue at the time was the fact all cell phones for communication were of no use, as all cell towers had been taken out by US Armed Forces during OIF I. I was talking with my roommate, Russ Hamilton, on this problem, and he mentioned that maybe detasked satellite phones may be a temporary answer. That was the answer. Why didn't I think of this? It was a simple thing to do. I made up my mind to attempt to get them. Let me explain what a detasked phone is. Insurgents were using satellite phones to set off IEDs from a distance by syncing the frequency of the IED to the phone. All they had to do was set the frequency, go back a mile or so from the IED, and wait for a passing convoy looking through binoculars. Once coalition forces captured the insurgent with the phone, information was obtained from the phone and then detasked, and placed in storage. I will not explain how information taken off the phone was obtained as this is classified. The telephones preferred by insurgents was the Thuraya satellite phone. Thuraya is an Arabic name for the constellation of the Pleiades. Thuraya is a company based in the United Arab Emirates and provides mobile coverage to more than one hundred ten countries. They were easily bought by insurgents and used only one time to set off an IED. Cell towers were later put back up, approximately in the late summer and early fall of 2004, with some safeguards. Meantime, satellite (sat) phones were the answer.

I contacted another Warrant Officer (WO) in the Camp Victory Signals Intelligence (SIGINT) community, whom I knew. I will not mention this individual's name, as this Officer may currently be operational, and I do not want to destroy any operational cover. This Warrant Officer is a very intelligent and highly-educated, capable, and knowledgeable SIGINT Officer and Soldier, a proven and tested leader of combat operations, and a good friend and battle buddy who was able to get me eleven detasked Thuraya satellite phones for my Teams. All I had to do was buy phone time through the local phone company. I went to the Battalion THOPS Major who was in charge of the Battalion Contingency Fund at the time and obtained permission to buy phone time for these phones from this fund. I obtained phone time from an Iraqi phone company in the Green Zone and distributed them to my THTs and the THTs in the other Battalion Company. My Teams used these phones in the field until the Battalion purchased Iraqi cell phones in the fall of 2004. The cell phones purchased by the Battalion were not issued to the THTs until September, two months before the Battalion rotated back to the States. This was because there was simply no cell service because there were no cell towers. The cell towers had all been blown down by explosives and bombs. Because of this, the satellite phones I obtained came in very handy in place of the SINGARS.

My List: You Don't Want On It

In the summer of 2004, I was able to get an Information Technology (IT) person assigned to my OMT. I had requested from the Commander someone who was knowledgeable of computers. I did not have time as the OIC to keep the computers online and in working order. I had three unclassified Nonsecure Internet Protocol Router Network (NIPR) for use by my teams for unclassified research and report analysis and for Internet usage. I had two classified SECRET Secure Internet Protocol Router Network (SIPR) also for use by my Teams for classified research. They were much in demand by my Teams, and I needed to keep them online. With no downtime, they were in use almost twenty-four hours per day. During the hours of approximately between eight o'clock in the evening to six o'clock in the morning, they were not much used except by my Records NCOIC for reporting from my outlying teams. I used one SIPR for my use for constant real-time enemy engagement. I needed this constant update to send my Teams outside the wire on Source Missions. This is when Tom Marley was assigned to my OMT. I also had access to Joint Worldwide Intelligence Communications System (JWICS) as needed but will not cover this access in this book.

Specialist (E-4) Tom Marley, whom I called Tom, was a very polite and well-brought up twenty-year-old young man. Tom did have his history though. Just prior to his deployment to Iraq, he had been involved in an incident that cost him one stripe, from Sergeant (E-5) to Specialist (E-4). This incident followed him to Iraq, where he had been doing gopher work for the First Sergeant, who kept him busy going for this and that for the Admin Section (S1). Tom was better than that and needed a more challenging position. Tom was later promoted to SGT and got his Stripe back Tom was very computer knowledgeable but lacked Army IT Regulation knowledge. He did do a good job of keeping my computers running. I had an SIPR at my desk that I used for real-time Command and Control (C2) updates. I got needed real-time information on IED, sniper, and insurgent activity right as it happened. I also had split screen Predator East and Predator West real-time drone cameras and action.

Drones are now known as Unmanned Aerial Vehicles (UAV). I did not have enough juice to call for strikes but did have enough juice to see in real time what the UAVs were up to. This allowed me real time outside the wire activity to direct my Teams for Source meets.

During my daily activities, Tom seemed to be there when and where I needed him. He reminded me of Radar on the old *M*A*S*H* TV series. He seemed to know what I needed before I did. I mentioned to Tom one time, after talking to an individual, that the individual was now on my shit list. This is when Tom decided to start my list in a separate pocket notebook that he kept. Whenever I became frustrated with anyone in the Admin area, any person whom I became concerned with, Tom would put him/her on my list. Whenever I came back into the OMT after a meeting (and it seemed like I was in constant meetings), Tom would always ask me if he needed to add someone to my list. There were always two to three people I had become frustrated with that deserved to be put on my naughty list. Over the course of several months, I had quite a few names on the list. The other Company Commander in the Battalion, my Company Commander, the Battalion Commander, the Brigade Commander, the Battalion Sergeant Major, Company First Sergeant, Executive Officer, and other distinguished individuals that deserved to be on my list. If I mentioned a name already on the list, Tom placed a tick mark by it. Some names had over ten check marks. It was a comical way to keep Tom engaged. If you are one of the individuals on my list, and reading my book, please don't take offense. I'm sure I was on other lists. But if you made my list, you should feel distinguished. A few months before Tom was due to rotate back to the States, he asked "Chief, what ya gonna do to these people on your list?" My answer was "Well, Tom, it's probably gonna be real bad, terrible in fact. You don't wanna know." "Yes, sir!" He always had my list handy just in case I became frustrated with someone, and there were several pages of people listed in his notebook by the time he left. I got to know Tom well while he was assigned to me, and I hated to see him rotate back to the States. Tom's father was a Veterinarian, and Tom was going to college to follow in his footsteps when his enlistment was over. The day before he left for home, Tom came up to me and asked if he could keep my list for a lifetime keepsake. Of course, I said yes. I think of Tom often and know he is now probably a Veterinarian back home. My list is probably in a place of honor in a drawer somewhere.

My Non Commissioned Officer in Charge (NCOIC)

I had just set the OMT up and had it started approximately in March 2004. By the way, I did so from scratch. The Source Files, Dossiers, Basic Source Data Sheets (BSD), Source Trackers, Convoy Trackers, and other operational guidelines, both classified and unclassified. In late March 2004, a young Sergeant First Class (E-7) walked into my OMT. She identified herself as Aggie Diaz, a Guam National Guard asset, and needed my help. Apparently, she had been assigned to a Direct Support Battalion that was supporting tactical operations in the Baghdad area, and they were using her outside her Military Occupational Specialty (MOS). (My OMT was General Support and not restricted to any particular Division, Operation, or Geographical location.) I should say, at this point, trained Counterintelligence Agents are not to be used for other jobs out-side their MOS by regulation. The Battalion she was assigned to was not an Intelligence Battalion and was simply unaware of how to use this asset. Sergeant First Class Diaz was wanting to know if I could help her transfer into my OMT. To this day, I don't know how she came to look at my OMT. I just never asked her. I took her contact information and told her I would see what I could do. When talking to her, I sensed a leader, and I needed an NCOIC. I could not tell her this, only that I would try to help. She thanked me and left. I immediately went to the Commander and relayed that I had found a good NCO and wanted Command help in getting her transferred to me. The process began, and a week later, I had one of the best NCOICs I ever served with. She took over NCO responsibilities and began providing needed NCO leadership to our assigned enlisted. When I arrived to work early mornings, she had already completed an Operational Situation Report (SITREP) that I was required to provide to Battalion Command Staff daily. At first, I reviewed her SITREPs for accuracy. After a few days, I stopped doing that and only reviewed for content for my knowledge and operational input. Aggie had my convoy trackers on my Teams going outside the wire for source meets done daily on her own initiative and for my review. My computers were ginned to the proper databases I needed for operations and tactical decisions, usually prior to my arrival. My source dossiers were always up-to-date, the proper Basic Source Data Sheets completed. She was also like the *M*A*S*H* Radar character. She knew exactly what I needed before I did and knew what I was going to say before I said or even asked for it. She saved me a lot of productive time and helped me run a smooth combat operation. If I needed classified maps, I sent Aggie. She got them and provided me with information I needed to make operational decisions. I took her to Command meetings and trusted her to help with some operational duties. She should have been the Company NCOIC, but I did not tell her this. I simply did not want to lose her leadership skill. We became lifelong friends. Aggie is currently a Sergeant Major (SGM) in the Guam National Guard. She would make a good Officer. Laura and I attended her graduation from the Sergeants Major Academy in Fort Bliss, Texas. I cannot tell you enough good things about this great friend and NCO.

Maps

On occasion, I obtained needed classified maps for operational planning. During the winter of 2004, I went to a restricted map processing center to obtain a particular area map I needed for review. This map facility was in a restricted area, surrounded by concertina wire on our compound. When in uniform, I did not wear a name tag, only my rank, for operational reasons. As I walked into the restricted classified map area, a civilian came up to me. He looked pale and out of breath. He asked me what my name was. I was hesitant in releasing my name because of what I did; however, I felt he was in a restricted area and couldn't be a bad actor. I told him, and he turned paler, and his mouth opened. He said, "You look exactly like my Great-Grandfather, whose picture I have on my wall at home." I thought this odd but didn't say anything I didn't feel old; maybe I looked it. He told me his last name was also Hurt, and he also told me his first name. We chewed the fat a little bit, and due to being in a hurry, I did not write his name down as I left. My thought was that I would return and talk with him when I had more time. I recall him telling me he was from North Carolina, but that is all I remember. I wish I had gone back to talk with him, but due to my Operational Tempo, I simply was never able to get back to the map room. Apparently, I have relatives in North Carolina. You just never know how small the world is.

Living Quarters

Shortly after arrival in Iraq, we were moved from our living quarters, the old Iraq Republican Guard Headquarters, into a mobile-home village. It was better than residing in tents, as some were. There were seven rows of seventeen trailers per row, each trailer divided into three separate living quarters, two per living-quarter section. The outside of these trailers were dirt at first. After two months of being in these trailers, the ground was rocked, making it a lot easier to walk to and from places. When it rained, mud was not easy to traverse through, especially to and from the restroom and shower facilities. The dirt was like silt and turned to mud real quick. The problem with putting rock down was this: when we were under mortar attack, the rocks became small pieces of shrapnel that could pierce our sleeping quarters. Blast barriers were placed around each mobile home, not only because of this but also helped if mortars or rockets landed directly right outside. There was nothing we could do if they came through the roof. Mobile homes were like being shielded with cardboard if they landed on the roof. On occasion, they did come through the roof, killing those Soldiers inside. My roommate and I were just blessed we were not hit in this manner.

Bounty on Intelligence Officers

After being in country for approximately two months, I learned through source meets and collection activity that Al-Qaeda had issued a fatwa proclaiming that Al-Qaeda fighters should attempt to capture and kill any Intelligence Officers and/or those working in or for U.S. Intelligence. I do not recall how much bounty was placed on us now due to time lapse; however, I recall it may have been five thousand dollars to ten thousand dollars. I think my life is worth more than that. I can tell you that they would have had a tough time collecting it. While in Iraq, I never learned or collected any information that an Intelligence Officer had been captured or killed; however, I always had this on my mind as my Teams or I was outside the wire on a mission. I always carried a folded U.S. Flag in my right front pants' pocket wrapped in plastic. I did so in the event I was ever captured, the symbol of Freedom would always be with me. Our daughter Janelle, now has this small flag, along with my "dog tags" and other memorabilia.

CHAPTER 19

Engagement

The sound of a Mortar, Rocket, or Machine Gun fire was cause to stop whatever one was doing and watch for any sign they were landing near. We were subject to rockets and mortar attacks all the time; the danger was always there. Ernie Pyle, the World War II writer, said it best: "Danger was like a hidden animal waiting to snare one along a path. The knowledge that peril was always possible was on one's mind constantly." It was an ever-ready presence that hung in the air. Often, we were in our quarters sleeping and awakened suddenly from a deep sleep by rockets or mortars. It is difficult to describe unless you have experienced it. One lives a more intense life in a combat environment. Being engaged is very loud, very fast, and very lethal. After a while, I became callus to the effects of "being engaged" and simply hoped that I did not get killed in my sleep it was just a matter of fact and part of life. Believe it or not, one does not think solely of self-safety when under attack. Sure, you run for safety and try not to be a casualty, but one thinks of his family and battle buddy over self-preservation. It was difficult going to sleep sometimes, knowing you may not awaken, especially when thinking of what might happen to your family if this happened. This is how it's done; just before going to sleep, you say a prayer asking God to take care of you during the night and to take care of your family if you don't make it through the night. Thank him for providing wise guidance and allowing you to lead your men through another day with no casualties. One more thing. There is a saying "there is no atheist in a foxhole." I believe that to be a very true statement; however, I have recently read on the Internet a thesis written by an atheist who served in combat. He was saying the exact opposite. I read his written report with a passing disinterest, and he did not make a believer out of me. I will just say this; I surmise that even an atheist who is under fire is deep down saying to him/herself that they hope there is a God. I have never understood how someone can believe there is no deity. Especially with the discoveries in Biblical Archeology proving the Bible correct in some areas, and then there is the miracle of birth. I do not feel Science will be able to prove everything in the Bible due to the passing of time. No matter how much proof exists, there will always be those that disbelieve established scientific biblical facts, even coming up with argument over established fact. There will always be those that skew biblical scientific facts to their belief system. The atheist will always have an argument trying to explain his view(s). "We walk by faith, not by sight" (2 Corinthians 5:7). They are wasting their time on me.

Improvised Explosive Devices (IEDs)

I will not say too much on these. Every time we went outside the wire, an Improvised Explosive Device (IED) was always on one's mind. Late in my Iraq tour, an Explosively Formed Penetrator (EFP) became more widespread by insurgents. EFPs were made in Iran and smuggled into Iraq to Al-Qaeda for use. (An EFP is a special type of shaped charge designed to penetrate armor.) This is what made our up-armored vehicles ineffective. EFPs were normally placed on bridges facing toward the road, so when a US Convoy went by, it could be set off from a distance, sometimes in a daisy chain to catch more than one or two vehicles. When on a convoy, you learned to drive a certain way: how to approach an overpass, how to go through an overpass, how to look for IED signs on the road, etc. Man's inhumanity toward man.

Rockets

One September 2004 day, while going to lunch, I heard an approaching rocket. *Katyusha* Rockets were being fired at us from Fallujah, a city some twenty plus miles from Baghdad, by Al-Qaeda for body count. Usually once to twice daily. A *Katyusha* Rocket is relatively simple and inexpensive to manufacture, compared with other artifacts of the genre. It was developed by the Soviets in World War I and used extensively by Al-Qaeda in Iraq. Handmade *Katyusha* Rockets are used by Palestinian fighters against Israel, although not equal to the models used by the Soviets who have seen improvements through the decades. An approaching rocket makes a shrill-like sound; however, if it's going to land near, that sound becomes less fuzzy and clear. It is hard to describe, but once you have been engaged by an enemy rocket enough times, believe me you learn the sound. As I was driving toward the Dining Facility (DFAC) in my jeep on that day, I was approximately two hundred feet from the DFAC drive-in when I heard an incoming rocket. I knew it was going to be close as it sounded like it was going to land on or near me. It landed about one hundred fifty feet or less away, causing no injuries, but the blast knocked down a female going to chow some one hundred feet to my left. She was very lucky. Had I not sped up to get into the DFAC drive-in, I may have been closer to impact. It did rattle me a little as this was one of the closest times I came to not being here. As I look back and think on this story, I feel seriously impressed I'm still alive. I continued to the DFAC as if nothing had happened other than a loud explosion. My ears were still ringing somewhat as I walked through the chow line. As I looked for a place to sit down and eat, I spied Captain Peck, the Battalion Chaplain, sitting and talking with a couple of troops. I sat down next to them. I figured that sitting next to the Chaplain would create more blessings for me, and I somehow felt safer sitting next to the Chaplain. There just had to be some kind of shield of protection around a chaplain. As I sit down to eat across the table from them, Chaplain Peck looked up at me and said, "Hey, Chief, did you just hear the explosion that incoming rocket just made?" I answered, "Yes, sir, I was just out there." I don't think he got the connection. I must have had a guardian angel assigned to me. I know they have had their hands full with me on many occasions. I somehow seemed to be around when the rockets started coming in. So what do you feel like when you evade death? Blessed and lucky at the same time. Adrenaline rush. Afterward, you tell your family you love them more often. You take nothing for granted. You laugh a little easier, and things seem to smell better. Nothing equals the life of survival in war; I am very blessed and happy to be back home unscathed. You never have friends like the ones you serve with in the military or in war. I don't think I can explain it any better than that. War will always be a part of me.

A little bit about Chaplain Peck. Chaplain Peck was a good Officer and Minister and former Enlisted service member in Military Intelligence. He often said a prayer for those of us leaving to go outside the wire. His prayers were not like ones you would hear in church on Sundays. A combat prayer is one that Chaplain Peck asked that if we had to shoot, that our aim hit its mark and that we come back alive and mission completed. You will not hear that type of prayer in church. Only in a combat environment. Chaplain Peck's prayers sometimes reminded me of what has become known as "Patton's Weather Prayer" by Monsignor James H. O'Neill, a retired Brigadier General. General Patton's Third Army Headquarters were located in the Caserne Molifor in Nancy, France, at the time the prayer was written. I have studied General Patton's tactics and have always felt General Patton was a great leader and was fortified by genuine trust in God, intense love of Country, and had a valued faith in the American Soldier. I have included "The Weather Prayer" in this book for those of you who have never seen it.

I made the mistake of relaying how close I came to being hit to my old buddy Russ—my roommate, my friend, my pal, my foxhole buddy, and trusted ally. Well.

Rocket Man

It was at about this time Russ felt I was a magnet for Rocket Fire. One September evening while coming out of the DFAC, I found a "Rocketman" Placard taped to the front of my jeep. (I still have that placard in my scrapbook.) I knew immediately Russ was up to tricks. He later wrote an e-mail, cc'ing me. This is the e-mail, verbatim: In the words of Chief Warrant Officer 4 Russ Hamilton:

> I can't wait to get out of this hellhole. I am sick of being mortared and rocketed, particularly at night in our trailers. It's not every single night (thank God) but often enough that everybody jumps when a loud noise is heard. We are just praying that the bastards don't get us before we go. I am tired of trying to claw my way through the floor to get lower while hollering at OJ that the bunker is too far away and to get his ass back down. He's such a daredevil and has been nick-named "Rocketman" for his propensity to attract indirect fire.

Russ is a lifelong friend and a retired Arizona State Trooper. We became fast friends because we both came out of the Law Enforcement environment, and we can tell war stories with each other, knowing they are not exaggerated. Russ is one of those guys who is a man's man. One of those guys you want to have a beer with. He has one of those gruff-and-tuff exterior personas, but he really is a teddy bear, a softie with a heart of gold. He is always there for you. If you need to get down in the mud to wrestle with pigs, he would be there with you. And he would enjoy it as much as the pigs would. I would jump in a foxhole with him anytime. Russ is a very brave, courageous, and experienced tactically and strategically proficient Soldier. I know he would have my six, as I would his. (I got your six or IGY6.) Russ and I are both getting long in the tooth now; however, don't take that as a sign of weakness. Neither one of us are soft targets. I will make one

249

caveat about friendship in a combat environment. One should not make friends in this type environment, in case a close friend becomes a casualty. Any combat loss is devastating, however, more so if it is a close friend. I made an exception to this rule with a few people, as I knew them prior to deployment. Russ was one of those exceptions.

A Trip from Baghdad International Airport

I'll relay one more friend and battle buddy, also an exception to the rule of making friends. When I first got to Iraq, I became acquainted with Sergeant First Class Edward Moran, now First Sergeant (1SG) Moran, Retired. Ed was a team leader of a TAC HUMINT team in the other Battalion Company OMT. I became interested in Ed when I learned he was a California State Trooper and a knowledgeable intelligence agent during a STANS fest. Ed is also one of those individuals who will also get down and play in the mud with you and like it. I would jump in a foxhole with him anytime. My teams were good at source development; however, I would have liked to have Ed assigned as one of my Team Leaders as he was also very good at developing sources. Ed was just one of those NCOs that developed into an exceptional NCO and leader and one that I kept an eye on. Not that he was doing anything I needed to keep watch on him for but I felt he knew what he was doing, and I found his tactics in combat exceptional in developing sources and conducting convoys to source meets. The Team Leaders assigned to me in my OMT were exceptional leaders and proficient in a tactical environment. However, Ed was one of the best Team Leaders in the other OMT and was well respected by his subordinates, peers, and Command Staff. I mention Ed for this reason. When I was medevaced (explained later in this book) out in July 2004 and returned in September 2004, I called my Commander upon my return when I landed at Baghdad International Airport (BIAP) and asked to be picked up for a ride back to our area in Camp Victory. I was told due to the current Operational Tempo, I would have to wait at BIAP for several hours until one of my teams could be turned loose to pick me up. A trip of only three miles. However, three miles can be a long way when traveling roads susceptible to attack. I was not at BIAP but an hour when Ed showed up with his Team to pick me up. Ed was not tasked to pick me up. He simply self-volunteered and wanted to retrieve me when he found I was stranded at BIAP. Ed was not one of my Team Leaders, and he went out of his way to retrieve me. This speaks volumes for his character. I have never forgotten his act of kindness and bravery traveling roads that could be dangerous just to pick me up. I think often and fondly of Ed.

I Awaken from a Deep Sleep

Combat operations make for a long day sometimes. One learns to work under intense stress, which becomes normal to daily life. When I laid my head down on my bunk at night, I was out. One night, I was dreaming. *OJ... OJ... OJ... OJ...* I thought I was dreaming at first and then realized Russ is hollering at me from his side of the room. "OJ, you awake?" My answer was "I am now." "You better get down. We're—BOOM—under attack." I was so sound asleep I was not hearing the falling incoming Rockets. The trailer was shaking from the blast noise. There was dust in the air. Things were falling off the shelves. Just as well I remained asleep. We made it through another attack without being hit this night. I could have slept through it not knowing we had ever been attacked. My guardian angel was at work again.

I Take One in the Windshield

One November 2004 evening while in route to the DFAC in my Jeep, I was traveling on the south edge of Camp Victory, when all of a sudden, there was a snap bang as if something big hit my windshield. It sounded harder than a simple rock strike and sounded loud enough to explode the windshield. I automatically ducked until I realized I was OK, and I sat back up, all while moving forward and accelerating. I didn't know if I had been shot at by sniper or just hit a large rock. I began checking my windshield and saw what looked like a small projectile that had struck at eye level on the windshield but had not penetrated. I was not injured and continued on to the DFAC. When I got back to my OMT, I reported being struck by something in the windshield to Command. I also reported the wind-shield damage to vehicle maintenance at the Motor Pool. The follow-ing day, Camp Victory Military Police reported that we were to be on the lookout for a sniper that was using what appeared to be a pellet gun hitting traffic on the same road I had traveled. I was apparently a victim. I was thankful it was a small arms and nothing bigger. I would have been hit in the face. To this day, I still don't know if it was an errant round or some type of pellet-gun round. It could have been either the way the windshield looked. I always seemed to have some type of incident happen to me on the way to the DFAC.

The Cobra

So I'm on the way to the DFAC on another day in early September 2004, I think, around noon. Ahead of me, I saw a big long black thing in the road. As I approached the darn thing, I realized it was a long black snake, about six feet in length, rather than a piece of trash or tire remnant. As I slowed and got closer, it slithered into a bunch of burnt trash on the side of the road. I learned when I got to the DFAC, it was probably a Cobra, which was apparently a common site on this particular road and area this time of year. Cobras on this day were the talk at mealtime. Well, I didn't know about it. I wished someone had warned me of such things. Goodness gracious. The following day, the Battalion Command Sergeant Major ordered everyone living in the old Republican Guard Headquarters being used for Troop Billeting that they were not to bring foodstuffs into the building. One of the Service Members had seen a small Cobra in the building. No one knew where it went, and all were on the lookout for several days. Apparently, the folks keeping snacks in the building were bringing in the rats. The rats were bringing in the Cobras. I hate snakes.

Incoming

From the time I arrived in Iraq in February 2004 up to November 2004, we were either rocketed or mortared approximately three times weekly or more, usually at night between the hours of twelve o'clock midnight to five o'clock in the morning. However, we were attacked sometimes during the day. Most of the incoming were coming from Fallujah where most of the insurgent activity was at that time. Once Fallujah fell in November 2004, the indirect fire went from three times weekly to once or twice monthly. It usually stopped at around five o'clock AM because that is the Muslim call to morning prayer time. The call to prayer was played over a loud speaker just outside our compound and usually woke us if we were not already awake. I'm sure on purpose. The loud speaker had to have been pointed in our direction. I can still hear it, and I've never liked it. We had more mortars lobbed into our compound than rockets. Mortars also have a distinct sound when close; one can tell after being engaged by indirect fire enough times. When we heard mortar explosions, we of course hit the deck, because one never knew if the insurgents firing the mortars were aiming for anything in particular. The Point of Origin (POO) from where a round had been fired could be determined within less than three minutes. That time has been cut significantly. All indirect incoming fire was for body count. It didn't make any difference who by the insurgents. During the November 2004 fighting in Fallujah, CH-54 Chinooks flew over our sleeping facility about fifty feet altitude as they were taking off from the airfield to deliver troops to the battlefield in Fallujah and returned with casualties. When the Chinooks came back, I just hoped that the casualties on board were not fatal. I knew some were but prayed for the survival of the wounded.

Airburst

One September 2004 morning, approximately three o'clock, we began receiving Rocket fire. *Katyusha* Rockets fired from Fallujah. At first, there were about three incoming, and we hit the floor from our beds, awakened out of a deep sleep. Trailer shaking, things falling from shelves, and dust. Then several more. You would be surprised how small of a ball you can become under a flak jacket on the floor. Russ and I both counted them. I recall now there were approximately seventeen. We learned later the last three or four were Airburst Rockets. Meaning the Rocket exploded in the air showering shrapnel below it into a kill zone. Another day in country.

The Errant Round

One January 2005 evening, Russ and I had occasion to be in the restroom facility at the same time. This particular evening happened to be the last night in country for Russ. I spent another seven days in country after Russ left for Kuwait the following morning. We were chitchatting, when all of a sudden, *whoosh*. Whizbang. A hole appeared in the wall, about a foot from where Russ was, about five feet from me. Had Russ not moved at an opportune time just prior, the round may have struck his head. A clinking noise on the floor drew our attention to it immediately. On the floor was a spinning AK-47 round that had come through the wall and luckily missed us both. Russ picked it up just as it stopped spinning and found the round to still be hot to the touch. One of the younger Service Members in the restroom asked Russ if he could have it as a souvenir. Of course. Take it. It was just another day in Iraq.

That's enough engagement stories. I don't like to think on them.

I Get Medevaced

Our drinking water in Iraq was from Egypt. The water was full of calcium, which caused me to get kidney stones. Believe me when I tell you, you don't want them. The medics placed me on a liquid drip, which took over two liters to get me back to normal water content, hoping I would eliminate them. I didn't. They were unable to help me on compound, and I was placed in a convoy to the Combat

Hospital in Baghdad. I was in a convoy with a Lieutenant Colonel Steve Jordan. Lieutenant Colonel Jordan was part of the Command structure of my IMIR team mentioned above. I remember this name, as I have a high school friend with the same name. At the time, there had been ambush activity on the road we were on, "Route Irish." It ran from Camp Victory to Baghdad, a distance of approximately ten miles, maybe a little more. Lots of IED placements and sniper activity on this road. Lieutenant Colonel Jordan took an AK-47 short-barreled rifle off the front seat beside him and handed it back to me in the back seat. I was in kidney pain but could still fire a weapon. He said, "Ya know how to use this, Chief? I said, "Yup." "Then if we come under fire, kill those sons a bitches." "Yes, sir! No problem." We were not attacked. Just as well. I hurt. Lieutenant Colonel Jordan dropped me off at the hospital, and I later underwent surgery in the Green Zone. I remember looking up at the paint peeling off the operating room ceiling as I was being put under. At the same time I was at the Combat Support Hospital (CSH), pronounced CASH, Saddam Hussein was also receiving treatment for heart issues. I didn't see him. Didn't want to. The surgery did not work, and I was Medevaced back to Fort Hood, Texas. I remember walking to the Blackhawk helicopter out the back door of the CSH while being medevaced to Fort Hood. It was a very hot July 2004 day, and the wind off the Blackhawk's rotors made it that much hotter. I was told it was one hundred forty degrees that day under the blades by the aircrew. From Fort Hood, I was later sent to Lackland Air Force Base, Texas. I had kidney surgeries at both Fort Hood and Lackland. From Lackland, I was sent back to Fort Hood to determine if I was going back down range. I wanted to go back to finish my tour, because I went to Iraq with my men, and I wanted to bring them home. Alive. I was released back to duty in early August 2004 and went back to Iraq. While I was at Fort Hood, Janelle, our daughter, wanted to visit me. I tried to discourage the visit, because if something did happen to me when I went back, I didn't want her last memory of me to be a weak bedridden Dad. She came anyway, and I'm glad she did. I had a nice visit with Justice, my Son-in-Law, Granddaughter Emily, and Janelle. It was during this visit that is the reason for writing this kidney stone story. While talking with Janelle on this visit, she says, "Hey, Dad. My co-worker's husband was in the military and wrote a book. Would you like me to have him sign a book over to you?" Of course, I said yes. Then I asked the name of the book. Janelle said, "He was a pilot called the *Flying Tiger*, which was the name of his book." I immediately sat up in my sickbed and was not quite as ill. I said, "Did you say *Flying Tiger*?" Long story short, Janelle worked with Maize Hill, General Tex Hill's wife. I said, "Get me a copy. I couldn't wait to read it."

I Meet a Flying Tiger

A brief history. As I was growing up, we studied World History while in high school. I was not a good high school student, but when any teacher mentioned anything about aviation, he had my attention. I love to pilot an aircraft; the thrill and challenge of it is exhilarating. In high school, I studied Hump Pilots, the Flying Tigers, and other heroes of World War II. Hump Pilots came about in early 1942. The Chinese Army had no supply route because the invading Japanese had cut all supply routes off. The Air Transport Command was born, flying supplies over the Himalayan Mountains, called the Hump by pilots flying the supplies. Thus, Hump Pilots. These pilots were heroic, flying in severe turbulence and crosswinds of one hundred to one hundred fifty Miles Per Hour commonly found on flights over the Hump. Flying these conditions takes a special kind of skill. The Flying Tigers were formed from the Army Air Corps, Navy, and Marine Corps Pilots by General Claire Chennault, who formed the American Volunteer Group (AVG), known as the Flying Tigers. The group was formed before the US entered World War II. I won't go into the Flying Tiger history. I could write a whole other book. But the Flying Tigers flew a Curtiss P-40 and painted the nose cones to that of a Tiger. Thus, the Flying Tigers were born. These were my boyhood heroes, and I dreamed one day of becoming a Pilot. Back on point. So when Janelle mentioned she knew General Tex Hill, I became very impressed very quickly. When I returned to Iraq and again became involved in Combat Operations, I forgot about the book until I returned home in early 2005. I was presented a signed copy of *The Flying Tigers* by David Lee "Tex" Hill by Janelle. A boyhood hero. "Would you like to meet him, Dad?" "Well, of course, absolutely," etc.

A brief history of Brigadier General David Lee "Tex" Hill. Tex was the Son of a Presbyterian Missionary in Kwangju, Korea. After receiving his Naval Aviator Wings, Tex was assigned to the USS *Saratoga* as a Torpedo-Bomber Pilot and later the USS *Ranger* and USS *Yorktown*. In early 1941, he resigned his Commission to join the American Volunteer Group (AVG), later known as the legendary Flying Tigers. Tex flew the P-408 Tomahawks as a Flight Leader. He Led the first strike force of fighters and bombers against the largest Japanese oil field on Formosa on Thanksgiving in 1941. Tex also earned the distinction of being the first P-51 Pilot to shoot down the nimble 43 Oscar fighter plane. Tex was a highly decorated World War II pilot, who later rejoined the Army Air Corps, later named the US Air Force. His decorations are too numerous to mention in this book. I am just very proud to have had the honor and privilege to have met and called BG Hill my friend. You only had to meet him once, and he was a friend for life. The same with his wife Maize.

Laura and I and Janelle had lunch with one of my boyhood heroes in San Antonio, Texas. I found Tex Hill one of the most humble men I have ever met, outside my Grandfather. Tex was eighty-nine years old at time. The Hills owned a farm in Kerrville, Texas, and Tex had just gotten off a hunting trip on his farm. He explained he was being overrun by javelinas and had rented a helicopter to shoot javelinas from with his .203-caliber rifle. I recall him telling me he had bagged over ninety of them. Pretty good for someone who is eighty-nine years old and from a helicopter. By the way, I should mention General Hill is credited with eighteen and a quarter shoot downs of Japanese aircraft over China. A real Triple Ace. Tex was a walking World War II history book and was still much in demand for speaking engagements throughout the US. He was the recipient of more Medals than I would want. After meeting Tex, he signed two Franklin Mint P-40s for me, along with a museum-quality "Blood

Chit." They are all in a place of honor in our home. Franklin Mint made the P-40J Aircraft after Tex Hill's Aircraft, detailed down to the cowboy symbol Tex had on his original Aircraft. A Blood Chit is a piece of cloth written in Chinese characters sewn on the back of their flight jackets in case they were ever shot down, which read: "This foreign person has come to China to help in the war effort. Soldiers and civilians, one and all, should rescue and protect him." You may recall the 1952 movie *The Flying Tigers* starring Marion Morrison, whose stage name is John Wayne. The movie was fashioned after a Squadron Commander, Tex Hill. Hill and Wayne were good friends from the time of that movie, and every year from that movie to the time of Wayne's death in 1979, Wayne hunted with Tex on his farm in Kerrville. I enjoyed meeting Tex and Maize Hill. It was one memory that will forever stay with me. It was as if we had known each other all our lives when we met. Tex and Maize were just those kind of people, both very personable and friendly. Once you meet them, you are lifelong friends. Both Maize and Tex have passed, Tex in October 2007 and Maize a year later in 2008, but both left a lasting American legacy. I think of our meeting often.

Me and Tex Hill

Me, Tex and Mazie Hill, and Laura

BG David Lee "Tex" Hill, earned the distinction of being the first P-51 Pilot to shoot down the nimble 43 Oscar fighter plane. Tex was a highly decorated WWII Pilot and Triple Ace, a real Flying Tiger who later rejoined the Army Air Corps, which later became the U.S. Air Force. His decorations are numerous. I am very proud to have had the honor and privilege to have met and called BG Hill my friend. You only had to meet him once, and he was a friend for life. The same with his wife Mazie. I highly recommend his book "Tex Hill FlyingTiger".

Sending People Outside the Wire

My Teams were responsible for developing actionable intelligence from developed sources. I rode with them on occasion outside the wire. I do not lead from the rear, never have.

We used the High-Mobility Multipurpose Wheeled Vehicle, commonly referred to as the HUMVEE. It has largely supplanted roles originally performed by the "original Jeep." My Teams made fun of me for calling the HUMVEE a Jeep, but that is a term I am used to. So when I said Jeep, they knew what I was talking about. In our Jeeps was a Blue Force Tracker (BFT). Making decisions that risk death is a very lonely feeling. You need all the information you can lay your hands on to send people in harm's way.

Blue Force Tracker (BFT)

BFT systems consisted of a computer used to display location information, a satellite terminal and antenna used to transmit location and other military data, a Global Positioning System (GPS), Command and Control Software used to send and receive orders, and mapping software used to plot the BFT on a map. The location of the host vehicle on the computer's terrain map display, along with the locations of other platform's (friendly in blue, enemy in red) BFT, can send and receive text and imagery messages and has a mechanism for reporting the locations of enemy forces. BFT also has route planning tools. By inputting grid coordinates, the BFT becomes both a map and a compass for motorized units. This system is now updated to a next-generation system.

Up-Armored Vehicles

Our Jeeps (HUMVEE) were not up-armored when we first arrived in Iraq. My Teams were going outside the wire on missions with vehicles that were essentially cardboard boxes if attacked. We did not receive up-armored vehicles until September 2004, three months before the 502nd Military Intelligence Battalion was due to rotate back to the States. One of my Green Zone teams was able to procure an up-armored Ford SUV from the Green Zone Motor Pool, approximately in June 2004. The vehicle was not being used, and they were able to sign the vehicle out to them. My team used this vehicle for source operation missions, and they naturally felt more comfortable in a vehicle that was up-armored during source meets. They had this vehicle for approximately forty-five days, when I was contacted by the Company Commander informing me that the State Department in the Green Zone had learned that my team was using an up-armored civilian vehicle, and they did not have one. The State Department had then gone through Command channels and was taking the vehicle from my Team. Apparently, their lives were more important than the lives of my men outside the wire. I had to inform my Team that they were to take the up-armored Ford back to the Motor Pool and began driving their original unprotected Jeep. It did not sit well with them, but they were Soldiers and followed orders. They did not get an up-armored vehicle until September 2004, but in the mean time, they were exposed on missions. I think back on this incident and begin to get frustrated all over again over the State Department's audacity.

Riding with the Teams

When I rode with the Teams (they called me affectionately "the ole man") in the Jeep, I became the Tactical Control (TC) of the Team Jeep, in place of the Team Leader, who sat behind me in the back passenger seat. The gunner stood in the middle of the Jeep manning a Squad Automatic Weapon (SAW) or .60-Caliber, and the last Team member sat behind me, and our interpreter sat behind the driver. This is how we convoyed to a source meet. Behind our Jeep was our assigned security team. I'll describe only two meets.

Bad Information

When a Source told you something, it had to be verified. We used an interpreter who translated all source meets. One of our interpreters' name was Sue. I liked her because she didn't mind playing in the mud with us and was not hesitant to get in a Source's face as needed. One summer day, a Source came in providing us information that, when checked, was found to already have been reported to one of my other Teams. When questioned further, we found the Source was trying to sell us the same insurgent information to get medical help for his Mother, or so he said. In Iraq, an Iraqi Doctor will only perform medical services on a cash-only basis. The Source's Mother needed lifesaving surgery, and he did not have enough funds to cover the cost of the surgery. The Source broke down emotionally during questioning and admitted he was trying to save the life of his Mother. I was unable to approve payout for information already received, as I was also responsible for classified and unclassified Intelligence Contingency Funds. I had the interpreter tell the Source to bring us better information, and then we may be able to help him. You simply felt bad by not being able to help a Source; however, on the other hand, a Source may not have been telling the whole truth.

Interview of Former Prisoners of War

On an unrecalled date, maybe around May 2004, my Foreign Military Intelligence Coordinating Authority (FORMICA) team was tasked with conducting the debriefing of individuals who had been released from Al-Qaeda to US Authorities. I will not mention what allied country the civilian detainees were from. A task that carried some responsibility and a task I knew my team was capable of doing. On the day of the scheduled debrief, an Intelligence Agency, I will not name, decided the debrief was too high profile for a Military Team and took over the debrief. My team would have done just as well. I mention this only to give you an idea of what a Military Intelligence Team is capable of. Even though the unnamed Intelligence Agency did not think so. My feeling was that we were operating in a combat environment and my team, being tactical, should have conducted the debrief they were trained for, and capable of.

The Illegal Rocket

I accompanied some of my individual Teams on a few source meets when I could get time from my OMT Operational Tempo. One of the Source meets I became personally involved was a source who was wanting to turn over a rocket to US Authorities. The Source had obtained and wanted twenty-five thousand dollars to do so. The rocket was supposedly a Russian-made missile, which was against Treaty to have in country. The Source was wanting my Team to meet him near Sadr City, where he would then turn over the missile to my Team. I don't think so. There was no way I was going to send a Team near Sadr City, for a possible ambush. I told my Team Leader to have the Source bring the missile to us at the compound. He agreed. Russ, who worked Battalion THOPS, and I went to the base operations and advised we may have a Russian-made missile coming on base and needed the Anti-Missile Defense sSstem used. This was a system that would detect live missiles or determine if the missile was inert. We did not need a blast on post. Long story short, through classified research, my Team Leader found this Source had tried selling this missile before and was trying to scam the Army. The Source meet was canceled and information passed to other teams of this scam and possible ambush tactic.)

We, of course, developed very good actionable intelligence on other Source meets, saving many American lives. The above meets are an example of the numerous types of sources we developed. As Fund Manager, I was able to get approval for a Contingency Fund payout of a large sum for a weapons and chemical cache for one of my Team Leaders. Thus taking it off the hands of individuals who would use it to kill Americans. Numerous reports requiring immediate action—such as sniper placements and placement of IEDs of an imminent danger to American personnel—called *Satellite Pour L'observation de ia Terra* or satellite for observation of earth (SPOT) reports were reported to the military Command handling that part of Baghdad were notified. Striker Teams were sent out as necessary by the notified Command. SPOT reports were on-the-spot actionable intelligence that needed to be turned over to a Command very quickly—i.e., impending short-suspense IED and sniper attacks waiting on a passing convoy. By the way, I don't know why (so don't ask) why a SPOT is called *Satellite Pour L'observation de ia Terra* or satellite for observation of earth.

Command Control Personal Computer

The Command Control Personal Computer (C2PC) is a Windows-Based Software application designed to facilitate Command Control functions to improve operational and tactical decisions and brings the tactical picture to a desktop. It exchanges tactical track data with combat operations systems. It also is an intelligence analysis system with decision aids and provides complete geographical situational awareness. It includes a robust track and overlay plot and route planning. It can produce operational graphics and input track data for synchronization. It is a powerful tool and provided me a common tactical picture of my teams. It is real eyes on system that I will not explain how it works because I received C2PC on my SECRET Internet Protocol Router Network (SIPRNet), a classified system. I will say it enhanced my HUMINT source operations for my Teams' source operations outside the wire. My computer technician and imagery analyst were able to get this system up and running during a badly needed operational phase, and I credit them with its success. I had some brilliant team members, the key to any successful operation. The system operated off my SIPRNet, which was up and running twenty-four hours a day, even when there were no teams outside the wire. My OMT was the only TAC HUMINT operation in theatre that had an up-and-running C2PC to my knowledge. It was so successful the Battalion S3 (operations) Section stole the Operational Console I had in my OMT to be placed in the S3 and was then piggybacked to my OMT. This was fine with me, as it cut down on the amount of space the console was taking in my operations area. I still had eyes on my Teams, which was my only concern. I was responsible for the lives of my team members, and I wanted any decision I made to be made with all available information. Dwight D. Eisenhower, another Kansan, had a saying: "Plans are nothing; Planning is everything." This is very true.

On Top of the Al-Rasheed Motel, Baghdad

The Al-Rasheed Motel (a five-star motel) sits downtown in Baghdad. It is surrounded by sandbags, blast barriers, and concertina wire in some places. It is approximately fifteen stories high and has an excellent all-around view of Baghdad. From the top of the Al-Rasheed, one can see a beautiful city of Mosques, homes, stores, and shopping—all trashed by war. Baghdad has its own smells: Cordite, Trash, Death, and Smoke. It's too bad what man has done to such a beautiful city. On the ground floor of the Al-Rasheed is an excellent restaurant. I have ate there several times and found the food very good. There is good shopping on the ground floor with small shops, and the hallways are lined with locals selling custom handmade local goods. The Al-Rasheed is the location where a Lieutenant

Colonel was murdered by a Rocket-Propelled Grenade Launcher (RPG) in early 2004. I do not recall the name of the Lieutenant Colonel, but on his last day in the country, he went shopping in one of the outdoor shopping centers near the Al-Rasheed to purchase keepsakes for his family back home. He decided to rent a room in the Al-Rasheed and be driven to the airport the following morning. Al-Qaeda learned of this, found out what room he was in, and, from a short distance, shot a Rocket-Propelled Grenade into his room, killing him on his last night in the country. That floor, the eighth, is blocked off, and the damage to the building can be seen from the road below. On a July 2004 day, I went to the top of the Al-Rasheed with the Battalion Commander, my Company Commander, the S3 (Battalion Operations), and some of my Walk-in Team members in the Green Zone. On the way to the top, we walked by this room and observed the damage to the room. One could see out through a large hole in the wall. Bed blown up, along with dresser drawers, etc. Nothing had been touched or attempted to be taken out of the room. One has to be very careful on top as there are snipers in the adjacent buildings. Also on the roof was a Man-Portable Air-Defense (MANPAD) team consisting of three Infantry personnel, who also warned us of sniper activity in the nearby buildings. No one from this team stood as we did. They knew and had been shot at before from adjacent buildings. This MANPAD team was there to fire on any reported sniper activity in the area and also protect against attacking aircraft if needed. My picture was snapped on the roof of the Al-Rasheed. I probably should not have taken this chance due to the activity known to be conducted in the area; however, it was a once-in-a-lifetime opportunity. In the background of this picture, one can see downtown Baghdad and the haze of War. Let me explain what a MANPAD is.

Man-Portable Air-Defense (MANPAD)

MANPADs are shoulder-launched weapons typically fired at one of two main target types—ground targets or air targets. MANPADs are small Surface-to-Air Missiles used to target helicopters and other low-flying aircraft. MANPAD weapons are also used against ground targets and come in a wide variety of types and sizes with smaller unguided weapons. MANPADs are generally used for close-range combat and larger guided systems for longer ranges. Most of these weapons are primarily designed for antitank warfare, although they are also effective against structures and a number of weapons have been designed specifically for such targets.

The Christmas Carolers

It is close to Christmas as I end this book. I think back to all the numerous holidays, including Christmases, I've missed with my family because of my Military assignments or past Law Enforcement duties. They are numerous. Christmas in a combat theater is much different than the lights and festive air with family at home. In a Muslim country, the Birth of Christ is not celebrated because it is a Christian holiday. Christmas is just another day in a Muslim country, and we worked; however, we did have Christmas dinner during our lunch break and small get-togethers with co-workers. During my time in Iraq, I would see the custodial staff on occasion coming and going, who were contracted to clean our buildings, our facilities, and clean and wash our laundry. I never took the time to talk with them. They were doing their jobs; I was doing mine. It's not that I did not care about them. Their job was just as important as mine. It's just that I was busy, and so were they. On one occasion, I did talk briefly with one custodian during a short visit just after I had showered in our facility trailer. He was there mopping and emptying trash and was genuinely happy. I learned in that brief time I talked to him that he was from Sri Lanka and had volunteered for Iraq for a salary I would not have accepted, but it was a lot of money to him, and his pay was going home to Sri Lanka to help support his family. He informed me that most custodial staff was from Sri Lanka, and all had volunteered to support their families. Over several months in Iraq, I had talked briefly with custodial staff coming and going and did not take a lot of time thinking about them. They were just there. In December 2004, around Christmas, there was a large tsunami in the Indian Ocean as the result of one of the largest earthquakes in history in Sumatra, Indonesia. The resulting Tsunami hit Sri Lanka, taking thousands of lives and causing billions of dollars in damage. Here's the point of this story. Christmas 2004 seemed lonely for me, as it did all men and women in harm's way and away from home. We were all thinking of our family who had to spend another holiday alone. I'm sure our families felt the same. There is a great deal of stress and anxiety that can bring sorrow to our hearts during Christmas. We become more contemplative and sensitive. Laura was home alone that Christmas, and this hardship is one I do not want her to go through again. My roommate Russ and I were in our trailer this particular evening, chitchatting, when all of a sudden, we heard Christmas Carolers? Were we hearing things? We went to the door and stepped outside to see the custodial staff from Sri Lanka singing Christmas songs to military personnel just outside our door. It was a dark, cloudless, and cold night but had celestial illumination. There was no sound of battle. No rat-a-tat of machine gun fire, no *pop pop pop* of small-arms fire, no explosions or noise, no smells of burning trash or cordite. It was silent but for the sound of Christmas coming to us from the Carolers. They stood outside our door and finished a song and began walking and singing to the other trailers. Russ and I came back inside our room and was silent for a moment, because we had just been talking about the lives lost in the Sri Lanka Tsunami. We realized that we had just been sung to by people who had lost family members in the Tsunami but had taken the time to sing to us, even though some were grieving for their own families. I did not feel so alone after that, and my respect for our custodial staff increased significantly. My thought was for the selfless act of the Sri Lankans who had taken time after a busy and hard day at work to think of us, even though they had lost family. I will never forget this Christmas because the Sri Lankans had sung of peace and hope and had just reminded me of what the Birth of Christ is all about. This is Christmas.

On Top of the Al Rasheed Hotel Baghdad

Front of Rasheed Hotel showing RPG Hits

In Uniform

In Kuwait

Me at Camp Slayer in front of Bombed out Castle

On C131 on way to Ft Hood (Medevac)

Iraqi Security Guards attached to my IMIR Team

My trailer with blast barriers. My room is third from right.

SFC Huerta – One of my former students and
later one of my THT Team Leaders

On Mission in Baghdad

Home of the ROCKET MAN!!

They're getting closer!

Nuff Said

Orders Ending Deployment

Upon leaving Iraq, we flew to Kuwait to await transportation back to the States on early February 7, 2005. We were there for seven days before we were manifested back. While in Kuwait, I had several of the men and women I served with come up to me and say things like "It was an Honor to have served with you, Chief," "I learned a lot from you, Chief," "I appreciated you taking care of me, Chief," "You taught me how to Lead, Chief," and "I hope I was not a disappointment to you, Chief." I was proud of them all. On occasion when I entered a room they were seated in or walking into my OMT, all stood as I entered, not because they had to but because they wanted to. The respect was mutual. No amount of awarded medals can equal these accolades placed on me by the men and women I served with. I can still see each of them in the cobwebs of my memory. They will remain with me forever. Some still keep in touch with me. It is an honor for me to have served with them. I did everything I could do to ensure all the men and women I served with came home. We left Kuwait on

February 7, 2005, and, at approximately two o'clock in the morning, arrived at Fort Lewis, Washington, for three days of outprocessing of the 502nd Military Intelligence Battalion. We left Fort Lewis on February 10, 2005, and landed in Sacramento, California, for three days' outprocessing of the 368th Military Intelligence Battalion where we were debriefed. I left Sacramento on February 14, 05, and arrived home to have Valentine's Day dinner with Laura. We had not seen each other for over a year.

I cannot describe to you what if feels like to step off an airplane onto free soil. It is simply indescribable. Sometimes one hears a noise, smells a smell, and remembers a sound. Memories, some good, some bad. Ever since returning, I now look at every day as a gift. For those who fight for it, Freedom has a special flavor the protected will never know. Freedom, do not take it for granted.

Most Units go home to a parade in their hometown, as did the Unit I was assigned to. I was cherry-picked from my home Unit and assigned individually. I flew to my assignment at Fort Hood, Texas in January 2004 and flew home individually in February 2005. I left home by myself and returned home by myself. It was more of an honor for me to be picked up at the airport by Laura than being in a parade and then fly home. Laura had endured far more than I had, and the best place for me was to be back home in her arms.

I ended my end of tour of duty After Action Report (AAR) to the commander with these words:

> We have the intent, and we are capable, of killing our enemies. Our great-grandfathers had this in World War I. Our fathers had this in World War II and Korea, and my generation had this in Vietnam. I see this same will and intent in these young warriors' eyes. It has been an honor and privilege to have served beside them. America can be proud of its sons and daughters.
>
> On those nights I am restless and can't sleep – memories of sights – sounds – smells. I think – could I have done it differently? Could I have

been a better Leader to the men and women I served with? Looking back, I feel I made the right decisions with the information I had available. I feel I served my purpose. But there is always that thought. My hope is that I left a shadow on the knowledge of Intelligence Operations of the men and women I served with. And so, it lingers…

CHAPTER 20

My Job Description

The Company Commander I worked with wrote this job description and evaluation. I thought I would include them:

> Operational Management Team (OMT) 52 Leader in a deployed Military Intelligence Company conducting Tactical HUMINT (TAC HUMINT) operations in support of Operation Iraqi Freedom II. Responsible for the technical control and mission management of six TAC HUMINT Teams (THTs) within Baghdad in support of Multi-National Corps-Iraq (MNC-I) and Multi-National Forces-Iraq (MNF-I). Provides mission focus, quality control of reporting intelligence oversight and threat analysis to THTs. Manages source administration, collection requirements, initial Sabotage and Espionage Directed Against the Army (SAEDA) investigations, and Intelligence Contingency Funds (ICF) to sustain operations. Provides single-source HUMINT analysis and administrative reports to the company Commander. Responsible for

equipment valued at over three hundred sixty thousand dollars.

My Company Commander Evaluation

Chief Warrant Officer 3 (CW/3) Hurt is a superb warrant officer. He was critical to Bravo Company's transition from its normal Modified Table of Equipment (MTOE) mission to its unprecedented wartime mission in support of OIFII. CW/3 Hurt's technical and tactical expertise in TAC HUMINT operations guided the unit in effective intelligence collection in a complex environment. He successfully forged thirty soldiers from ten different National Guard and Reserve Component Units into a highly productive, cohesive combat-ready intelligence team. CW/3 Hurt efficiently leveraged his leadership, experience, and expertise to effectively maximize THT's collection abilities and survivability resulting in quality reporting with no casualties. His tireless efforts helped acquire critical information on Al-Qaeda, Iraqi former regime loyalist, and anticoalition forces, which was instrumental in identifying, locating, capturing, and eliminating threats to coalition forces and the stabilization of Iraq. Under CW/3 Hurt's direction, OMT 52 processed over seven hundred Iraqi Military Intelligence Reports, one hundred ninety Contact Reports, one hundred seventy-five Basic Source Data Reports, fifty-two SPOT reports, three hundred Draft Intelligence Information Reports, of which one hundred fifteen were published nationally. CW/3 Hurt's solid framework for success included the creation of new operation databases, evaluation and report tracking mechanism, Techniques, Tactics, and Procedures (TTPs) and Standard Operating Procedures (SOPs), and source registry. He also built a strong professional working relationship with the Battalion's Tactical HUMINT Operations Section (THOPS) and other intelligence agencies facilitating an open, collaborative environment where intelligence and resources are readily shared. He is a proven combat intelligence officer.

My Battalion Commander Evaluation

Superb performance by an excellent Warrant Officer in a combat zone. CW/3 Hurt trained the personnel in the Company OMT and established TTPs from scratch. He was instrumental in the construction of numerous operational databases to facilitate smooth and orderly TAC HUMINT operations. He established a source registry and managed the company collection plan. As the intelligence contingency fund (ICF) manager, he effectively and efficiently established the company's contingency funds program and provided oversight to ensure strict compliance with published regulations. CW/3 Hurt guided OMT 52 in the production of over seven hundred sixteen intelligence reports of which one hundred fifteen were published nationally. His leadership and guidance led to the production of installing Command Control Personal Computer (C2PC) to enhance situational awareness in the company Tactical Operations Center (TOC).

I am including a copy of my Combat Action Badge (CAB) recommendation. I am hesitant including this in my book because what I experienced is not anything compared to what others experienced. This recommendation is part of my experience in Iraq and is the only reason I place it in this book, which will give you an idea of the operational environment we operated in.

Narrative for Award of the Combat Action Badge (CAB)

CW/3 Oliver J. Hurt served in Operation Iraqi Freedom II from February 2004 through February 2005 while assigned to the 502nd Military Intelligence Battalion and later the 250th Military Intelligence Battalion at Camp Victory, Iraq, near the Baghdad International Airport. While on Camp Victory, CW/3 Hurt was routinely subjected to enemy mortar, rocket, and direct fire. In particular, CW/3 Hurt's office and quarters were in areas of Camp Victory that were routinely targeted by insurgent indirect fire, sustaining numerous close impacts of fifty to one hundred meters or less from mortar and rocket fire while in or around the proximity of his work and living areas. CW/3 Hurt also subjected himself to the hazards of insurgent activity by traveling in vehicular convoys to the Baghdad International Zone.

Specific occurrences include: (1) On the night of 20 January, 2005, CW/3 Hurt was in his quarters when a sniper in a nearby mosque fired a round from an AK-47-type rifle that pierced a multi-use trailer approximately fifty feet from his quarters. (2) On an unrecalled day in November 2004, CW/3 Hurt was in the dining facility (DFAC) on Camp Victory when a rocket impacted just outside the building, peppering the facility with shrapnel. (3) On an unrecalled day in October 2004, while en route to the DFAC, a rocket impacted approximately one hundred feet from him, injuring one soldier. (4) On an unrecalled day in November 2004, a rocket impacted approximately six hundred feet from his quarters, killing two soldiers. (5) On an unrecalled day in June 2004, a rocket impacted approximately two hundred meters from his quarters, killing two soldiers. (5) On an unrecalled day in April 2004, three mortars impacted two hundred feet from his exposed position, peppering shrapnel on adjacent quarters. Additionally, CW/3 Hurt was subjected to dozens of near-proximity indirect fire attacks (within one hundred meters), which is not specifically documented for this report. During each of these incidents, CW/3 Hurt could have easily been killed or seriously wounded.

CW/3 Hurt served with distinction during his tenure as the 502nd and 250th Military Intelligence Battalions tactical HUMINT Operations Management Team 52, Officer in Charge (OIC), earning an Army Commendation Medal for his actions.

Sacrifice

The following paragraph was written by an author unknown to me, but I find it very pertinent. I have added a sentence or two making it part of my thought.

It's hard for people to fathom the numbers of battlefield deaths. They're so huge. They seem so detached and faceless from far away. They were—no doubt—wet, cold, and scared as they struggled through lethal fire. Another American has paid the ultimate price for our Freedom. Another American Soldier, another dusty corner of an unforgiving battlefield, another one of us. Each battlefield loss diminishes me, because it diminishes America. Only those who have seen combat know of the indescribable feelings one has during combat. No matter what military service one serves, or amount of awarded medals, there can be no other honor bestowed on one than to be called a Soldier.

There is a saying by George Orwell I find particularly true: "People sleep peaceably in their beds at night only because rough men stand ready to do violence on their behalf."

After the horror and bravery has dimmed and passed and these memories fade further and further away and the people and participants pass away, we are forced increasingly to rely on books. These thoughts will always be in my thought and memory.

Military Mentors

I have had numerous Leadership Mentors over the years of my military career and those I have emulated. All were good leaders. There are some that stand out. I'll tell you about one, but there are many. When I was assigned to the 368th Military Intelligence Battalion in Phoenix, Arizona, as a TAC HUMINT Team Commander, there was a young Captain named Larry Lamb, assigned to the S3 (Operations) Section. Captain Lamb was a very knowledgeable, intelligent, and capable Officer. Captain Lamb had the responsibility of putting THT Teams together and assigning team members to an operational Team Commander. Darn if he didn't frequently change team members around. This made it sometimes kind of cumbersome for Team Commanders to work a cohesive team. Over the years, we were assigned to different Units but always knew who each was. Then, in 2008, now Lieutenant Colonel Lamb took over as Battalion Commander (CO) of the 5/104th Military Intelligence Instructor Battalion in Fort Huachuca, Arizona, the battalion I was assigned to. We both had been promoted up through the ranks in the command staff. When he became the Battalion Commander, I then became his S2 (Security and Intelligence) Officer. Lieutenant Colonel Lamb took over a Battalion that needed a good leader, because the outgoing Commander had in effect made the Battalion ineffective. Lieutenant Colonel Lamb changed that and, after approximately less than six months, had a very effective instructor staff and Battalion. He is one of those rare individuals who became a very good tactical and technical commander and valued leader. Over the course of two years in the Command Staff working together, I found him one of the best Commanders and Leaders I have ever worked with. Lieutenant Colonel Lamb is now Colonel Lamb and is a proven wartime tactical and strategic leader. It was an honor to have served with him. He was a good mentor and fair to his Command Staff. I would be surprised if he does not make Brigadier. When I retired, he presented me with the Knowlton Award and nominated me for the Legion of Merit (LOM).

As I end this book, I learned that COL Lamb recently retired. I called him and asked him about his retirement and he informed me that he was ready. He was an excellent leader and soldier. Taking off your uniform for the last time can be an experience. I'm sure he felt this experience.

Knowlton Award

Established in 1995 by the Military Intelligence Corps Association (MICA), in support of the Military Intelligence Corps, the Knowlton Award recognizes individuals who have contributed significantly to the promotion of Army Intelligence in ways that stand out in the eyes of the recipients, their superiors, subordinates, and peers. These individuals must also demonstrate the highest standards of integrity and moral character, display an outstanding degree of professional competence, and serve the Military Intelligence Corps with distinction. The MICA is the sponsoring agency and provides financial resources, administrative control, and publicity.

Lieutenant Colonel Thomas Knowlton's distinguished military service during the Revolutionary War was recognized by General George Washington, who appointed him to raise a regiment, expressly for desperate and delicate intelligence services. Knowlton exemplifies the gallantry, bravery, and strong determination to succeed associated with the Military Intelligence soldier. As a brave warrior soldier and the first intelligence professional in the Continental Army, Lieutenant Colonel Thomas Knowlton embodies courage and dedication to duty.

Knowlton Award Narrative

Lieutenant Colonel Larry Lamb

Chief Warrant Officer Four (CW4/) Oliver J. Hurt enlisted in the United States Army as a Military Police Officer (MP), serving in Korea and Germany as a Military Police Dog Handler. His duties were critical to Force Protection and Anti Terrorism efforts for the Command, placing him in close proximity to exchange of fire between the Republic of Korea and Korean National Police Agency (NKPA) elements. CW/4 Hurt cross-trained as a US Army Counterintelligence (CI) Agent and became the Non Commissioned Officer in Charge (NCOIC) of the Counterintelligence Section, First Military Intelligence (MI) Center in Phoenix, Arizona. In this position, he was responsible for producing target country studies to support three combatant commands. He also established a Military Intelligence Library for the First Military Intelligence Center, supporting the fifteen subsections of the center. CW/4 Hurt then embarked on a career as a Warrant Officer becoming a Counterintelligence Technician and Team Commander, Company C, 368th Military

Intelligence Battalion, supporting the 501st Military Intelligence Brigade in Korea. CW/4 Hurt was instrumental in helping to produce a target country study on the NKPA, which was used by the 501st Military Intelligence Battalion as a base of reference document. CW/4 Hurt worked as a Special Agent in Charge on active duty for training for the 501st, Taegu, South Korea, and later as an Operations Officer during a North Atlantic Treaty Organization (NATO) exercise. In this position, he was responsible for strategic intelligence reporting between five separate Military Intelligence detachments. Subsequently, CW/4 Hurt became the Senior Counterintelligence Instructor, Fifth Battalion, 104th Regiment (Military Intelligence), Third Brigade, 104th Division, and oversaw the US Army Reserves (USAR) Counterintelligence Agent training program providing dozens of qualified agents to the Army Reserve. On several occasions, CW/4 Hurt served as Course Manager, overseeing the successful completion of numerous student courses of instruction often extending his orders to ensure mission completion. Upon Mobilization Chief, CW/4 Hurt became the Officer in Charge, Operational Management Team 52, Baghdad, Iraq, where he planned, coordinated, and synchronized hundreds of Human Intelligence collection operations in support of Operation Iraqi Freedom with USAR soldiers he had trained. OMT 52 conducted split-based operations, with six Tactical Human Intelligence (HUMINT) Teams supporting the US and Coalition Forces with critical Counterintelligence/Human Intelligence capability.

Receiving the Knowlton Award, Dec 2010 at
BN Awards Banquet, From LTC Lamb

Retirement

I retired from the US Army as a Military Intelligence Warrant Officer 4 (CW/4), specializing in Counterintelligence. My Uniform is now proudly displayed in the Valley Center, Kansas, Historical Society Museum. I would still be wearing an Army Uniform if the Army would let me. I retired with twenty-eight years of service to our Country. I loved it. I have lived life to pursue noble undertakings, to live life to the fullest, having used all my talents with no regrets. I still miss the adrenaline flow though. So I will continue life's journey with my beloved Laura, and when I sing my death song, I will do so like a warrior going home.

I hope you have enjoyed reading about some of my exploits, and I would like you to know I am extremely proud to have served in the Military for our Freedom. For those who fight for it, Freedom has a special flavor the protected will never know.

The words of General Douglas MacArthur in his last speech to West Point in May 1962 come to mind as I write to end this book.

> Duty, Honor, Country
>
> These words build basic character. They make you strong enough to know you are weak and brave enough to face yourself when you are afraid. They teach you to be proud and unbending in honest failure but humble and gentle in success.
>
> The shadows are lengthening for me. The twilight is here. My days of old have vanished—tone and tints. They have gone glimmering through the dreams of things that were. Their memory is one of wondrous beauty, watered by tears, and coaxed and caressed by the smiles of yesterday. I listen then, but with thirsty ear, for the witching melody of faint bugles blowing reveille, of far drums beating the long roll.

In my dreams, I hear again the crash of guns, the rattle of musketry, and the strange mournful mutter of the battlefield. But in the evening of my memory, there echoes and re-echoes: Duty, Honor, and Country. But I want you to know that when I cross the river, my last conscious thoughts will be of the Corps and the Corps and the Corps.

God bless America.

Retiring My Uniform, Valley Center, KS Historical Society

WHAT IS A CHIEF WARRANT OFFICER 4?

Chief Warrant Officer 4 (CW4) is the fourth Warrant Officer rank in the United States Army. Those who rise to this rank join a class of determined and skillful commanders. CW/4s are senior-level technical and tactical experts who perform the duties of technical leader, manager, maintainer, sustainer, integrator, and advisor and serve in a wide variety of branch level positions. Warrant Officers are highly skilled, single-track specialty Officers, and while the ranks are authorized by Congress, each branch of Uniformed Services selects, manages, and utilizes Warrant Officers in slightly different ways. Warrant Officers are bold decision makers and known for their proven performance. They are trained in and possess analytical skills, and a hands on approach to problem-solving. Warrant Officers are commissioned by the President of the United States and take the same oath as regular Commissioned Officers. As Warrant Officers become more senior they focus on integrating branch and Army Systems into Joint and national-level systems. Experienced leaders, they possess a proven ability to meet challenge head on. Warrant Officers can and do Command detachments, Units, Activities, Vessels, Aircraft, and Armored Vehicles; as well as lead, coach, train, and counsel subordinates. However, the Warrant Officer's primary task as a leader is to serve as the technical expert, providing valuable skills, guidance, and expertise to Commanders and Organizations in their particular field.

I thought I would include a basic job description of a CW4 Counterintelligence Technician/Agent, which is not an entry-level position. This will give an idea of what an Army Senior Counterintelligence Agent does, and will shed some light on some of the training to agents I instructed as mentioned in this book.

The Counterintelligence Agent/Officer is primarily responsible for supervising and conducting counterintelligence surveys and investigations to detect, identify, assess, counter, exploit and neutralize adversarial, Foreign Intelligence Service and terrorist threats to National Security.

Basic Duties:

Conducts investigations/operations to detect and prevent acts of espionage, sabotage, and terrorism. Supervises all operations in field office and above; manages counterintelligence elements that support all Army organizations and activities up to including the Chief of Staff, Army, Secretary of the Army, and the Secretary of Defense.

Conducts investigations/operations by applying sound judgment and analytical reasoning methods to detect and prevent acts of espionage, sabotage, and terrorism directed against Army activities; supervises investigative, operational, and administrative personnel; manages investigative/operational elements of varying size commensurate with skill and experience level; prepares, reviews, and approves investigative/operational reports of investigations and inspections; performs terrorism counteraction analysis and threat analysis; investigates national security crimes of Army interest as defined by regulation, the UCMJ, or applicable US Code; conducts and supervises both overt and covert investigations; supervises the technical performance of subordinate military and civilian personnel in related job skills; develops, evaluates, and manages sources and informants of military intelligence; develops and approves investigative plans; obtains and executes arrest and search warrants in coordination with the Criminal Investigations Division or the FBI; interviews and interrogates witnesses, suspects, and subjects, and obtains written statements executed under oath; represents the Army's interests in investigations conducted collaterally with the Department of Defense, Department of Justice, and other federal, state, or local investigative agencies; writes, reviews, and approves reports of investigation; provides security and operations security advice and assistance to Army elements; conducts threat analysis and vulnerability estimates.

Provides guidance and technical input to subordinate counterintelligence elements or other staff elements; manages counterintelligence elements providing counterintelligence support to combat commanders up to and including Theater Army level.

About The Author

Oliver J. Hurt, known as OJ, is currently a Sr. Special Agent, National Background Investigations Bureau (NBIB) and has over 30 years of investigative experience. He is a graduate of Wichita State University (WSU), and is a former Police Officer Wichita, KS, Police Department (WPD), and small-town Police Chief. He is a former Helicopter Pilot, WPD, and was a Chief Pilot. OJ was the Counterintelligence Point of Contact (POC) for the Southwestern Region, Defense Investigative Service, and is a CW/4 (Retired) Military Intelligence Officer, specializing in Counterintelligence, with both Strategic and Tactical assignments. OJ is also a former Certified Counterintelligence Instructor. As an Intelligence Officer, Oliver spent one year in Iraq, as Officer in Charge of six TAC HUMINT Teams responsible for actionable intelligence collection in Baghdad and the surrounding areas. OJ is a graduate of numerous Intelligence schools and is also a graduate of the Army Command and General Staff College. OJ is the recipient of the following Army Ribbons and Medals:

Combat Action Badge
Knowlton Award
Legion of Merit
Army Commendation Medal with 4 Device
Army Achievement Medal w/4 Device
Good Conduct Medal with 2 Device
Army Reserve Component Achievement Medal
National Defense Service Ribbon with 3 Device
Korean Defense Medal
Armed Forces Expeditionary Medal-1
Iraq Campaign Medal

Global War on Terrorism Expeditionary Medal-1
Global War on Terrorism Service Ribbon
Non Commissioned Officers Professional Development Medal with
   3 Device
Army Armed Forces Reserve Medal-1 with M Device
Army Reserve Component Overseas Training Service Ribbon with
   4 device
Overseas Service Medal with 4 Device
Army Service Ribbon with 2 Device
Overseas Service Bars-4
UNIT CITATIONS
Meritorious Unit Citation
Army Superior Unit Citation

ORGANIZATIONS

Masonic Lodge

Rainbow Girls Grand Cross of Color
Order of Eastern Star (Past Patron)
Hero of 76 (Past Commander)

Scottish Rite Valley
of Wichita (32d Degree)
Midian Shrine
Sojourner

CPSIA information can be obtained
at www.ICGtesting.com
Printed in the USA
FSOW04n0030030617
34678FS

9 781681 979850